"A lucid guide to male and female[...]"

—*New York Times*

"Until recently, there have been two groups of people: those who argue sex differences are innate and should be embraced and those who insist that they are learned and should be eliminated by changing the environment. Sax is one of the few in the middle—convinced that boys and girls are innately different and that we must change the environment so differences don't become limitations."

—*TIME*

"Convincing... psychologist and family physician Leonard Sax, using twenty years of published research, offers a guide to the growing mountain of evidence that girls and boys really are different.... This extremely readable book also includes shrewd advice on discipline, and on helping youngsters avoid drugs and early sexual activity. Sax's findings, insights, and provocative point-of-view should be of interest and help to many parents."

—*New York Post*

"Using studies as well as anecdotes from his practice and visits to classrooms, [Sax] offers advice on such topics as preventing drug abuse and motivating students.... The book is thought-provoking, and Sax explains well the science behind his assertions.... [*Why Gender Matters*] is a worthy read for those who care about how best to prepare children for the challenges they face on the path to adulthood."

—*Scientific American*

"*Why Gender Matters* is an instructive handbook for parents and teachers . . . to create ways to cope with the differences between boys and girls."

—*Boston Globe*

"*Why Gender Matters* pulls together wide-ranging findings on everything from how girls respond to stress, to how antidrug ads actually encourage teenage boys to use drugs, and how all of these differences are hardwired from birth."

—*National Post* (Canada)

"A potent new book . . . [Dr. Sax] cites a cascade of research that shows the many ways boys and girls differ, from how their brains develop to how they handle stress."

—Margaret Wente, *Globe and Mail* (Canada)

"[Sax] challenges parents and teachers to acknowledge the latest evidence of lifelong gender differences or risk their children's educational success and emotional health."

—Joanne Good, *Calgary Herald*

"Sax presents a reader-friendly, persuasive argument, challenging many basic assumptions by interspersing hard data with numerous case studies."

—Mary Ward Menke, *January Magazine*

"Fascinating . . . This book takes an 'outside the box' position on gender. Paradoxically, Sax says, gender-neutral education favors the learning style of one sex or the other, and so only drives men and women into the usual stereotyped fields. The best way to raise your son to be a man who is caring and nurturing, says Sax, is to first of all let him be a boy. The best way to produce a female mathematician is to first of all let her be a girl. . . . I think Sax is on to something. Mature men and women do draw on qualities that stereotypically belong to the opposite sex. But the easiest way to get them to that point is to first make them confident about being a man or a woman. . . . Sax adds that children are less happy and confident nowadays because no one is teaching them how to be men and women. This is a powerful, even obvious insight, once you dare think it."

—Stanley Kurtz, *National Review Online*

"As the principal of an elementary school, I am constantly on the lookout for outstanding articles and books about gender-specific learning differences. *Why Gender Matters* is the best I've read."

—John Webster, Head of School, San Antonio Academy

"*Why Gender Matters* is an outstanding work of scholarship. I am going to make it our 'faculty read' this summer."

—Paul Krieger, Headmaster, Christ School, Arden, North Carolina

"Extremely interesting . . . Challenged many of my basic assumptions and helped me to think about gender in a new way."

—Joan Ogilvy Holden, Head of School, St. Stephen's and St. Agnes School, Alexandria, Virginia

"*Why Gender Matters* is a fabulous resource for teachers and parents. Dr. Sax combines his extensive knowledge of the research on gender issues with practical advice in cogent, highly readable prose. I am eager to have my colleagues at school read this book and discuss it!"

—Martha Cutts, Head of School, Agnes Irwin School,
Rosemont, Pennsylvania

"In this reader-friendly book, Dr. Sax combines his comprehensive knowledge of the scientific literature with numerous interesting case studies to argue for his thesis that single-sex education is advantageous."

—Sandra Witelson, Ph.D., Albert Einstein Chair in
Neuroscience, McMaster University

"I simply will never be able to express how eye-opening this book has been for me. Yes, me—even though I thought I was a boy-raising specialist. After all, I have produced four healthy, smart athletes. I must know what I'm doing. But many of my boy-raising days I thought I was going mad. I'd come home from some sports event trembling because of the way the coach yelled at my kid. I'd ask my husband and whichever son it happened to be that day how they could stand being yelled at like that. Almost every time husband and son would look at me and not have any recollection of being yelled at during the game. Now I understand!"

—Janet Phillips, mother, Potomac, Maryland

"As the father of a four-year-old daughter and now new twin boys, this particular book looked intriguing. Well, I couldn't put it down. Not only is it well written, with engaging anecdotes, but it presents the latest scientific findings in gender research (with lots of footnotes so you can read the studies yourself if you are so inclined) and relates [them] to the job of parenting. It helps that the author is a family doctor who has seen his share of dysfunctional situations that in hindsight might easily have been prevented with a little knowledge. The book is more than just informative about gender differences in children—he relates this information to such parenting topics as disciplining your child, gender specific education strategies, dealing with problem children, kids and drugs (both the legal and nonlegal kind), and teenage sex."

—Phillip Trubey, father, Rancho Santa Fe, California

"As a high school administrator, I am leading a book study on *Why Gender Matters* with my faculty this fall. As an aunt to a newborn, this was the shower gift to my sister. As a mother of two boys and one girl, I hung on every word. There is simply no category of individuals who are in contact with children of any age who should not read this book. I cannot recommend it strongly enough."

—Leone Langseth, Deer Park, Texas

Why
Gender
Matters

Nonfiction by Leonard Sax, M.D., Ph.D.

*Boys Adrift: The Five Factors Driving the Growing Epidemic
of Unmotivated Boys and Underachieving Young Men*

*Girls on the Edge: The Four Factors Driving the New Crisis for Girls—
Sexual Identity, the Cyberbubble, Obsessions, Environmental Toxins*

*The Collapse of Parenting: How We Hurt Our Kids
When We Treat Them Like Grown-ups*

SECOND EDITION

Why Gender Matters

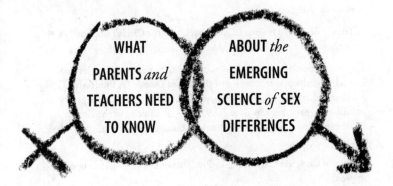

WHAT PARENTS *and* TEACHERS NEED TO KNOW

ABOUT *the* EMERGING SCIENCE *of* SEX DIFFERENCES

Leonard Sax, M.D., Ph.D.

HARMONY
BOOKS · NEW YORK

Published in the United States by Harmony Books, an imprint
of the Crown Publishing Group, a division of Penguin Random
House LLC, New York.
crownpublishing.com

Harmony Books is a registered trademark, and the Circle colophon is a
trademark of Penguin Random House LLC.

The first edition of this work was published in hardcover in the United
States by Doubleday, an imprint of the Knopf Doubleday Publishing Group,
a division of Penguin Random House LLC, in 2005; and subsequently
published in paperback by Broadway Books, an imprint of the Crown
Publishing Group, a division of Penguin Random House LLC, New York,
in 2006.

Library of Congress Cataloging-in-Publication Data is available upon
request.

ISBN 978-0-451-49777-2
Ebook ISBN 978-0-451-49778-9

Printed in the United States of America

Book design by Ralph Fowler
Cover design by Jennifer Carrow

10 9 8 7 6 5 4 3 2 1

Second Edition

For my wife, Katie
And our daughter, Sarah

CONTENTS

Why Gender Matters

CHAPTER 1

Differences

Jason is sixteen. His sister Sonya is fourteen. They come from a stable home with two loving parents. Mom and Dad are concerned about Jason, their son: He's not working hard at school and his grades are sliding. He spends most of his free time playing video games like *Grand Theft Auto* or *Call of Duty*, or surfing the Web for pictures of girls.

Both parents are actually quite proud of Sonya. She is a straight-A student and an athlete, and she has many friends. But when I meet with Sonya, she tells me that she isn't sleeping well. She wakes up in the middle of the night, feeling guilty about having eaten one whole slice of pizza at supper. She often has palpitations and shortness of breath. And she has just started to cut herself with a razor blade, secretly, on her upper inner thigh so her parents won't see. She hasn't told her parents any of this. On the surface she is the golden girl. Inside she feels that she is falling apart.

Her brother Jason, on the other hand, is happy as a clam. He can eat a whole pizza without the slightest remorse. He has no difficulty sleeping: in fact, his parents had to kick him out of bed at noon on a Saturday. He likes to spend his free time hanging with his two buddies who are just like him, playing video games and looking at pictures of girls online.

Matthew turned five years old in August, just before kindergarten started. He was looking forward to it. From what he had heard, kindergarten sounded like one long playdate with friends. He could hardly wait. So his mother, Cindy, was surprised when, in October, Matthew started refusing to go to school, refusing even to get dressed in the morning. More than once Cindy had to dress him, then drag him writhing and thrashing into the car, force him into the car seat, and then pull him out of the car and into the school.

Cindy decided to investigate. She sat in on his kindergarten class. She spoke with the teacher. Everything seemed fine. The teacher—gentle, soft-spoken, and well educated—reassured Mom that there was no cause for alarm. But Cindy remained concerned, and rightly so, because major problems were just around the corner.

Caitlyn was a shy child and just the slightest bit overweight all through elementary school. In middle school she underwent a metamorphosis from chubby wallflower to outgoing socialite. She lost weight so quickly that her mother, Jill, worried she might be anorexic. For the next four years, though, everything seemed great—in a frantic and crazy sort of way. Caitlyn was juggling a heavy academic load, had lots of friends, and maintained a full schedule of after-school activities, staying up until midnight or later doing homework. But she seemed happy enough—often frenzied and frazzled, sure, but still happy. Or at least that's what everybody thought until the phone rang at 3:00 a.m. that awful, unforgettable November night. A nurse told Jill that Caitlyn was in the emergency room, unconscious, having tried to commit suicide with an overdose of Vicodin and Xanax.

These stories share a common element. In each case problems arose because the parents did not understand some differences between girls and boys. In each case trouble might have been averted if the parents had known enough about boy/girl differences to recognize what was really happening in their child's life. In each case the parents could have taken specific action that might have prevented or solved the problem.

We will come back to each of these kids later in this book. Right now it may not be obvious to you how each of these stories illustrates a failure to understand sex differences. That's okay. Later on we'll hear more about Justin and Sonya, Matthew, and Caitlyn. Armed with some knowledge about boy/girl differences, you will be able to recognize where the parents made the wrong decision or failed to act, and you will see how the stories might have ended differently.

The Dubious Virtue of Gender-Neutral Child Rearing

I enrolled in the Ph.D. program in psychology at the University of Pennsylvania way back in September 1980. Governor Ronald Reagan was challenging President Jimmy Carter for the presidency. The original Apple computer had recently come on the market. "My typewriter is working fine" was the answer the department secretary gave me when I asked her whether she would be getting a computer anytime soon. Nobody I knew had ever heard of e-mail or the Internet. The invention of the World Wide Web still lay ten years in the future.

Among the courses I took that fall was a graduate seminar in developmental psychology. "Why do girls and boys behave differently?" my professor, Justin Aronfreed, asked rhetorically. "Because we *expect* them to. We *teach* them to. Imagine a world in which we raised girls to play with tanks and trucks, in which we encouraged boys to play with dolls. Imagine a world in which we played rough-and-tumble games with girls while we cuddled and hugged the boys. In such a world, many of the differences we see in how girls and boys behave—maybe even *all* the differences— would vanish."

In another seminar my fellow graduate students and I learned about the extraordinary work of Professor John Money at Johns Hopkins. Professor Money had been consulted by the parents of an unfortunate little boy whose penis had literally been sizzled off during a botched circumcision. At Dr. Money's recommendation, the boy had been raised as a girl, with excellent results (according to Dr. Money). The child loved to play dress-up, enjoyed helping Mom in the kitchen, and disdained "boy toys" such as guns or trucks. "Dr. Money's work provides further evidence that most of the differences we observe between girls and boys are socially constructed," Professor Henry Gleitman told us. "We reward children who follow the sex roles we create for them while we penalize or at least fail to reward children who don't conform. Parents create and reinforce differences between girls and boys."

We nodded sagely. In clinical rotations we often encountered parents who still clung to the quaint notion that girls and boys were different from birth. But we knew better.

Or so we thought.

I graduated with my Ph.D. in psychology, as well as my M.D., in 1986. When I left Philadelphia to begin my residency in family practice, I got rid of most of the papers I had accumulated during my six years at the University of Pennsylvania. But there was one folder I didn't throw out: a folder of papers about sex differences in hearing, showing that girls and boys hear differently.

Four years later, after I finished my residency in family medicine, my wife and I established a family practice in Montgomery County, Maryland, just outside of Washington, DC. Several years passed. I wasn't thinking much about gender differences. Then, in the mid-1990s, I began to notice a parade of second- and third-grade boys marching into my office, their parents clutching a note from the school. The notes read: "We're concerned that Justin [or Carlos or Tyrone] may have attention deficit disorder. Please evaluate."

In some of these cases I found that what these boys needed wasn't drugs for ADHD (attention deficit hyperactivity disorder) but rather a *teacher* who understood the differences in how girls and boys learn. Upon further inquiry, I found that nobody at the school was aware of girl/boy differences in the ability to hear. I reread the papers in that manila folder, documenting hardwired differences in the ability to hear, showing that the average boy has hearing that is less sensitive than the average girl. In the next chapter we will look more closely at evidence for sex differences in hearing.

Think about the typical second-grade classroom. Imagine Justin, six years old, sitting at the back of the class. The teacher, a woman, is speaking in a tone of voice that seems about right to her. Justin barely hears her. Instead, he's staring out the window or watching a fly crawl across the ceiling. The teacher notices that Justin isn't paying attention. Justin is demonstrating a deficit of attention. The teacher may reasonably wonder whether Justin perhaps has attention deficit disorder.

The teacher is absolutely right about Justin showing a deficit of attention. But his attention deficit isn't due to attention deficit disorder, it's due to the fact that Justin isn't hearing the soft-spoken teacher very well. And very few six-year-old boys will raise their hands and say, "Excuse me, Ms. Gentlevoice, I do hear you, but not very well. Could you please speak more loudly?" The teacher is talking in a tone of voice that seems comfortable to her, but some of the boys are zoning out. In some cases we might be able to fix the problem simply by putting the boy in the front row.

"You should write a book, Dr. Sax," one parent told me. "Write a book so that more teachers know about the differences in how girls and boys hear."

I allowed myself a patronizing smile. "I'm sure that there must already be such books for teachers, and for parents," I said.

"There aren't," she said.

"I'll find some for you," I said.

That conversation took place nearly twenty years ago. Since then I've read lots of popular books about differences between girls and boys. And guess what. That mom was right. Not only do most of the books currently in print about girls and boys fail to state the basic facts about innate differences between the sexes, but many of them promote a bizarre form of political correctness, suggesting that it is somehow chauvinistic even to hint that any innate differences exist between female and male. A tenured professor at Brown University published a book in which she claims that the division of the human race into two sexes, female and male, is an artificial invention of our culture. "Nature really offers us more than two sexes," she claims, adding, "Our current notions of masculinity and femininity are cultural conceits." The decision to "label" a child as a girl or a boy is "a *social* decision," according to this expert. We should not label any child as being *either* a girl *or* a boy, this professor proclaims. "There is no either/or. Rather, there are shades of difference."[1] This book received courteous mention in *The New York Times* and *The Washington Post*. America's most prestigious medical journal, *The New England Journal of Medicine*, praised the author for her "careful and insightful" approach to gender.[2]

I soon assembled a small library of books that counsel parents that the best child-rearing is *gender-neutral* child rearing. These books tell parents that true virtue is to be found in training your child to play with toys traditionally associated with the opposite sex. You should buy dolls for your son, to teach him how to nurture.[3] You should buy an Erector set for your daughter. The underlying assumptions—that giving dolls to boys will cause boys to become more nurturing, or that giving girls Erector sets will improve girls' spatial relations skills—are seldom questioned.

On the same bookshelf you can find books that do affirm the existence of innate differences in how girls and boys learn. But these books often promote antiquated and inaccurate gender stereotypes. "Girls are more emotional than boys." "Boys have a brain-based advantage when it comes to learning math." Those notions turn out to be false.

On one hand, you have books claiming that there are no innate differences between girls and boys, and that anybody who thinks otherwise is a reactionary stuck in the 1950s. On the other, you have books affirming innate differences between girls and boys—but these authors interpret these differences in a manner that reinforces gender stereotypes.

These books have only one thing in common. They are based less on fact and more on their authors' personal beliefs or political agendas—either to deny innate sex differences or to use sex differences in child development as a justification for maintaining traditional sex roles. After waiting for somebody else to write a book about girls and boys based on actual scientific research and clinical experience, I finally decided to write one myself.

Every child is unique. I will not suggest that all boys are the same or that all girls are the same. I know that they are not. I have been a medical doctor for more than thirty years. I am the veteran of thousands of office visits with girls and boys. But the fact that each child is unique and complex should not blind us to the fact that gender is one of the two great organizing principles in child development—the other principle being age. Trying to understand a child without understanding the role of gender in child development is like trying to understand a child's behavior without knowing the child's age. Pick up a book with a title like *What to Expect from Your Two-Year-Old*. That book is very different from *What to Expect from Your Eight-Year-Old*. Of course, nobody is saying that all two-year-olds are alike or that all eight-year-olds are alike. While recognizing diversity among two-year-olds, we can still have a meaningful discussion of the ways in which two-year-olds and eight-year-olds differ, categorically, in terms of what they can do, what they're interested in, how they relate to their parents, and so on.

At least with regard to how children hear and speak, gender may be even more fundamental to learning than age is. When the noted linguist and Georgetown University professor Deborah Tannen compared how girls and boys of different ages use language, she "was overwhelmed by the differences that separated the females and males at each age, and the striking similarities that linked the females, on one hand, and the males, on the other, across the vast expanse of age. In many ways, the second-grade girls were more like the twenty-five-year-old women than like the second-grade boys."[4]

The analogy to age differences provides a good way to think about sex differences. No two girls are alike, just as no two boys are alike. Seven-year-old Stephanie, who likes to roll in the mud and play soccer, is very different from seven-year-old Zoe. Zoe's favorite hobby is playing with her Barbies. Zoe also insisted on joining the Junior Poms, a sort of cheerleading group. Zoe was asking for lipstick at age five. Her mother, Barbara, a sincere old-school feminist, was horrified. "Where is this coming from?" she asked me, bewildered. "I only own one lipstick and I haven't used it in six months. And I loathe and despise Barbies. I've never even bought one for Zoe. She gets all that trash as gifts from her aunts and uncles."

Despite their differences, Stephanie may share more with Zoe than you might imagine. In their ability to listen, in their visual system, and in their willingness to affiliate with adults, as we will see, Stephanie may have more in common with Zoe than she has in common with her brother or with most boys.

The first edition of this book was published in 2005. In the years since, much new research has been published demonstrating important, hardwired differences between girls and boys. But few parents and teachers are aware of this research, because very little of it has been reported in the news media. In this updated edition I will share some of that research.

We will start with some astonishing new research showing big sex differences in the ability to smell, as well as new research on girl/boy differences in hearing and in vision. Next we will look at research on girl/boy differences in risk taking and in aggression.

In chapter 5 I will share some of what I have learned from my visits to more than four hundred schools over the past sixteen years about girl/boy differences in the classroom. When teachers understand those differences, the result is more boys who love Emily Dickinson and *Jane Eyre* and more girls who want to do computer coding.

In chapter 6 we will consider some recent research on girl/boy differences in sex itself: how girls and boys experience sexual motivation differently and often have different sexual agendas. The link between romance and sex appears to be constructed differently in most girls compared with most boys, as we will see. In chapter 7 we turn our attention to drugs and alcohol. Girls and boys both get addicted, but they get addicted in different ways and often via different pathways. The more you know about those differences, the better equipped you will be to safeguard your daughter or your son.

Chapter 8 is completely new for this edition. It's all about social media and video games. Snapchat and Instagram didn't exist when the first edition of this book was published in 2005. And in that bygone era, "playing a video game" meant playing on a console against another gamer using the same console, or against the computer itself. Online gaming as we know it today did not exist. Over the past decade, a great deal of research has been published on the effects of video games and social media. The more time girls spend on social media such as Snapchat and Instagram, the more likely they are to become anxious or depressed; but that's much less true of boys. Boys, on the other hand, are more likely to be spending many hours a week playing video games, which can undermine their social skills.

Chapters 9, 10, and 11 are devoted to girls and boys who don't fit gender-typical patterns. In chapter 9 we look at the latest research on gender-atypical girls and boys: the kinds of kids who used to be called "tomboys" and "sissies." Girls differ from one another. Boys differ from one another. Differences among girls and differences among boys are not just noise in the data. The differences are meaningful and consequential. Gender is complicated.

In chapter 10 our focus is on lesbian, gay, and bisexual kids. And in chapter 11 I will share with you my understanding of the research on intersex and transgender individuals. These three chapters—9, 10, and 11—form a unit. In order to understand some of the research that I present in chapter 11 on transgender individuals, it's helpful to know about the research in chapter 9 on the androgen receptor. So if you are going to read these three chapters, I hope you will read them in order.

In the final chapter, chapter 12, I try to make sense of how we as parents can use all this information to help our children grow up to be all that they were meant to be. There's no going back to the bad old days of the 1950s, when girls and boys were pigeonholed into pink and blue cubbies. But what does it mean to affirm and cherish gender differences in the modern era, when girls and boys can be anything they want to be? That's one of the questions we will consider in the closing chapter, and throughout the book.

In the twelve years since the publication of the first edition, a world of new research on gender differences has been published. Much of this research is not well known outside of scholarly circles. You will discover that new research here. Gender is complicated, as I said. But gender matters.

There is more at stake here than the old question of nature versus nurture. The failure to recognize and respect sex differences in child development has done substantial harm—such will be my claim throughout this book. I will try to convince you that the lack of awareness of gender differences has had the unintended result of reinforcing gender stereotypes. The result is more girls uploading sexualized and provocative photos to their Instagram and Snapchat and more boys spending hours playing violent video games in which they pretend to be macho warriors or villains. You may not yet see the connection between gender-blind upbringing and gender-stereotyped outcomes. In this book I will show you that connection. Just as important, the growing confusion about gender is contributing to a rise in anxiety and depression among girls and disengagement among boys.

I have been encouraged by all the readers who have contacted me over the past twelve years to tell me how valuable the first edition of *Why Gender Matters* has been to them—in parenting, in working with troubled youth, in teaching, in pastoral work, in juvenile justice. I have written this new edition with you in mind: the mother, the father, the social worker, the teacher, the school administrator, the pastor, the rabbi, the imam, the probation officer. I hope you find it useful.

CHAPTER 2

Smelling, Seeing, and Hearing

A marriage is risky business these days . . .
History and experience both make clear
That men and women do not hear
The music of the world in the same key . . .
So what is left to justify a marriage?
Maybe only the hunch that half the world
Will ever be present in any room
With just a single pair of eyes to see it.
Whatever is invisible to one
Is to the other an enormous golden lion . . .

—Bill Holm, "Wedding Poem for Schele and Phil"

Smelling

For eighteen years I practiced in a suburb of Washington, DC, in Montgomery County, Maryland. A husband and wife I knew—let's call them Jennifer and Tom—went away for a one-week vacation in August. Shortly after they returned home, Jennifer came to see me. "When we got home from vacation, I stepped into my kitchen and I thought I would die from the smell," Jennifer said. "It reeked. It's hard to describe the stench. Imagine a rotting carcass on a pile of chicken poop." (Actually Jennifer didn't say "poop"; she used a different word.) "And it was hot. We had left the air-conditioning off while we were away. But when we turned the air-conditioning back on, that just seemed to make it worse. It blew the smell all through the house. And I'm pretty sure whatever died—something must have died—was in the ductwork somewhere. I think I smelled that smell, or just a trace of it, before we left. But whatever it was, it was a million times more powerful when we got back home. So I told my husband, 'We need to hire somebody, a contractor or a ductwork person, to come out and find out what died and *clean it out.*' And do you know what my husband said?"

"No," I said.

"He said, '*I* don't smell anything.' Can you believe it? I think he must just be trying to annoy me. Either that or he truly is a pig raised in a barn."

Two days later, Tom came to see me. He said, "My wife is being a witch." (Actually he didn't say "witch"; he used a different word.) "She keeps going on and on about how we have to hire somebody to clean out our ductwork or rip open the wall or something, to figure out where some godawful smell is coming from. But *I do not smell anything.* And I'll be darned if I'm going to spend a pile of money trying to get rid of a smell I can't even smell." (Actually he didn't say "darned.")

I told Tom the same thing I told Jennifer. The sense of smell is different between women and men. It's entirely plausible that a woman could perceive an odor that is—for the woman— overpoweringly awful, while the man doesn't smell anything. The best approach is for each partner to respect and trust the other's report. If you're a woman and your husband says he doesn't smell anything, don't call him a pig. Explain to him that even though he doesn't smell the horrible stench, you do smell it.

If you're a man and your wife says that there is an overpowering odor that is giving her a headache, don't call her a witch. Respect the fact that under certain circumstances, women may perceive odors that men can't detect.

What's the evidence?

In the laboratory Dr. Pamela Dalton and her colleagues exposed men and women to several smells. Not just once, but over and over again. Dr. Dalton and her coworkers found that with repeated exposure, the women's ability to detect the odor improved. How much did it improve? By a factor of 50 percent? Or maybe by 500 percent—a fivefold improvement? No, the *average* improvement for women was an improvement of 100,000-fold: the women were able to detect the odor at a concentration one 100,000th of the concentration they had needed at the beginning of the study.

What about the men? Did they show a similar improvement—a 100,000-fold increase in sensitivity? No, they did not. Okay, how about a thousandfold improvement? Nope. How about just a hundredfold improvement? Sorry. The men, on average, showed *no improvement at all* in their ability to detect the odor.[1]

Jennifer hired a service to clean out the ductwork. The men did indeed find two dead rats, which were the source of the pungent odor. The rats had died in a small puddle of trapped water, which seemed to have made the smell worse.

Here's what I think happened. The rats must have died at least a few days before the family left on vacation: Jennifer said there was a trace of the odor before she left. Each time Jennifer came into the house before she left on vacation, she was being exposed to the odor, something like the subjects in Dr. Dalton's study. With each successive exposure, she was becoming more sensitive to the odor. Then she and Tom and their kids went away on vacation. When she came back, the odor was much stronger because the rats had been rotting in the warm ductwork. But Tom didn't smell anything at all.

How is that possible? What's going on in the anatomy of the olfactory system—the system we use to smell—that can account for such huge differences between female and male?

Quick anatomy lesson: Smell receptors in the nose send their signals via the olfactory nerve to the olfactory bulb. The olfactory bulb is located on the bottom side of the brain. The olfactory bulb is the first stop for information about smell.

There are two kinds of cells in the brain: *Neurons* are considered the most important, because they seem to play the most important role in sending information via electrical signals. But *glial* cells are essential too, because they provide structure and may also modulate information processing in the brain.[2]

On all counts women beat men. Women have more cells in the olfactory bulb: 16.2 million in the average woman, compared with 9.2 million in men. When you look just at the neurons in the olfactory bulb, the average woman has 6.9 million, compared with just 3.5 million in males. When you look at the glial cells, women again have more: 9.3 million in the average woman compared with 5.7 million in the average man. All these differences are highly statistically significant.[3]

When I read this report about sex differences in the olfactory bulb, I thought of my visit to girls' schools and boys' schools near Hastings, New Zealand (single-sex schools are very popular in New Zealand). I met with girls from Nga Tawa, a girls' school.

The school leaders had arranged an optional cocurricular activity with a nearby boys' school, a ballroom dancing club, which met in the evening. But administrators at both schools were discouraged, because the club was not popular with the girls. There were many more boys than girls in attendance. The boys refused to dance with other boys, so half the boys were sitting and watching other boys dancing with the girls. Each week there were fewer girls in attendance.

I asked the girls, "Why don't you want to go to the ballroom dancing club?" One of the girls answered, "I can't stand those *smelly* boys putting their hands on me!" Then I met with the boys. I asked them, "Do you take a shower before you go to the ballroom dancing club?" All the boys shook their heads no. I asked, "Why not?" One of the boys answered, "No need. I don't smell bad." I told that boy and the other boys: "You have *no idea* how you smell to a girl. You're not a girl. You can't smell odors the way a girl can smell odors. You need to go home and shower, *with soap*, before you go to the ballroom dancing club!"

If you're a mother, and you have a son, and his room stinks, don't say: "What's wrong with you? How can you stand the stench?" If your son's room doesn't smell good, begin by asking your son whether he thinks his room smells bad. If he says no, explain to him that his room *does* smell, but he can't smell it. Explain that good hygiene means keeping the room clean, even if he doesn't think it smells bad. And "clean" may mean something different to you, his mother, than it does to your son. Explain that your definition, not his, is the standard that will be enforced. Explain that learning to conform to a woman's standard of cleanliness is a useful life skill for any man, if he hopes someday to live with a female partner.

As I said, I have been a medical doctor for more than thirty years. I have seen many marriages end. On television, when marriages end, there's often a romantic affair going on: one of the partners is cheating on the other. In the real world, in my observation, romantic affairs are less often the cause of divorce. Many busy parents just don't have time for that sort of thing. The disintegration of a marriage often begins with miscommunication of just the sort that I described between Jennifer and Tom. Before they met with me, they were angry with each other. Jennifer thought Tom was belittling her concern about the bad smell. Tom thought Jennifer was being unnecessarily fussy, complaining about an odor that he couldn't smell. That sort of problem, repeated over and over, can lead to a loss of affection. But once Tom and Jennifer understood what was going on, they could understand each other better, with good humor and with an understanding of their differences.

Hearing

Remember that story I shared in chapter 1, about the second-grade boy in "Ms. Gentlevoice's" classroom who wasn't paying attention? I have been involved in many cases like that over the years. Some of those boys did better, as I mentioned, when you moved them to the front row, or when you moved them to a classroom with a teacher who spoke more loudly. (Simply asking Ms. Gentlevoice to speak more loudly seldom works, I discovered; Ms. Gentlevoice may make an effort for a day or two or even a week or two, but eventually she is likely to revert to her usual style.)

In the first edition of *Why Gender Matters*, I tried to understand why some boys do better with a teacher who speaks more loudly. I didn't do a very good job. I cited research on hearing *thresholds*: the softest tone that can be heard. The threshold for the average girl or woman is quieter than for the average boy or man, but the girl/boy difference is not huge and there is lots of overlap between the sexes. And it turns out sex differences in hearing *thresholds* aren't really relevant to differences in how girls and boys experience midrange sounds well above the threshold.

In my defense, the first study to adequately explain this phenomenon—of boys not hearing the quiet-voiced teacher—was not published until 2007, two years after the publication of *Why Gender Matters*. The research is a bit technical, so I have put my discussion of the research into the Extra Stuff: Sex Differences in Hearing at the end of the book (page 317). Here's the bottom line: For the average boy to hear you as well as the average girl, you have to speak about eight decibels more loudly. A difference of eight decibels is about three clicks on the volume dial of a typical car radio. It doesn't mean shouting. It does mean speaking more loudly. If you're a mother and you feel that your son is ignoring you, try speaking just a bit more loudly.

This works the other way as well. A girl in my practice complained that her father was always shouting at her. It wasn't what he said that bothered her but the way that he spoke: He was too loud. "Annoying," she said. She told me that she just slips into her bedroom and closes the door. She was avoiding contact with her own father because she didn't like to be shouted at.

A few days later I spoke with Dad. I mentioned that his daughter indicated that he sometimes raised his voice with her. "I have never *ONCE* raised my voice to that child! You hear what I'm sayin' to you?!" Dad said to me, very loudly, almost shouting. I explained that sensitivity to loudness varies as a function of age and also of biological sex. Girls and women are—on average—

more sensitive to sounds than boys or men of the same age (again, see the Extra Stuff at the end of the book for more data on this point). Also, children and teenagers are more sensitive to sounds than middle-aged people are. I explained that as a middle-aged man speaking to a teenage daughter, he was much less sensitive to sound than she was. He didn't think he was shouting. But his daughter was experiencing something close to shouting. I suggested that the next time he spoke to his daughter, he should make an effort to speak much more quietly.

A few weeks later I saw his daughter again. "Totally amazing," she said. "My dad can actually talk like a normal person." She wasn't avoiding him anymore.

Seeing

Twenty years ago, a little boy named Andrew Phillips (his true name) came home from school on the brink of tears. The teacher had given each of the children in the class a small box of crayons and a blank sheet of white paper. "Let's have a little creative time. Draw whatever you want," the teacher had said.

Andrew had used his black crayon to draw two stick figures stabbing each other with knives. Other kids in the class (who happened to be mostly girls) had drawn colorful pictures of people and pets and flowers and trees. The people in the girls' pictures had hair on their heads; they had clothes on their bodies. Andrew's stick figures had none of these adornments. The teacher praised the girls' drawings but not Andrew's.

Andrew came home upset. His mother, Janet, arranged to speak to the teacher, who was unapologetic. "Actually, I considered making a referral," the teacher said.

"A referral? What do you mean?" Janet asked.

"A referral to mental health. After all, he did draw two people attacking each other with knives."

"But he's a six-year-old *boy*," Janet said.

"Of course he is, and that's why I decided against initiating the referral."

A child's choice of what he wants to draw says something important about him. A boy who wants to draw pictures of warriors fighting is a different sort of child from the girl (or boy) who wants to draw friends or pets or flowers.

Here's an old fable:

> *Nasrudin was the chief keeper of ornamental birds for the king. One day, walking about the royal grounds, he saw a falcon that had alighted on a tree. He took out his scissors and trimmed the claws, the wings, and the beak of the falcon. "That is at least some improvement," he said. "Your keeper had evidently been neglecting you."*
>
> *Moral: You cannot turn a falcon into a robin or a dove. You will merely succeed in ruining the falcon.*[4]

The teacher had said, "Why can't you draw something less violent? Something more like what Melissa drew, or Emily?" But what Andrew heard was *Why do you have to be who you are? Why can't you be someone else?* Why do you have to be a falcon? Why can't you be a robin or a dove?

Andrew's mom pulled him out of the well-regarded private coed school he was attending and transferred him to Mater Dei, an all-boys school in Bethesda, Maryland. Before long he was drawing again. The teachers at the boys' schools weren't so insistent on the boys using lots of different colors or drawing faces with eyes and mouths and hair. Instead, the teachers helped the boys to make their action pictures more exciting, more vivid. And they asked the boys to tell the stories behind the pictures. Andrew loved telling stories about heroes and dragons and battles. One of his drawings, from second grade, is shown below. The caption reads "He shook his lance and it shot a lazer and it cilled the dragon. But it was stilt ULIV."

Andrew blossomed at the boys' school. He became not only an artist but also a writer, an actor, and an athlete. And what an athlete. Andrew grew into the most talented athlete I have seen in my three decades as a physician. By the time he graduated from high school, he was six feet four inches tall, 290 pounds of solid muscle. He was recruited by many of the top NCAA Division I football programs. He chose Stanford because it had the best academics of any program offering him a scholarship. At Stanford

He shook his lance and it shot a lazer and it cilled the dragon.
But it was stilt ULIV.

he majored in the classics, studying Latin and Greek. And he was a starting lineman on the astonishing Stanford team that rose into the top 10 during Andrew's years at Stanford, helped not only by Andrew but also by Andrew's friend, another Andrew named Andrew Luck.

You don't need a boys' school to achieve results like Andrew's. You do need teachers who understand and respect the differences between girls and boys.

What happens when you give girls and boys a blank piece of paper and a box of crayons and ask them to draw whatever they want to draw? Researchers who have conducted such studies consistently find that girls are more likely to draw flowers and trees and pets, with lots of colors. The people in the girls' drawings have eyes, mouths, hair, and clothes. A few boys do draw pictures just like the girls draw. In chapter 9 we will learn that those gender-atypical boys—boys who draw pictures like those the girls draw—have other features in common with other gender-atypical boys.

But the great majority of boys draw pictures that are quite different from the girls' pictures: Most boys draw a scene of action at a moment of dynamic change, like a monster eating an alien or a rocket smashing into a planet. Human figures, if present, are often just stick figures, lacking eyes, mouth, hair, and clothes.

Some teachers have figured out these boy/girl differences on their own. But many teachers have not. And you can't blame the teachers. I have met teachers who have master's degrees in early elementary education from leading universities such as the Harvard Graduate School of Education or the University of Texas at Austin, and yet those teachers have never been told about these boy/girl differences. On the contrary: the teachers have been taught that when a six-year-old draws a human figure, that figure should have eyes, a mouth, and hair; and if those features are lacking, then the student should be corrected. The underlying, unspoken assumption is that there is just one right way for children to draw: with lots of colors and detail. The boys' pictures often don't fulfill these criteria. And boys who draw pictures with violent themes—such as a knight killing a dragon—are often told, subtly or not, that they are out of bounds. Sometimes the correction is gentle: "Andrew, why do you have to draw something so violent? Now look at Emily's pretty picture of the cute puppy—why can't you draw something like that?" Sometimes the correction is more emphatic. I heard from one parent whose young son was disciplined because the boy's drawing of a Roman gladiator beheading another gladiator violated the school's "zero tolerance" policy on violence and depictions of violence.

One result is that many boys disengage from visual arts. I visited a second-grade classroom in an American elementary school. The teacher said "Free time! You can do whatever you want!" Some of the girls sat in the center of the classroom and began coloring. One boy started running around the room making buzzing noises. After watching him for a minute, I got in his way and I stopped him. I pointed at the girls and I said, "How come you don't want to sit and draw?" The boy responded, without hesitation or apology: "Drawing is for girls."

Drawing is for girls. Where did he get that idea? I'm sure the teacher never said, "Drawing is for girls." But she might as well have. By praising and *understanding* pictures of people, pets, flowers, and trees, with lots of colors—but not really comprehending the point of a picture all in black crayon of a knight killing a dragon—that teacher is unintentionally sending the message that drawing is for girls. **The lack of awareness of gender differences has the unintended consequence of *reinforcing* gender**

stereotypes. The result is a culture in which many boys believe that "drawing is for girls." Last year, fewer than one in four students who took the AP Exam in Studio Art were boys.[5] There's nothing innate about that. Men are perfectly capable of creating great art. But in modern American culture, very few boys *want* to study art. They have been turned off by a gender-blind culture that—because of its gender blindness—inadvertently sends the message that "drawing is for girls."

While there may not be any innate difference in the *ability* to draw, I do think the evidence clearly demonstrates a big difference in what kind of drawings girls and boys *want* to draw. In every culture researchers have studied—in Africa, Asia, Europe, and North America—girls are more likely to draw pictures of flowers and pets, using lots of colors; while boys are more likely to draw scenes of actions, using fewer colors.[6] In my visits to more than four hundred schools over the past sixteen years, I have learned that when teachers understand these differences, they can break down gender stereotypes, and the same boy who loves football and video games will also love to draw.

There is now growing evidence that these differences in the kind of drawings boys and girls like to make may derive in substantial part from hardwired differences in the visual system. I present some of this evidence in the Extra Stuff: Sex Differences in Vision at the end of the book (page 325). All of us humans have two visual systems inside our heads. One system is devoted to color, detail, and texture. The other is devoted to speed and direction—especially to changes in direction. The evidence I cite in the Extra Stuff section suggests that girls and women have more resources in the system that specializes in color, detail, and texture. Boys and men have more resources in the system that specializes in speed and direction.

There has been a feminization of American education, especially in the early years. The result is that the female perspective has become normative. That's a fancy way of saying that the female way of seeing things is now so ingrained that nobody's even aware of it. *Of course* a picture of a human figure should have eyes, a mouth, hair, and clothes. How could anyone suggest otherwise?

But here's the good news: I have seen firsthand how dramatically the classroom can change when teachers (both women and men) have one day's training in these differences. Just explain to the teacher that most boys want to draw *action*, not color and texture. Remind teachers that the job of the teacher is to help the boy draw the picture *he* wants to draw: more vivid, more evocative of the action. Sometimes just drawing a few lines to signify the wind or the whoosh of the car can brighten the boy's face. Women teachers can do this just as well as men can. We'll talk more about some of these strategies in chapter 5.

CHAPTER 3

Risk

The secret to getting the most fun out of life is: to live dangerously.
Build your cities on the slopes of Vesuvius! Send your ships into
unknown seas! Live at war with your peers and with yourself!

—Friedrich Nietzsche, 1887[1]

Tossing the Ring

Let's suppose you're a college freshman taking introductory psychology. One of the course requirements includes "volunteering" as a subject in a study. You choose the ring-toss study, because the course guide says it will take only twenty minutes and no needles are involved.

You show up for the study. The technician shows you what you're supposed to do. There's a one-foot pole standing upright on the floor. You are given six rubber rings, each about the size of a horseshoe. The technician tells you to toss the rings at the pole, one ring at a time. The object of the game is to land the ring right on the pole.

"Where do I stand?" you ask, noticing that the floor is marked off one foot from the target, two feet, five feet, ten feet, fifteen feet, and twenty feet.

"Anywhere you like," the assistant says.

"You mean I could do all the tosses from one foot away?" you ask.

The technician nods.

"Do I have to hit the target a certain percentage of times?"

"No," the technician answers. "Just toss the six rings, and we'll move on to the next part of the experiment. I'll step out of the room to give you some privacy."

"Privacy?" you ask, but the technician is already gone.

What do you do now? Most young women will stand one or two feet away from the target, toss the rings, and move on. Most young men stand five or ten feet away from the target, even though doing so greatly increases their risk of missing the target.[2]

You toss the rings.

"Okay, now we move on to the next part of the experiment," the assistant says. A door opens and in step two of your classmates. You nod and say hello. The sex of the two classmates is the same as yours. (If you're a woman, they're female.) The two classmates are asked to sit in chairs along the wall, facing you.

"Okay, now we do it again," the assistant says, handing you the rings again.

Most young women will toss the rings just the same when other women are present as they do when they are by themselves. But most young men behave differently. When other young men are watching, most young men will demonstrate what psychologists call a "risky shift."[3] If the man tossed the rings from two feet when he was alone, he'll back up to five feet when other men are in the room. If he tossed the rings from five feet when he was alone, he'll back up to ten feet when other men are watching—

even if he's never met the men before and never expects to see them again. "I guess I didn't want them to think I was a wuss" is the way one explained the change in his behavior.

Living Dangerously

Many boys enjoy taking physical risks. And the majority of boys are impressed by other boys who take risks, especially if the risk taker succeeds. Girls are less likely to enjoy physical risk taking for its own sake and are much less likely to be impressed by risk-taking behavior in others.[4] In another study boys and girls both engaged in the same risky activity, but girls experienced the risk as less fun and more stressful.[5] Girls may be *willing* to take risks, but they are less likely to *seek out* risky situations just for the sake of living dangerously.

Imagine yourself back in middle school. Suppose you heard about a friend who rode a bicycle off of a twelve-foot-high board-walk and landed on a sandy beach. Just for fun. Boys who engage in that kind of risk-taking behavior will likely raise their status in the eyes of their peers. "Did you hear what Brett did? Rode his bike off the top of the boardwalk! Awesome!" Even if they fail, those boys are likely to earn the respect of other boys for trying.

If girls heard about another girl who rode her bike on purpose off the top of a twelve-foot-high boardwalk, they would be less likely to ooh and aah. They might even be critical. "She must be totally nuts to do something like that. What a weirdo," another girl might say.

Another example, this time with high school kids. Suppose a twelfth-grade boy goes to a party Friday night and has un-protected sex with a college woman he's just met, and then on

Saturday night he goes to another party and has unprotected sex with a different young woman. His buddies will be impressed, especially if the boys glimpsed the two women and consider them to be pretty. "You da *man*," they might say, and give him a high five.

Suppose now that the same thing happens, but with the genders reversed. A twelfth-grade girl goes to a party Friday night and has unprotected sex with a college man she's just met, and then on Saturday night she goes to another party and has unprotected sex with a different man. If her girlfriends find out about her exploits, they are *not* likely to be favorably impressed, regardless of whether the men in question are good-looking or not: they are more likely to think she's a slut, or insanely reckless, or both.[6]

Girls and boys assess risk differently, and they differ in their likelihood of engaging in risky behaviors. As soon as kids are old enough to toddle across the floor, boys are significantly more likely to do something dangerous: put their fingers in an electric socket, try to stand on a basketball, jump off a chair onto the floor.[7] And when parents try to stop their child from doing something risky, boys are less likely to comply. Studies in the United States and around the world universally find that boys are more likely to engage in physically risky activities.[8] Boys are more likely than girls to be seriously injured or killed in accidents such as drowning, misuse of firearms, or head injury related to riding a bicycle.[9]

Psychologist Barbara Morrongiello interviewed children ages six through ten who had been injured or who had been in "close calls." She found that compared with the girls . . .

- boys were more likely to attribute their injuries *erroneously* to "bad luck" rather than to any lack of skill or foresight on their part;

- boys were less likely to tell their parents about the injury;

- boys were more likely to be around other boys at the time the injury occurred.[10] A boy is more likely to do something dangerous or stupid when he's with a group of boys than when he is by himself.

Lizette Peterson and her associates at the University of Missouri wanted to study sex differences in children's responses to risky situations. They set up a video game in which kids rode a stationary bicycle while watching an interactive video screen. The simulation was so realistic that when the bicycle on the screen went under the branch of a tree, some kids ducked their heads. Then the kids suddenly confronted a hazard: in some cases just a coiled garden hose blocking the path; in other cases more dangerous situations, such as an oncoming car swerving suddenly from the opposing lane so that the car was about to hit the kid head on. The bike was wired so that Peterson and her colleagues could measure how quickly the kids stepped on the brake to avoid a collision.

I wouldn't want to be sitting on the back of a bike if one of those boys was riding it. The boys were much slower to brake than the girls were. If the simulation had been real, many of the boys would have sustained life-threatening injuries. The boys were also more likely to report feeling *exhilarated* by the simulated collision, whereas girls were far more likely to report feeling *fearful*.[11]

So one reason many boys engage in physically dangerous activities may be that *the danger itself* gives the activity a pleasant tingle. That's a tough concept for some women to grasp. A mother who warns her son, "Don't ride your bike off the boardwalk. You might get hurt," has missed the point. Her son knows it's dangerous. He's riding his bike off the boardwalk *because* it's dangerous.

Researchers at Boston University asked a simple question: why are most drowning victims male? The data are striking. Among teenagers fifteen to nineteen years of age, boys are 9.8 times more likely to die in a drowning accident than girls are. Among young adults twenty to twenty-four years of age, young men are 10.4 times more likely to die in a drowning accident than young women are. In other words, among young people fifteen to twenty-four years of age, boys and young men are about *ten times* more likely to die in a drowning accident than girls and young women are.[12] How come?

Imagine a group of girls walking along a Florida beach in summertime. They see a sign that says WARNING: RIP TIDE ZONE! DON'T SWIM HERE! GO OVER THERE → AND SWIM WHERE THE LIFEGUARD IS. Most girls will say, "Hey, we probably shouldn't swim here. Let's go swim over there, where it's safer." Now imagine a group of teenage boys walking along the same beach, looking at the same sign. There's a good chance that one of the boys will snort and say, "Rip tide? Ha! That's just water! I'm stronger than water!" He plunges in—and he may be washed to his death.

The Boston University psychologists concluded that a major contributor might be that boys and young men "probably overestimate their swimming ability . . . placing themselves in riskier aquatic situations than women."[13] By the time the boy discovers his error, it may be too late.

Likewise, epidemiologists at the University of Pittsburgh have found that males are much more likely to die in thunderstorms than females are. Many of those deaths occur when a flash flood blocks a road. A female driver, encountering a stretch of road under water, is likely to do the sensible thing: turn around and find another way. Male drivers, on the other hand, are more likely than female drivers to drive right into the water—and die.[14]

So that may be another reason why boys are more likely to engage in physically risky activities. It seems that boys systematically *overestimate* their own ability and/or *underestimate* risk.

Gender stereotypes may be playing a role here. When kids are asked which child—a girl or a boy—is most likely to get hurt when riding a bike, climbing a tree, etc., girls and boys agree that the girl is more likely to get hurt. In fact, the reality is just the opposite: *boys* are more likely to get hurt.[15] The majority of our entertainment, of our television and movies and novels and stories and video games, continues to show the boy saving the girl or the man saving the woman. There are some exceptions—one of my favorites is the character of Rey in the latest Star Wars movies—but they remain exceptions. That bias toward risk-taking males in the majority of cultural programming may be partly to blame for boys' overestimation of their abilities.

But we should be careful before we march down the same road as those 1970s-era scholars who believed that sex differences derive primarily from cultural influences. For one thing, a similar phenomenon—the male taking greater risks—has been observed in primates such as monkeys, baboons, and chimpanzees. Studying a wildlife refuge for Japanese macaque monkeys, researchers Linda Marie Fedigan and Sandra Zohar wanted to find out why there were so many more adult females than males. Although the ratio of female to male monkeys was roughly 1:1 at birth, by adulthood there were as many as *five* females for every one surviving male. What happened to all the other male monkeys? And why isn't a similarly imbalanced sex ratio seen in zoos? Fedigan and Zohar considered many possible explanations, such as:

- The "fragile male" hypothesis: maybe the males are just more susceptible to illness and disease;

- The predator hypothesis: maybe the males are not as good at escaping predators;

- The risk hypothesis: maybe the males engage in more dangerous behaviors;

- The mutant hypothesis: maybe the males are more likely to carry harmful mutations (this is actually a variation on the "fragile male" hypothesis).

After carefully reviewing twenty-one years of data, Fedigan and Zohar found support only for the risk hypothesis. "Males are mainly lost to the population because of their risk-taking behaviors." Male monkeys do wild and crazy things, just like teenage boys. For example, these researchers found that male monkeys take stupid risks around highways: they try to scamper across a highway, only to be crushed by an oncoming truck. Female monkeys are much less likely to take the same risks. They tend to avoid highways.[16]

These differences appear to be largely inborn. It's hard to argue that male monkeys overestimate their abilities because they've been watching too much James Bond or playing too many video games. We have to consider the possibility that the tendency for male primates—including boys and young men—to do insanely dangerous things may be at least in part innate, rather than culturally programmed.

Dare Training

If you have a son, you need to understand his motivation so you'll be able to keep him from riding his bike off a cliff. Parents of daughters need to understand this issue too, from another perspective. Most young girls need some encouragement to take risks, the right kind of risks, and to raise their estimation of their own abilities.

Many gender-based inequities persist in our society. Men remain far more likely to be CEOs of major corporations, despite the fact that there is now a substantial cohort of equally well-trained women. Only twenty-six of the *Fortune* 500 companies are led by women CEOs, a proportion that hasn't changed much in the past thirty years.[17]

Consider the gender gap in income. The average woman in the United States working full time still earns less than the average man earns. Some of that difference is explained by differences in occupation. The average software engineer with a master's degree in software engineering earns more than the average elementary school teacher with a master's degree in elementary education. Most software engineers are men. Most elementary school teachers are women.

But even when you control for occupation, education, and hours worked, a significant gender gap in pay persists: about ninety-two cents for women for every dollar earned by a man in the same job, according to the most recent estimates.[18] Men are still getting paid more than women do for doing the same work, on average, in most fields, with a few exceptions: actuarial and accounting work, for example, is one of the few fields where men and women do earn the same.[19]

Economist Linda Babcock studied students graduating from Carnegie Mellon University with a master's degree in a business-related field. She found that the starting salaries of the men were about 8 percent higher on average than those of the women: the men were paid about $4,000 more. Babcock then looked to see who had *asked* for more money during the job-finding process. It turned out that only 7 percent of the female students had asked, compared with 57 percent of the men. Controlling for gender, Babcock found that students who asked for more money received a starting salary that was $4,053 higher on average than students who didn't ask. In other words, the gender gap could be explained by the fact that the women *hadn't asked* for more money.[20]

Asking for more money when you've just received a job offer is taking a risk. You might give offense to a prospective employer. You might give the impression of being greedy. You might conceivably lose the job or start off in your new job on the wrong foot. So most women don't ask. And those who don't ask don't get.

To be successful, *really* successful in business, you have to be willing to take those kinds of risks. You want your daughter to be able to do that. To take a risk when the moment is right. How can you empower her to have that kind of self-confidence?

My first suggestion: *don't* do what your neighbors do, if your neighbors are typical North American parents. Parents in North America are more likely to shield their girls from risks and less likely to praise them for engaging in risky activities such as climbing trees or riding a bike hands free. I myself have observed enormous differences in the way parents respond when their child is injured. Fourteen-year-old Jason injured his back playing JV football. He could barely walk. Dad helped his wounded warrior stagger into my office. Dad was concerned, of course, but I also detected a note of pride. "It was a goal-line stand. They had the ball on our two-yard line. Fourth down. Fourth quarter. Jason just threw himself at the running back. Sacrificed his body totally. Stopped the other guy cold. We took over on downs and won the game." I checked the X-rays: everything was fine. Neurological exam was normal. I reassured Dad that Jason just had a bad muscle spasm from the injury. I recommended a few days off from sports, soaking in a warm bath, and a muscle relaxant. Dad's first question: "So when can Jason get back on the field?"

I saw a very similar injury in a fourteen-year-old girl playing field hockey. Tracy also could barely walk. *Both* Mom and Dad accompanied Tracy to my office. Once again the X-rays were normal. The neurological exam was normal. I reassured the parents that Tracy just had a muscle spasm. I recommended a few days off from sports, soaking in a warm bath, and a muscle relaxant, just as I had for Jason. Parents' first question: "Do you think Tracy should give up field hockey? Maybe she's just not cut out for it. Or at least she should take the rest of the season off?"

The difference in the parents' reaction is striking. It's so remarkable, I've begun calling parents' attention to it. "Suppose Tracy were a boy with the exact same injury. Would you be thinking about taking your child out of the sport?" I ask them. "No, you wouldn't," I say, while they're still hesitating. "You'd be saying things like 'Walk it off. Work it out. You can do it.'"

What are good ways to get girls to be more comfortable with risk taking? Margrét Pála Ólafsdóttir, an educator in Iceland, has developed a program for young girls that she calls "dare training." The idea first occurred to her during a field trip for girls only. It was a warm day, and some of the girls took off their shoes and socks. On an impulse, she encouraged *all* the girls to take off their shoes and socks and run around on the stones and pebbles in the park (you have to wonder whether a teacher in our more litigious American society would have had the courage). Then she dared them to dance. One girl moaned when a stone hurt her foot. "What can we do instead of complaining when it hurts?" Ólafsdóttir asked the girls. "Sing," suggested one of the girls. "And so we did," Ólafsdóttir says. "Sang and danced all the way [back to the school]—barefooted. We felt like superwomen."

The girls were "joyful and proud that they had discovered a new world," Ólafsdóttir wrote. Inspired, Ólafsdóttir hauled mattresses into the girls' kindergarten. She stacked the mattresses on the floor, put a table next to the mattresses, and encouraged the girls to jump from the table onto the mattresses, with an invitation to scream as they jumped. Because "an important part of the [stereotypical] female role is to keep quiet and because noise is not integrated into girls' play, it became obvious that training in making noise and using the voice should be part of the 'daring' exercises," Ólafsdóttir wrote. Soon the girls' room was almost as loud as the boys' room. When the girls said it was too easy to jump from a table onto a mattress, "we just put another table on top of the first one—and at last a chair on top of everything."

Once the girls understood that they had a teacher who *wanted* them to take risks, they started creating their own challenges. They tossed raw eggs high in the air and caught them without breaking them (sometimes). They squirted one another with water pistols. One girl built a high wall out of sponge-foam bricks. "What are you going to do?" Ólafsdóttir asked the girl. "Jump over the wall!" the girl shouted back. The wall was obviously too high. But "how could I destroy her faith after months of developing a new self-image?" Ólafsdóttir asked herself.

> [The little girl] climbed up, took a deep breath and jumped directly on to the wall, which collapsed. The whole group laughed but our heroine was not sure how she should react and looked to me for help. . . . I thought of my own experience of not feeling good enough no matter how hard we try, until at last we stop trying, lose our confidence and stop taking risks. . . . That is how we are kept in the old role of passivity and stopped from trying new things. . . . [That little girl] had found the perfect way. We have to train away the old fear of mistakes that holds us back. . . . I gave the girls exactly this speech though in different words.[21]

This story highlights a problem with this approach. If a girl takes a risk and fails, she may end up being *more* risk averse, not less. Ólafsdóttir acknowledges this hazard. "The feeling of weakness and inability and the tendency to low self-esteem are so integrated into girls' thinking, that [this] training can be counterproductive if we do not know exactly what we are doing." Start with something the girls know they can do, then gradually let them build up that wall, stretch their abilities to the limit.

Freycinet

Let's go back to Lizette Peterson's study, where she rigged up a stationary bike so kids could "ride" through a hazardous environment. Peterson then asked all the *parents* whether their kids had ever been injured riding a bike, injured badly enough to require medical attention. She found that kids who had been injured were *less* fearful doing the simulation than kids who had never been injured—even after controlling for the degree of confidence kids felt riding bicycles. She calls this the "invulnerability" effect. When a kid has fallen and (let's say) scraped a knee or gotten a cut, they recover. One week later that kid is thinking, *Hey, that wasn't so bad. I got hurt and now I'm fine.*

Girls in particular benefit from "dare training," to use Ólafsdóttir's term once again. Trying to jump over the wall, and failing, and getting bruised, and then discovering that she can *get over it* is a good way to build your daughter's courage and inner strength. Let me give you another example of a "dare training" program, which I observed on my six trips to Australia—except that they don't call it "dare training." They call it "abseiling." In the United States we call it "rappelling down a cliff."

Lauriston is a girls' school in Melbourne, Australia, that I have visited on two occasions. (Girls' schools are much more common in Australia than in the United States.) When the girls are in Year 9—our ninth grade—every girl is required to spend the year at the school's facility at Howqua, a remote area in the mountainous forest three hours north of Melbourne, near Mansfield. It's a year of rugged hikes and no mobile-phone service. The girls live in cabins in the woods. And *every* girl is required to participate in the abseiling program.

Jen Willis, who was then director of outdoor education at Lauriston, told me about a Lauriston girl who was quiet and shy. The girl was very bright and did well in classroom work, although she didn't speak much in class. She didn't like to raise her hand or to speak in front of others, and when she did speak she spoke in a very quiet voice, almost a whisper. And this girl, let's call her Kyra, was terrified of heights. She begged Ms. Willis not to make her do the abseil down the cliff. But Ms. Willis insisted—and besides, Ms. Willis didn't have the authority to excuse Kyra. *Every* girl is required to do the training for the abseil and to do the abseil itself. No exceptions.

When the big day came, Ms. Willis told Kyra, "You go first." That seemed unkind to me, but Ms. Willis explained it to me this way: "If you're standing at the top of the cliff, watching your friends drop over the side one by one, it can be scary. The cliff is so steep that you can't even see them once they drop over the side, unless you lean over the side yourself, which I knew Kyra would never do. And if you're afraid of doing the abseil, you may just get more afraid watching each of the other girls drop over the side. I knew it would be best for Kyra for her to go first."

Ms. Willis must have been right. Kyra did the abseil without any difficulty. And the very next day, teachers started to notice a difference in the classroom. Kyra began raising her hand.

She began speaking in public—and when she spoke, it wasn't a whisper anymore; you could hear what she was saying. She literally "found her voice," to borrow a phrase from Carol Gilligan. When a teacher asked her why she was now more comfortable raising her hand and speaking out, she said, "After doing the abseil, it's not so scary to speak in class anymore."

Note that the Lauriston program at Howqua is *mandatory*. There are similar programs at American schools, but in my experience the American programs are almost always optional, not mandatory. As a result, the girls who need them most do not participate. Kyra would never have signed up for this program. On the contrary, she begged to be let out. So if you think your daughter needs a boost to find her voice, I suggest that you find a program like Lauriston's and sign her up—even if she says she doesn't want to. In my book *The Collapse of Parenting*, I explained that parents must sometimes push their kid to do things the kid might not want to do. If your daughter is timid, sign her up for a rock-climbing program. (American parents typically blanch in horror when I suggest that they sign up their risk-averse daughter for a rock-climbing program, over her objections. I examine this failure to exercise parental authority, and how that failure contributes to the growing fragility and anxiety of American kids, in *The Collapse of Parenting*.)

St. Michael's Collegiate School is a girls' school in Tasmania, Australia, where the leadership has made a real commitment to the abseiling program, again believing that it can empower girls to find their voice and take appropriate risks. Once again, *every* girl is required to participate in the program, beginning when the girls are six years old. Nine years later, the girls can do the abseil down the cliffs at Freycinet National Park, four hundred feet above the Pacific Ocean. Here's one of the photos the school

The right kind of training can empower girls to take risks. Photo courtesy of St. Michael's Collegiate School, Hobart, Tasmania.

gave me. Look at the girl's face. She is calm. Put me in that same situation, and I would be a quivering mass of Jell-O.

Such programs are common in Australia. They are less common here, but you can find them. And not every girl needs such a program. You have to know your child. When it comes to risk taking, individual differences can be huge. I met a girl who rides her ATV down a steep, rugged, heavily wooded mountain about five miles north of my office. I know a little boy who doesn't want to finger-paint because he's worried the paint won't come off his fingers. The girl on the ATV could use some of the "hazard precautions" that I will describe in a moment. The boy who doesn't even want to finger-paint could use "dare training" or something like Lauriston's program at Howqua.

Hazard Precautions

What about the boy who gets a thrill out of taking risks? He skateboards down a banister, or tries to. He rides his bike off a brick ledge onto the sidewalk. At the swimming pool, all he wants to do is run at top speed off the highest diving board. You've already taken him to Urgent Care three times with injuries, but the injuries have not fazed him. Now he's doing aerial skateboard tricks and asking for skydiving lessons. Each year he wants to do something even more hazardous. You have nightmares about spinal-cord injuries. What to do?

There are at least three basic principles involved in decreasing the risk of your child experiencing a severe injury. The first principle: **remember the "risky shift."** Boys in groups do stupid things that they don't do, or are less likely to do, when other boys are not around. Your boy wants a thrill. Great. Take the whole family skiing or snowboarding. Insist on everybody having a lesson first, no matter what their level of expertise. Taking a lesson from an expert will keep your boy in touch with reality and give him a more accurate assessment of his skills. He may think he's ready to tackle the black-diamond "expert" slopes. The teacher can show him that he'll actually have more fun, and be able to do more, on slopes that are better suited to his skill level. A family trip to the ski slopes is a much safer undertaking than a group of teenage boys going to the same mountain.

The second principle: **supervised is better than unsupervised.** I've seen parents who refuse to let their boy play football because they think it's too dangerous, but they allow him to practice his skateboarding with his buddies in the parking lot. I've got news for those parents: your son is at much greater risk of injury in an unsupervised setting with other boys than in any setting where there's a responsible adult in charge. Boys who enjoy taking risks will take risks. Yes, there is a risk involved when your son runs out onto a football field. He's going to collide with players who are bigger and stronger than he is. But a football practice supervised by a competent coach is a lower-risk environment for serious injury than a parking lot with a bunch of boys and no adults around. YouTube is crammed with videos of boys in parking lots doing stunts on the hoods of moving cars—with nobody at the steering wheel. Your boy will be safer on a football field than he would be in the parking lot with other boys.

The third principle: **assert your authority.** Years ago, Dallas Cowboys cornerback Deion Sanders suffered a concussion during a game with the Washington Redskins. The team doctor correctly advised Sanders to stay out for the rest of that game. When you've suffered a concussion, the brain swells just a bit. You may feel okay an hour later. But if you're hit in the head again, the swelling can be massive, leading to death in minutes if the increased pressure causes the hind part of the brain to squirt down into the spinal column. That's why the doctor told Sanders to sit out the rest of the game.

Sanders disregarded the doctor's advice. When he felt better, he went back out on the field. When Sanders returned to the sideline, the doctor didn't scream or yell. He simply took Sanders's helmet and walked away. The doctor kept Sanders's helmet tucked under his arm for the rest of the game. (And today, of course, the NFL has new rules in place that would formally prohibit Sanders from returning to the game—but this took place back in 1999.)

That's an example of how to assert your authority with a boy who likes to take risks and who hasn't abided by the guidelines you have set. Don't argue. Don't negotiate. Just do what you need to do. If you've told your boy that he's not allowed to ride his mountain bike down the steep mountain without your permission and without a grown-up in attendance, and he's broken that rule, don't ask him to "promise." When his friends come by and ask him to go riding down the steep hill again, he'll look like a wimp if he says, "I can't go because I promised my father I wouldn't unless we have a grown-up with us." In the "boy code," honoring a promise made to a parent may be a sign of weakness. But the "boy code" respects a heavy-duty woven-steel cable lock.

So go to the hardware store and buy a sturdy lock. That way, when his friends come by and ask him to go riding, he can say, quite honestly, "*I can't*. My dad put this monster lock on my bike." When you've decided that your son can ride his bike again—and you know when, where, and *with whom* he'll be riding, including at least one adult—then unlock it.

CHAPTER 4

Aggression

Real men like to fight.
—General George S. Patton[1]

The surface of a girl fight can be as silent and smooth as a marble.
—Rachel Simmons[2]

Jeffrey

Jeffrey, age fourteen, was moody, irritable, and depressed. School annoyed him. Sports didn't really interest him. He didn't have many close friends. The psychiatrist had prescribed an anti-depressant plus Ritalin for attention deficit disorder. Even with the medication, Jeffrey was still withdrawn and despondent. Getting through the school day was a struggle, even though his parents had enrolled him in a private school where the classes were small and the teachers were caring and attentive.

That summer Jeffrey's father arranged for him to spend two months in Zimbabwe. Jeffrey had been hired as an assistant to

Cliff, a professional hunter. Cliff made his living taking North American and European men into remote areas of Africa to hunt wild game. Jeffrey's parents packed enough medication to last Jeffrey all summer.

After three days with Jeffrey, Cliff told him to stop taking the pills. "You don't need them," Cliff said. And he was right—at least as far as hunting in the African bush was concerned. Jeffrey could sit for hours, motionless in the tall grass, waiting for prey to appear.

The local Ndebele tribesmen took a liking to Jeffrey. They could see that he was different from other American and European tourists. Jeffrey was comfortable with the locals, and the locals were comfortable with him. More than anything else, Jeffrey wanted to learn to hunt the way the Ndebele men did. So they taught him to use their hunting javelin.

Have you ever tried to hit an archery target using a bow and arrow? Imagine that you are trying to hit that target, but instead of a bow and arrow you have only a wooden spear—twice as long as a baseball bat—and you have to *throw* it at the target from a distance of thirty yards. After an hour of practicing, Jeffrey told the tribesmen that he was ready to hunt. They chuckled and pointed at a grouse about thirty yards away. Jeffrey stared at the bird, nodded to himself, then hurled the javelin with all his might. The bird, transfixed by the spear, was killed instantly. Everyone was amazed—except for Jeffrey.

Cliff snapped a picture of Jeffrey standing on a pile of rocks, his arms raised in triumph, holding the dead bird in one hand and the javelin in the other. Jeffrey gave me a copy of that picture when he came back home.

"That summer was a turning point," his mother, Jane, told me later. Jeffrey still had to take medication in order to function well

Jeffrey, triumphant, after killing the grouse

in school. But his whole attitude had changed and his depression lifted. He no longer saw himself as a failure. "That summer gave him confidence," Jane said.

Now suppose Jeffrey's parents had not sent him to Zimbabwe. Suppose they had sent him instead to "Camp ADD," a summer camp where boys (and girls) diagnosed with attention-deficit/hyperactivity disorder spend their summer working on reading and writing skills. There are many such camps today. Six weeks indoors in July and August. Then you go right back to school in September for more of the same. If Jeffrey's parents had done that, he might not have grown up to be the outgoing and amiable man he now is.

"The great moments of our life come when we find the courage to rechristen our 'evil' as the best within us," Friedrich Nietzsche once wrote.[3] The same hidden intensity and impulsiveness that had been liabilities for Jeffrey at school in Maryland became advantages when he was hunting in the wilds of Zimbabwe. The experience of feeling himself to be a genuinely gifted and talented hunter changed his whole outlook on life. After he nailed a grouse at thirty yards when nobody thought he could do it, schoolwork didn't seem so hopelessly difficult anymore.

If you're opposed to hunting, here's the part that may not sit well with you: if Jeffrey had hurled his spear at a target on a wall, it wouldn't have had the same effect. Hitting a target on a wall wouldn't have changed his life. The fact that he had *killed a living thing* was crucial. Most women (and some men) recoil from that idea. And I'm not necessarily endorsing it. But the reality is that most girls and women relate to violence very differently from how most boys and men do.

Lessons from the Playground

Ever watch kids playing on a playground? Psychologist Janet Lever spent a whole year at elementary school playgrounds, watching girls and boys play. Boys fight a lot, she noticed: boys engage in physical violence about twenty times as often as girls do. To her surprise, though, she found that boys who fight each other usually end up being *better* friends after the fight. They are more likely to play together in the days after the fight than they were in the days before.[4]

Girls seldom fight, but when they do—often with words rather than fists—the bad feelings last. "I hate you! I'm never ever *ever* going to play with you again!" Katie says to Amy; and the older she is, the more likely that she will be true to her word. After a big fight between Katie and Amy, "Amy's group" may not play with "Katie's group" again for the rest of the school year.

Before you claim that these differences are just an artifact of human culture, consider that Lever's reports are similar to what scientists have found with chimpanzees. Male chimpanzees are about twenty times as likely to fight as females are, but the fights don't last more than a few minutes and rarely result in major injury. Two male chimps who fight each other this morning may be grooming each other this afternoon. According to Frans de Waal, a primatologist at the Yerkes National Primate Research Center in Atlanta, "Picking a fight can actually be a way for [male chimps] to relate to one another, check each other out, and take a first step toward friendship." Female chimps rarely fight, but when they do, their friendship is over. The hostility that results can last for years. Serious injury is also *more* likely to occur when female chimpanzees fight. Female chimps who have fought each other are "vindictive and irreconcilable," according to Dr. de Waal.[5]

In our species these differences are apparent as soon as children can talk. Boys as young as two years of age, given a choice between violent fairy tales and warm and fuzzy fairy tales, usually choose the violent stories. Girls as young as two years of age most often choose the warm and fuzzy stories.[6] In another study psychologists found that five- and seven-year-old girls who like to make up violent stories are more likely to have significant behavior problems than girls who prefer warm, nurturing stories. However, among boys, a preference for making up violent stories is *not* an indicator of underlying psychiatric problems.[7] A preference for violent stories seems to be normal for five- to seven-year-old boys, while the same preference in five- to seven-year-old girls suggests a psychiatric disorder.

Psychologists Louise and David Perry interviewed girls and

boys (average age ten years), asking them how they might respond to certain situations. For example, suppose you're playing soccer with your friends, and some other kid comes and grabs the ball from you. Would you hit the other kid? If you did hit the other kid, do you think hitting the kid would get you the ball back? And how would you feel afterward? Most boys said that they would hit the kid who tried to steal the ball. The older the boy, the more confident he was that he would succeed in getting the ball back by hitting the other kid. And the boys who said that they would hit the other kid also said that they would feel absolutely no guilt about hitting him. "Why should *I* feel guilty? He took my ball!" They were confident that other boys would approve of their action. For good reason: boys who act aggressively usually *raise* their standing in the eyes of other boys, as long as their action is provoked, that is, as long as it's not bullying.

Girls respond differently. Not only were girls less likely to respond aggressively to the kid who stole the soccer ball, but they were also more likely to have misgivings about responding aggressively and be less confident of a successful outcome. They were more likely to anticipate feelings of guilt and emotional upset about hitting someone else, even in response to the provocation of someone taking away their soccer ball. And they did not expect other girls to approve of their action, even though it was provoked. Girls who respond to provocation with an act of physical aggression may *lower* their standing in the eyes of their peers.[8]

There's good evidence that at least some of these differences are biologically programmed. Some of that evidence comes from studies of girls with congenital adrenal hyperplasia (CAH). Owing to a genetic defect in the adrenal glands, the adrenal tissues of a girl with CAH produce high levels of male hormone while the girl is still in her mother's womb. That male hormone partially masculinizes the girl's brain. When young girls who have CAH are offered a toy—given the choice of an airplane, a ball, military action figures, Barbie dolls, or Magic Markers—CAH girls are more likely to choose an airplane or a ball or the fighting action figures and less likely to choose the Barbie dolls or Magic Markers, compared with girls without CAH. When CAH girls are tested at age four, they are found to have preferences about halfway between those of non-CAH girls and typical boys: CAH girls are more likely to choose games of simulated violence than non-CAH girls are, but less likely to choose violent games than typical boys are.[9] In fact, the masculinity of a CAH girl's choice of toy is proportional to the severity of that girl's CAH. The more severe her CAH—that is, the more male hormone her brain was exposed to before birth—the more masculine her behavior and her toy preferences will be.[10] These researchers also found no evidence of parental influence on the children's play behavior. Parents who encouraged their daughters to play with more "feminine" toys had zero effect on their children's play behavior.

Studies with laboratory animals show similar sex differences. Among most higher mammals, and especially among our closest relatives, the primates, juvenile males are more likely to engage in rough-and-tumble play than females are. In one study of long-tailed macaques, for example, the "boy" monkeys were six times more likely to engage in rough-and-tumble play than the "girl" monkeys were.[11] "Girl" monkeys, on the other hand, are more likely to engage in what primatologists call *alloparenting*. They're babysitting.[12] Young female monkeys are far more likely than young males to look after a baby monkey, allowing the baby's mother time off to forage. The mother returns to retrieve the baby from the "babysitter" when it's time for the baby to breast-feed.

Among other primates, you will find that young females show much more interest than young males do in taking care of babies. That's true for baboons[13] and for rhesus monkeys.[14] Among wild chimpanzees, young females are more likely to cradle a stick in their arms the way a chimpanzee mother cradles her baby; young male chimpanzees are more likely to use the same stick as a weapon.[15] Likewise in our species: girls, on average, are much more likely to be interested in babies than boys are. And researchers find that the difference in interest level *diminishes* throughout the human life span. Girls are much more likely to be interested in babies than boys are. Male interest in babies is roughly constant across the life span, but women over forty-five appear to be less interested in infants compared with younger women, teenage girls, or younger girls. The researchers who documented this finding concluded that these differences suggest "a biological adaptation for parenting," a hardwired difference.[16] That sex difference does not appear to be affected by parents' attitudes toward their child's behavior. Sons whose parents encourage them to nurture babies are no more nurturing than sons of parents who make no such efforts.[17]

If a similar behavior is observed across many different primate species, including humans, then that behavior probably serves some biologically useful purpose. It's not hard to see a biologically useful purpose of young female primates feeling drawn to caring for little babies. Formal studies have demonstrated that the more practice a young female monkey has taking care of a little baby, the better she will be at it.[18]

But what about rough-and-tumble play? What useful purpose is served when young males chase one another and wrestle, sometimes for hours on end? Primatologists have suggested two reasons why young males spend so much more time than young females in rough-and-tumble play. One reason is that in many primate species—including our closest relative, the chimpanzee—the male is much more likely to pursue and kill moderate-size prey. In the wild, the adult male chimpanzee commonly hunts, kills, and eats monkeys while the adult female chimpanzee very rarely hunts such prey, instead preferring nuts, berries, and small invertebrate species such as termites. Adolescent male chimpanzees often kill monkeys; adolescent female chimpanzees never do.[19]

But there's another reason, researchers believe, why it's useful for young males to engage in play-fighting. Wrestling and fighting with other males teaches them the rules of the game. If young male primates are deprived of the opportunity to fight with other males, those males grow up to be *more* violent as adults, not less.[20] They have never learned how to get along with other males in a playful, aggressive way. The rage seems to get bottled up inside until it explodes. And if it's true for our cousins, it may be true for us. In just a moment we will consider proposals offered by well-intentioned reformers to ban dodgeball and snowball-throwing on the grounds that such activities are "violent" and "aggressive." The irony is that if our sons are anything like their primate cousins, such measures may not decrease the likelihood of serious violent acts: it might even *increase* the likelihood of the kind of violent outburst the reformers are trying to prevent.

Affirm the Knight

Aggression has a different meaning for most girls than it has for most boys. For many boys, aggressive sports—such as football, boxing, wrestling—may not only be fun; they may actually form the basis for a lasting friendship. The concept "aggression = fun" doesn't come naturally to most girls. Aggression between girls doesn't build friendships; it destroys them. So it's hard for girls to imagine any positive consequences from aggressive play.

These differences also affect how children *talk* with one another, especially with same-sex peers. Put a tape recorder in a boys' locker room and listen to the banter.

"Your momma's so fat, she sat on an iPad and turned it into a flat-screen TV!"

"Your momma's so fat, they used Google Earth for her school photo."

"Your momma's so dumb, she thinks Taco Bell is a phone company in Mexico."

"Your momma's so old, I told her to act her age and she died!"

Playful aggression as a mode of relationship is hardwired into many males, not just in our species but in other primates. Differences between girls and boys are natural. Evidence from monkeys and chimpanzees suggests that those differences are hardwired to a substantial degree. Those differences should be acknowledged, accepted, and used appropriately. Instead, many educators today seek to eradicate gender-specific behaviors.

In particular, many schools now actively discourage and punish "aggressive" play. Many school districts have banned kids from playing dodgeball on school playgrounds in the belief that it encourages violent behavior.[21] Some schools are taking these prohibitions to the extreme, banning even games like tag. "Body contact is inappropriate for recess activities," asserts Doris Jennings, principal of Woodlin Elementary School in Silver Spring, Maryland.[22] Other school districts threaten expulsion for kids who throw snowballs.[23]

It's getting crazy. Ten-year-old Johnny Jones walked to the front of the classroom to get a pencil. On his way back, his friend pretended to "shoot" at Johnny. In response, Johnny pretended to pull back on an imaginary bow and arrow and "shoot" an arrow back. A girl promptly told the teacher that the boys were shooting at each other. The teacher took the two boys into the hall and reprimanded them. The teacher then sent Johnny to the principal. The principal suspended Johnny and informed Johnny's mother, Beverly, that her son could be *expelled* on the grounds that Johnny had violated the school's weapons policy. Beverly Jones retained an attorney. After three months of legal back-and-forth, the school agreed to back down and remove Johnny's suspension from his record. John Whitehead, an advocate for the child, observed that the school's actions amounted to "criminalizing the imagination."[24] Whitehead also advises kids, "Don't joke around in school." Being a boy—doing things boys have always done, like saying, "Bang, bang, you're dead"—can now get you in deep trouble.

The basic premise underlying the arguments against dodge-ball and saying "bang bang" and throwing snowballs is this: if you prevent boys from engaging in pretend violence, then boys will *be* less violent. In my book *Boys Adrift*, I explored the evidence on this point in greater depth, with attention to boys who have engaged in actual violence, boys such as Dylan Klebold and Eric Harris, the two school shooters at Columbine High School in April 1999. In fact, there is no evidence that preventing boys from engaging in pretend violence will in any way decrease the likelihood that they will engage in actual violence, such as the massacre perpetrated by Klebold and Harris at Columbine High School. Instead, prohibiting playful boy games may actually increase the likelihood that the suppressed aggression will manifest itself in less healthy ways. "You can try to drive out nature with a pitchfork, yet nature will always return," according to the old Latin proverb.[25] The boy disengages from school and devotes his energies to getting to the next level in *Call of Duty* or *Grand Theft Auto*, games that reward the boy's enthusiasm for aggressive play.

The solution to taming a boy's aggressive drive is *not* to squelch the drive every time it appears. Banning dodgeball from the school yard makes as much sense as Prohibition. Instead, you want to *transform* the boy's aggressive drive. Sublimate it into something constructive. Julie Collins, a counselor at Georgetown Prep, a high school I visited, explains it this way: "You can't turn a bully into a flower child. But you *can* turn a bully into a knight."

Her motto: affirm the knight.

Here is a true story that exemplifies Julie Collins' principle. A small town in rural Illinois was being terrorized by a local gang of teenage thugs. Storekeepers who refused to pay tribute saw their stores vandalized. One storekeeper made a wager that his clerk could beat the gang leader in a fight. The gang leader accepted the challenge.

Most of the town turned out to watch the fight. The storekeeper's clerk and the gang leader fought each other for what seemed like hours. Finally the clerk backed away and proposed that they call it a draw. "The fight ended in friendship," we are told, and the clerk "not only earned the group's respect but became their informal leader." The name of the clerk: Abraham Lincoln.[26]

In 1831 the town organized a militia to fight in the Black Hawk War. The militia, comprised mainly of the young gang members, elected Lincoln to be their captain. They remained loyal to him throughout the next thirty years as he rose from storekeeper's clerk to president of the United States.[27]

This archetypal-but-true story of the young Abe Lincoln reso-
nates with ancient traditions of male friendship. "The youthful
leader often establishes his authority by besting the strongest
young tough in the neighborhood," one writer observes. "King
Arthur beats the undefeated Lancelot, and Robin Hood knocks
Little John off a bridge."[28] I would add that this tradition is even
more ancient than King Arthur and Robin Hood. It goes back
to the very roots of recorded history. The Epic of Gilgamesh,
dating back roughly five thousand years, begins with a similar
fight between Gilgamesh and Enkidu. As in all these stories, the
two protagonists become close friends after the fight. Indeed, the
fight provides a solid foundation for the friendship and makes it
lifelong.

It's a guy thing. Many young boys get a thrill from violent or
pretend-violent confrontation. Most young girls don't. I'm not
saying that girls are never violent or aggressive, just that girls seldom *enjoy* physical aggression and confrontation the way many
boys do. Girls are aggressive in their own way. We'll get to that
in a minute.

Sex Differences Diminish as a Function of Age

I was giving an evening presentation to parents on this topic.
More than three hundred parents were in attendance. When I
said, "Many boys enjoy confrontation in an aggressive setting,
but most girls don't," I saw a woman my age raise her hand. I
didn't call on her, though: With an audience of more than three
hundred, you have to do the Q&A at the end of the talk. If you

take questions all through the talk, you might not get to the last slide before the ninety minutes are up.

When this woman saw that I wasn't going to call on her, she got out of her chair and began stomping down the stairs toward the front of the auditorium where I was speaking. The stairs were not carpeted and her boots were making a racket as she *stomp stomp stomped* down the stairs toward me. Finally I stopped trying to talk and waited a moment for her to get down to the front.

"Yes?" I said.

"Dr. Sax, I just want you to know something," she said, coming quite close to me. "I'm a litigator. I *enjoy* confrontation. I *enjoy* being aggressive. And I'm a woman! So that pretty much blows your theory to pieces, doesn't it?"

I wasn't sure what to say. "Let me ask you a question," I said, trying to phrase the question in my mind. "When you were nine or ten years old, when you were in elementary school, did you enjoy confrontation then?"

Her face worked strangely. I suspect that she wanted to say, *You're darn right I did!* But she couldn't say it. Finally she shook her head no. I handed her the microphone.

"I was different when I was little. I didn't like people to shout at me. If my teacher looked at me the wrong way, I'd burst into tears," she said. "When I first began work as a litigator, I wasn't any good at it. The opposing attorney would mock me in open court. I'd go into the ladies' room, hide in a stall, and just cry." She took a breath. "But then I saw how these attorneys who would attack each other in court would hang out in the bar afterward and trade jokes. One afternoon they invited me to join them, and I did. That's when I began to figure it out: that the name-calling and the mocking is a *game*. So I started playing the game. I started making fun of them in open court, just the way they had done to me. And I started winning cases. That was about ten years ago. Now I'm just about the best there is in my field. And I enjoy it. But I see your point. It took me . . . some time to get to where I am."

Sex differences diminish as a function of age. As a practicing physician, I see middle-aged women who are bold and aggressive, and I see middle-aged men who are not. But it's unusual to find a ten-year-old girl who enjoys physical confrontation, or who loves to spend her free time playing violent games such as *Call of Duty* or *Grand Theft Auto*.

Violence, Girl Style

Mary is the mother of fifteen-year-old Julie. Mary told me how Julie came home from her riding lesson with a funny look on her face. Over supper, Mary asked what was wrong.

"Nothing," Julie said.

"Come on. You're upset. Tell me."

Julie looked as though she might cry. "It's all the girls at the barn. They *hate* me."

"That's silly. They're some of your best friends," Mom said.

Julie said nothing. She gripped her spoon and looked at her soup.

"You all went out together last Saturday, to the horse show and then to dinner afterward," Mary reminded her. "You told me you all had a great time. That was just five days ago. What makes you think they don't like you all of a sudden?"

"The moment I walked in the barn. They were all talking about me. As soon as they saw me, they stopped," Julie said.

"How do you know they were talking about you?" Mom asked.

Julie rolled her eyes. "It's obvious," she said. She stirred her still-untasted soup. "They *all* hate me now. I said hi to Lisa and she acted like I wasn't even there. Lisa, of all people! Can you believe that? If it weren't for me, Lisa wouldn't have a single friend at the barn. She wouldn't even be *at* the barn." Tears welled in Julie's eyes. "It's all Karen's fault. Karen hates me. She's *always* hated me. She's jealous of me because I'm a better rider and I have a nicer horse. And now she's gotten the other girls to be mean to me."

The next morning, Julie announced she didn't want to ride anymore. She'd been riding since she was six years old. "Don't make me go back to that barn," she begged her mother.

Many parents in this situation might make the mistake of assuming that the problem is all in their daughter's head. They think that because the signs of aggression are absent, nothing is really going on. Don't be deceived. Odds are your daughter is right.

Girls and boys both fight, but they tend to fight differently. Boys can be mean to one another, but the meanness is usually right there on the surface. Riley puts a wad of sticky used chewing gum on Mike's seat at the cafeteria table when Mike isn't looking. Mike sits down, realizes he's got somebody else's chewing gum on his butt, and looks around to see who did it. Somebody points at Riley. Mike hauls off and slugs him. The two boys roll on the floor, hitting and kicking, until Mike pins Riley down. The teachers pull them apart and send both of them to the principal's office. One day later, Mike and Riley may be sitting together at lunch—better friends than they were before.

Provocation, leading to a violent response, followed by resolution. That's the pattern with many boys. But that simple pattern is less common among girls. "The surface of a girl fight can be as silent and smooth as a marble," observes Rachel Simmons.[29] Tension can arise so subtly that even the girls themselves sometimes can't honestly tell you how it started. A violent response is seldom appropriate and seldom made, because the provocation may be hard to define:

- *She ignored me in the hall even after I said hello to her.*

- *She sat with Sophia instead of me at lunch, and she knows Sophia hates me.*

- *She sighed when I spoke up in English class, like I had said something stupid.*

Tensions can simmer and build for weeks or months, corroding a friendship until there is no friendship left.

Simmons uses the phrase "alternative aggression" to describe these ongoing wars among adolescent girls. It's a useful term because it reminds us that these ongoing tensions *are* a form of aggression. Parents sometimes don't recognize the damage that alternative aggression can cause. For one thing, the perpetrator is often a "good girl," polite to adults and clever at hiding the clues. A girl who victimizes other girls in this manner is often the *most* socially skilled and may even be one of the most popular girls— just the opposite of the typical boy bully.

Girl bullies are different from boy bullies. Boys who bully often have few friends, may be socially inept, may not be doing well in school. The boy bully picks on his victim as a way of improving his own status, at least in his own eyes. *I can't be the biggest loser in the school if Jacob is terrified of me*, he thinks. But he probably doesn't know Jacob very well. His bullying is motivated not so much by anything Jacob has done or said as by his *own* insecurities, his vague hope that he will feel better by making someone else miserable. He may also hope to ingratiate himself with other boys by picking on the victim. "When an unpopular kid is harassed by someone from a popular crowd, wanna-bes and posers may take the incident as a signal that their own status can be improved by going after that victim," observes Professor John Bishop of Cornell University.[30]

The situation is almost completely reversed for girls. Whereas boys often bully kids they barely know, girls almost always bully girls within their social group. These girls are intimate enemies. They know each other. They know where it hurts most.[31]

Here's a summary:

GIRLS who bully typically . . .	BOYS who bully typically . . .
have many friends	have few friends
are socially skilled	are socially inept
are doing well in school	are below-average students
know the girls they bully	don't know the boys they bully

My workshop for schools on this topic is titled "The Four Bullies." In that workshop we identify four different kinds of bullying:

1. boy-on-boy bullying

2. girl-on-girl bullying

3. sexual harassment

4. hate-based bullying

Boy-on-boy bullying is what you might call "classic" bully-ing, where the big bully smashes the geeky boy into the wall or smushes him into a locker. *Hate-based bullying* refers to bullying based on race, ethnicity, sexual orientation, etc. If white kids at a majority-white school are picking on a Hispanic kid because he is Hispanic (or if Hispanic kids at a majority-Hispanic school are picking on a non-Hispanic child), that's an example of hate-based bullying. Even if it's all boys, it's not typical boy-on-boy bullying. The strategies that are effective in stopping boy-on-boy bullying are different from the strategies that work to stop hate-based bullying. Boy-on-boy bullying often means the gender-typical boy is picking on the gender-atypical boy: the jock beating up the geek, for example. In chapter 9 we will talk more about the gender-atypical boy and why he is often the target of bullying.

Sexual harassment is a form of bullying, but the motivation is different. The most common form of sexual harassment is a boy harassing a girl who has rejected his advances. In my observations at more than four hundred schools, the schools that are most effective in preventing sexual harassment are those that teach girls and boys to be ladies and gentlemen. A gentleman does not harass a lady, and a lady will not tolerate harassment. In chapter 12 I will have more to say about that.

Our focus at the moment is girl-on-girl bullying. Why do girls do it?

I had the pleasure of having dinner, one on one, with Rachel Simmons, author of *Odd Girl Out*. I told her that my favorite chapter in her book was "The Bully in the Mirror," in which she admitted that she herself had been a bully in middle school. "Yeah, everybody says that's their favorite chapter," Rachel told me. But Rachel said that it was the hardest chapter for her to write, because she had to portray herself in a very unfavorable light, as the mean girl. Nevertheless, it's an immensely important chapter, because it teaches an important lesson: *any girl can be a bully*. Only a small subset of boys will ever bully. But any girl can be a bully.

The motivation for boy-on-boy bullying is pretty straightforward: the boy bully gets a visceral pleasure out of beating up the smaller boy. There have always been a small minority of boys and men who take pleasure in inflicting pain. There are some girls who take pleasure in inflicting pain, but they are rare, much rarer than boys who take pleasure in inflicting pain.[32] But any girl can be a bully. So why is this girl being a bully?

The answer: to defend her social niche. Let's say you're the popular, athletic girl who's also really funny. That's your niche. Then another girl moves into town and enrolls at your school. She's also athletic and she's also funny. Everybody's talking about how funny the new girl is and what a great athlete she is. You may feel that your niche is threatened. So you might feel tempted to start spreading stories about how the new girl is arrogant and conceited, to turn your friends against her.

A grown-up would understand that there is room for more than one funny, athletic girl in the social structure of any school. But a thirteen-year-old girl is not a grown-up. She's a thirteen-year-old girl.

The most effective strategies to prevent and to rectify girl-on-girl bullying are, in my observation, strategies that are employed schoolwide. I share some of those strategies in chapter 5 of my book *Girls on the Edge*. If you are a teacher, counselor, or school administrator, or if you are planning to talk with a school employee, I hope you will take a look at the strategies I share there. But what are you supposed to do if you're a parent, and you discover that your daughter is the "odd girl out," the girl who's being ignored and ostracized by other girls?

Start by taking the problem seriously. Don't dismiss or minimize it by telling her she's just imagining things. Maybe she is being oversensitive, but maybe she's not. It pays to find out. When did the problems begin? Who are your daughter's "enemies"— who's taking part in the campaign against her? What might be motivating those girls? Remember that other girls might ostracize your daughter not because of anything she has done but because she prompts other girls' envy. As Simmons observes, "the girls who get ostracized are usually the ones who have what most girls are expected to want: looks, the guy, money, and cool clothes."[33] Make an appointment to talk face to face with the guidance counselor. Sometimes the counselor really knows the situation at the school. Sometimes, unfortunately, the counselor is clueless. Either way, you need to be sure that the counselor understands your level of concern.

Consider signing your daughter up for after-school activities that would involve her with a different group of girls. Team sports are one option, if she is so inclined. Dance or drama may be a good choice. Or horseback riding, or swimming. Of course, girls in these other activities can be just as prone to cliques and rivalries as the girls at her school. But girls need connection with other girls. By showing your daughter that you understand her situation and that you're taking the problem seriously and doing your best to help—instead of trying to talk her out of it—you're already helping her feel better.

In extreme cases you may need to talk with your daughter about other options. Ask her how she would feel about transferring to another school. If you're in the public school system, the guidance counselor can often facilitate this transfer. That's another reason why you'll want to be in touch with the guidance counselor throughout the process. Sometimes a transfer can be accomplished seamlessly over a semester break.

Watch for signs of clinical depression. If your daughter is

CHAPTER 5

School

Melanie

Melanie was an academic superstar all through high school. In eleventh grade she took Advanced Placement (AP) English, AP Spanish Language, AP American History, and AP Biology, as well as trigonometry. Not only did she get straight A's that year, but she also really seemed to enjoy each class. She was especially interested in the environmental science unit of her biology class. Her biology teacher, Ms. Griffith, recognized Melanie's talent and encouraged her. With Ms. Griffith's help, Melanie devised a science project to test and correlate levels of pollutants in samples of water taken from the Potomac River at different points, from Harpers Ferry in West Virginia all the way down to Georgetown and Anacostia in Washington, DC. Her project won second place at an environmental science fair. "You're more than just smart," Ms. Griffith told Melanie after the fair. "Lots of scientists are smart. The great scientists are those who have imagination." Melanie beamed.

At Ms. Griffith's suggestion, Melanie signed up to take AP Physics in her senior year. Ms. Griffith assured her she wouldn't have any problem. "Physics will come naturally to you," Ms. Griffith said. "You have an analytical mind."

The first day of physics class seemed to go okay. The instructor, Mr. Wallace, plunged right in, presenting formulas and equations relating distance, velocity, and acceleration. At the end of class, as students were standing up and gathering their books to leave, he called out, "First seven problems in chapter 1, due tomorrow"—the class groaned—"in writing. Show your work, make it neat, hand them in at the start of class!"

Melanie looked at the problems that evening. The first five weren't too difficult. The last two were harder. They didn't seem to fit any of the formulas in the book.

That semester, Melanie was also taking AP Spanish Literature, AP English, AP European History, and AP Calculus. She had homework assignments in each of those subjects as well. She wrote out the answers to the first five physics problems. Then, rather than waste time trying to figure out the two remaining problems, she decided to do her homework in her other subjects and to meet with Mr. Wallace for help during her morning study period.

She didn't have any trouble finding Mr. Wallace during second period the next morning. He was in the physics lab, checking the equipment for the first experiment. She introduced herself and then asked: "About the homework assignment . . . I had a question. The first five problems were pretty easy, but I had trouble with the last two. They didn't fit any of the problems that were solved in the chapter. Like the problem where the boy is trying to catch the bus. The bus is pulling away from the bus stop; it's accelerating at a constant rate, which means that its speed is increasing, and we're supposed to figure out whether the boy can catch the bus, and if so how long it will take him to catch up with the bus." She paused to give Mr. Wallace a chance to say something, to suggest how to solve the problem.

Mr. Wallace said nothing. He glanced at her, then looked out the window. It was almost as though he hadn't heard anything she had said.

"Would you like me to show you the problem?" she asked, taking her book out and flipping to the page.

He shook his head.

"It's right here on page twenty-two," she began.

Mr. Wallace interrupted. "I think maybe you're in the wrong class," he said.

"What?" Melanie asked.

"Physics isn't for everybody," Mr. Wallace said. "Ms. Griffith told me what a hardworking student you are. In subjects like biology, students who work hard will do well. But physics is different. Either you have the right kind of mind for it or you don't."

"But you don't even know me," Melanie protested. "How do you know what kind of mind I have?"

"I just don't want you to hurt your grade point average," Mr. Wallace said. "Ms. Griffith told me that you're a straight-A student, that you might be the class valedictorian. I'd hate for you to lose that by staying in this class."

"You're saying I should drop this class?" Melanie said in disbelief. "After one day? One homework assignment? Which we haven't even discussed yet?"

Mr. Wallace nodded. "I'm sorry," he said.

Melanie slammed her book shut and left the room without another word. She wanted to go to Ms. Griffith and ask: *What is wrong with this guy?* Or maybe she would go to the school counselor and complain.

But she did neither. Instead, she dropped the course. "If he doesn't want me in his class, then I don't want to be in his class," Melanie told me later. "I mean, what if he gives me a lower grade just because he doesn't like me? I have to think about my college transcript. I don't want a B on my transcript in the last semester that colleges will see."

Some people would say that this incident illustrates the way in which sexist male teachers drive well-qualified girls out of physics classes. Those critics would point to the fact that Melanie was one of only six girls in a class of twenty-three students as evidence that the school was biased against girls taking physics. Those critics might also mention the fact that the homework problems in this particular textbook refer to boys, almost never girls, chasing after buses, hitting baseballs, driving race cars, and so on.

That analysis has some merit, but I don't think it's the whole story, in part because I know Melanie. Melanie was a victim, yes, but not primarily a victim of sexism. She was more a victim of Mr. Wallace's lack of understanding of the differences in how girls and boys learn.

Here's my assessment of what happened and why.

First, here's the "why": Girls and boys, on average, have different expectations for the teacher-student relationship. Because teachers are often unaware of those differences, male teachers especially often misunderstand and misinterpret the behavior of their female students. Most girls will naturally seek to affiliate with the teacher. They expect the teacher to be on their side, to be their ally. Most girls won't hesitate to ask the teacher for help when they need it. Educational researchers have found that girls are more concerned than boys are with pleasing the teacher and more likely than boys to follow the teacher's example.[1] Remarkably, a similar finding has been described in our closest genetic relative, the chimpanzee. Anthropologists who have spent many years observing chimpanzees in the wilds of Tanzania report sex differences in learning similar to what we see in human children. Girl chimps follow their teacher's example—in this case, regarding the proper way to dig for termites—while boy chimps disregard the teacher, preferring to do it their own way—or they ignore the teacher's example altogether and go off to swing from a nearby tree or wrestle with another male chimp. The boy chimps are consequently much slower to master the task than the girls are—a year or two slower, on average.[2]

Sex differences in how students relate to their teacher give rise to sex differences in motivation to study and in the weight that students give to their teacher's opinions. As a result, according to educational psychologist Eva Pomerantz, girls are at greater risk of being harmed by a negative assessment from a teacher:

> Girls generalize the meaning of their failures because they interpret them as indicating that they have disappointed adults, and thus they are of little worth. Boys, in contrast, appear to see their failures as relevant only to the specific subject area in which they have failed; this may be due to their relative lack of concern with pleasing adults.[3]

Girls are more likely than boys to do their homework even if the particular assignment doesn't interest them. Girls want the teacher to think well of them. Girls earn better grades than boys do, in every subject, not because girls have higher IQ scores—there are no sex differences in general intelligence[4]—but because girls *work harder* than boys do; they don't want to disappoint the teacher.[5] Boys, on the other hand, will be less motivated to study unless they find the material intrinsically interesting. Likewise, most boys will consult the teacher for help only as a last resort, after all other options have been exhausted.

The teacher I described at the opening of this chapter, whom I called Mr. Wallace, was a student himself once, of course. When he was a student, he probably asked the teacher for help rarely and only after he had worked long hours over a problem. When Melanie asked him for help on the second day of class, Mr. Wallace may have assumed that she had been working on the problem for hours. He knew from Ms. Griffith that Melanie was a smart, hardworking student. He may have thought: *If this smart, hardworking student has worked on this problem for hours and she still can't figure it out, then she probably doesn't belong in my class.* When he suggested that she drop the class, he may have been sincerely trying to act in her best interests.

If Mr. Wallace had taken a few minutes to ask Melanie how much effort she had put into solving the problems on her own, he would have realized his mistake. She hadn't spent even five minutes on those problems. However, Mr. Wallace and Melanie would still have had to reconcile their conflicting educational styles. If she had explained to Mr. Wallace that she was asking him for help *before* making a sustained effort to solve the problem on her own, he might have been surprised, even annoyed. He might have concluded that maybe she wasn't such a hard worker after all. Melanie would most likely have sensed his annoyance and been irked by his response. *Why* shouldn't *I ask the teacher for help? Isn't that what the teacher is there for? Why should I waste hours working on the problem the wrong way when the teacher can show me the right way?* That's what other girls have told me in similar situations.

Melanie went on to get straight A's again that semester. She was accepted at her first-choice school, the University of Maryland, and she went on to earn a four-year degree in business. There's nothing wrong with business, except that Melanie never expressed any interest in it when she was in high school. She was really on fire in that biology class. I can't help wondering whether she might have gone on to become the great scientist Ms. Griffith predicted she could be, if only her high school physics teacher had known more about the different educational styles of girls and boys—if he had encouraged her instead of pushing her out the door.

Face to Face, Shoulder to Shoulder

Friendships between girls are typically different from friendships between boys. Girls' friendships are about being together, spending time together, talking together, going places together. Friendships between boys, on the other hand, usually develop out of a shared interest in a game or an activity. We might characterize the difference this way: Girls' friendships are *face to face*, two girls talking with each other. Boys' friendships are *shoulder to shoulder*, a group of boys looking out at some shared common interest.[6]

Conversation is central to most girls' friendships at every age. Girlfriends love to talk with each other. When they start having trouble talking, the friendship is in trouble. The mark of a truly close friendship between two girls or two women is that they tell each other secrets they don't tell anyone else. They confide in each other about their most personal doubts and difficulties. *Self-disclosure* is the most precious badge of friendship between females. When she tells you a secret she's never told anyone else, then you know that you are truly her dear friend.

Boys are different. Most boys don't really want to hear each other's innermost secrets.[7] With boys the focus is more often on the activity, not on the conversation. Four boys can spend hours playing a video game without exchanging a single complete sentence. You may hear screams of agony and shouts of exultation, but you may not hear much that qualifies as conversation.

Girls' friendships are, on average, more intimate and more personal than most boys' friendships. That has advantages and disadvantages. The advantage, of course, is that each girl derives strength from the intimacy of the friendship. When a girl is under stress, she looks to other girls for support and comfort. When girls are under stress, they want to be with their friends *more*. When boys are under stress, they may just want to be left alone.[8] (Many mothers don't know about these differences. When a mother sees that her son is under stress, she often tries to comfort him. Often she will be rebuffed, and she may take the rebuff personally. She shouldn't.) Psychologist Shelley Taylor, who has specialized in the study of gender differences in the response to stress, summarizes her findings this way: "Women maintain more same-sex close relationships than do men, they mobilize more social support in times of stress than do men, they turn to female friends more often, and they report more benefits from contact with their female friends and relatives."[9]

Girls' Friendships Have Different Values Compared with Boys' Friendships, on Average

	Girls	Boys
Friendships focus on . . .	One another	A shared interest in a game or activity
Games and sports are . . .	An excuse to get together	Often central to the relationship
Conversation is . . .	Central to the relationship	Often unnecessary
Hierarchies and rank	Destroy the friendship	Organize the camaraderie
Self-revelation is . . .	A precious badge of friendship	To be avoided if possible

These differences are relevant to education for many reasons, chief of which is that girls and boys relate to teachers differently. For many boys, being friends with a teacher may be a sign of geekdom. (The coach is often an exception to this rule. It's usually okay for boys to be friends with the coach—as long as the coach himself is a real jock, not a dork or a geek.)

Professor John Bishop at Cornell University writes:

> In the eyes of most students, the nerds exemplify the "I trust my teachers to help me learn" attitude that prevails in most elementary school classrooms. The dominant middle school crowd is telling them that trusting teachers is baby stuff. It is "us" [the boys] versus "them" [the teachers]. Friendships with teachers make you a target for harassment by peers. . . . Boys are not supposed to suck up to teachers. You avoid being perceived as a suck-up by

avoiding eye contact with teachers, not raising one's hand in class too frequently, and [by] talking or passing notes to friends during class (this demonstrates that you value relationships with friends more than your reputation with the teacher).[10]

Girls are less likely to think friendship with teachers equals geekiness. On the contrary, a girl student may actually raise her status in the eyes of her friends if she has a close relationship with a teacher—especially if the teacher is young, "cool," and female. I knew a young teacher at an all-girls school who occasionally invited her favorite girl in her class to go to the movies with her. Being invited to see a movie with that teacher is a major status booster. (Being friends with a teacher is less likely to boost a girl's status if the teacher is male, as other girls may suspect that she is using her sexuality to get a better grade.) But I think that teacher was making a big mistake. You don't want to have "favorites" because if you do, every kid who is not your favorite may disengage. If Sonia is your favorite, Vanessa may feel, or even say out loud, "You don't care about *me*, so I don't care about your stupid algebra." By contrast, if the girl believes that you really care about her, then she is more likely to work hard in your subject, not because she suddenly loves algebra but because she doesn't want to let you down. She doesn't want to disappoint you.

With boys it's different. A boy who is buddy-buddy with the teacher does not thereby raise his stature in the eyes of his peers. On the contrary, being friends with the teacher can *lower* a boy's status in the eyes of other boys, if that boy comes to be seen as the teacher's pet. And the average boy is likely to be less concerned about disappointing the teacher's expectations, compared with the average girl.

Girls are more likely to assume that the teacher is an ally and a friend. Boys are less likely to share that assumption. So, when encountering difficulties, girls are more likely to consult the teacher early. Boys, as I said a moment ago, usually consult the teacher only as a last resort. And girls are much more likely than boys are to ask a teacher for advice about personal matters, totally unrelated to the academic material.

Girls' friendships work best when the friendship is between equals. If you're a girl or a woman and you think your friend believes herself to be "better" than you, then your friendship with her is not likely to last. Boys are more likely to be comfortable in an unequal relationship, even if they are the lesser party. The third-string linebacker may relish being the best buddy of the star quarterback. He may not resent the quarterback's higher status. He may even try to magnify his friend's status in the eyes of others. This male characteristic has roots that go very deep. If you know the stories of Gilgamesh and Enkidu, Achilles and Patroclus, David son of Jesse and Jonathan son of Saul, or Don Quixote and Sancho Panza, then you've heard this story before. Those friendships were not less strong because of the difference in status between the friends. On the contrary, the hierarchical character of the relationship defined and even ennobled the friendship. "Jonathan made a covenant with David because he loved him," we read in the biblical book First Samuel. "Jonathan took off the robe he was wearing and gave it to David, along with his tunic and even his sword, his bow and his belt." David didn't give him anything in return, and Jonathan didn't expect him to. Jonathan said to David, "You will be king over Israel and *I will be second to you*" (emphasis mine).[11] Jonathan's dream was a world in which his hero, David, would be king and he, Jonathan, would be the king's right-hand man. And Jonathan is fine with that.

These differences explain a useful tip that several teachers have shared with me. If you're working with a girl, *smile and look her in the eye* when you're helping her with a subject.[12] That's the way girls interact with their own friends. Too many teachers, especially men, don't make eye contact with their female students. "I asked him a question, and he answered it, but he just seemed to be talking into empty space. Or he was looking at his shoes. He didn't look at *me*," one girl said to me. "He didn't care about *me*. It was almost like I wasn't even there."

I was leading a workshop for teachers in Yuba City, California, talking about the importance of making eye contact with students. A young man, a teacher, raised his hand. "I'm sorry, I'm not going to do that. I think it's inappropriate," he said.

"Inappropriate?" I repeated.

"Yep." The young man explained that he is single and he is straight. He is teaching high school seniors, which means seventeen- and eighteen-year-old girls. He explained his concern that if others see him smiling and making eye contact with an eighteen-year-old female, they might think he is flirting.

"I understand what you're saying," I answered. "But I'm not suggesting that you *touch* her. You can keep ten feet of distance between you, and always make sure that there are other people in the room. But you must make eye contact and smile." With support from the other teachers, we gradually persuaded the young man not to look at his shoes when he was talking with a female student.

If you're working with a boy, sit down *next* to him and spread out the materials in front of you, so you're both looking at the materials, shoulder to shoulder. Don't hold an eye-to-eye stare with a boy you don't know well. There are different kinds of eye-to-eye contact, of course. But sustained eye-to-eye contact among males who are not already good friends can easily be perceived as a prelude to a fight. It may make the boy uncomfortable or even provoke a hostile response.

Another application of these differences is that small-group learning is a good teaching strategy for girls but seldom for boys. I was visiting an eighth-grade classroom in Columbia, South Carolina. Science class. The teacher said, "Now I'd like you to break into your small groups. I'd like you to discuss the differences between cell *walls* in plants and cell *membranes* in animals."

I was standing next to a table with four boys at the back of the class. The four boys looked at one another. One boy said to another, who was apparently new to the class, "So, how long you been living in Columbia?"

Imagine if the boy responded, "Oh! We're not supposed to talk about that! We're supposed to talk about cell walls in plants and cell membranes in animals!" If a boy were to say such a thing, the others would be astonished by such a display of geekiness. The boy would be branded a teacher's pet. But of course the boy said no such thing. He said, "My folks and I just moved here from Dallas, and I'm telling you, I miss Dallas. You folks don't have no football here!"

The other boys gaped at him. Then one said, "What do you mean, no football? What about Clemson? What about U of SC?"

The boy from Dallas waved his hand with an air of dismissive superiority. "That's just college football. That's not *real* football."

Now the four boys embarked on a lively debate about the comparative merits of NCAA Division I football versus the National Football League. And that was the end of the day as far as cell walls in plants compared with cell membranes in animals.

Why is small-group work less likely to be an effective strategy for boys, at least in elementary school and middle school, compared with girls?

First reason: Girls are more comfortable asking the teacher for help when they need it. If you give four girls a group assignment, you can be confident that if they get stuck, at least one of them will come to you for help.

Not so with boys. If four boys get stuck, there's no guarantee that any of them will ask the teacher for help, unless one of the boys is a geek, and even geeks know that asking the teacher for help lowers their status in the eyes of the other boys. If the boys get stuck, they may just throw spitballs and get rowdy instead of asking for help.

That leads us to a second reason why small-group self-directed learning works better for most girls but not for most boys. Boys can raise their status in the eyes of other boys by disrupting the teacher's program. If the teacher breaks the class into small groups and two boys in a group of four start being disruptive, those boys raise their status in the eyes of at least some of the other boys in the room, no matter how puerile their behavior. (Incidentally, the word "puerile" is derived from the Latin word *puer*, meaning a young boy. There is no pejorative word corresponding to the Latin *puella*, young girl.)

Like many sex differences relevant to education, these differences diminish as a function of age. You can often use small-group work once boys are seniors in high school. But you can't be confident that those strategies will work with boys in elementary school or middle school.

Hearing the Difference

In chapter 2 we noted that the average girl hears better than the average boy. Anytime you have a teacher of one sex teaching children of the other sex, there's a potential for a mismatch, if only in decibel level. If a male teacher speaks in a tone of voice that seems normal to him, a girl in the front row may feel that he is yelling at her. Conversely, if a boy is at the back of the room with a soft-spoken female teacher at the front, he may not hear her very well.

Recall our earlier discussion of the misdiagnosis and overdiagnosis of attention deficit disorder. Some boys who are not paying attention may just need the teacher to raise her voice a bit—about eight decibels, as we discussed in chapter 2. This fundamental fact is not taught in most schools of education. When I speak to teachers, they are fascinated to learn that girls and boys do indeed differ, on average, in how they hear. Experienced teachers often figure this out on their own—after five or ten years of teaching. One veteran teacher told me that she puts the boys in the front of the class and the girls in back. That's pretty much the opposite of how girls and boys normally seat themselves. Here's the most common arrangement when kids are allowed to seat themselves: you will have two or three highly motivated boys sitting in the front row, the rest of the boys at the back, and the girls in the middle. That's the "natural" way for kids to seat themselves, because most girls like to affiliate with the teacher and most boys don't. (In chapter 9 we will talk more about the two or three boys who do.)

The Teacher's Guilty Secret

The differences in how girls and boys hear is one hardwired reason why both girls and boys are shortchanged by a lack of awareness of gender differences. Another reason has to do with differences in the way girls and boys respond to threat and confrontation.

"I yelled at one of my students one day," Kate, a middle-school teacher, confessed to me. "I was going from desk to desk, collecting the homework. I got to his desk and he said, 'I didn't do it.' There was something about his tone of voice. So insolent. I was just so frustrated with him, because Sam is a smart boy, but he just wasn't doing the work. He never did the homework. And that day he seemed to be boasting about it. So I just lost it. I really let him have it. I yelled at him, in class, in front of the other students. I didn't mean to but I did.

"Right afterward, I was worried he'd never speak to me again," Kate said. "I expected to get an angry phone call from the parents. To be honest, I was worried I might get fired. I mean, I yelled at him in front of the entire class. But the next day Sam turned in his homework, perfect and on time, for the first time ever. He even asked me whether I would like to look at his collection of baseball cards. Those baseball cards are his most prized possession. He'd never shown them to me, or to any adult at the school, before.

"Then, three weeks later, his mom finally did call. I was so nervous! I was sure she was going to be angry with me for screaming at her son. But she wasn't. She was calling to thank me. She didn't seem to know anything about that episode. She wanted to know what magic I had used to get Sam so energized about his schoolwork. I didn't know what to say. I didn't feel I could tell her what really happened."

I am not recommending that you ever yell at a student in class. You should never lose your cool in front of your students. But I think this difference illustrates some of the girl/boy differences that teachers need to understand. "If I had done that with a girl, I'm sure she wouldn't have spoken to me for the rest of the semester, at the very least," adds Kate. "Plus she probably would have gotten half her friends not to talk to me either."

Female Brains, Male Brains?

There was recently a flood of news reports about an Israeli study of the brains of men and women. According to the study authors, there's no such thing as a "male brain" or a "female brain." We are all a mosaic, a mix of male and female.[13] The article received extensive, positive coverage in the media. Kate Wheeling, a reporter for *Science* magazine, breathlessly enthused that the report "could change how scientists study the brain and even how society defines gender."[14]

Other scientists were more critical of the Israeli study. Researchers at Yale and Massachusetts General Hospital pointed out that if one were to apply the standards of the Israeli study to animals, it would be difficult to distinguish cats from dogs. After all, there are few characteristics that reliably distinguish every cat from every dog. And the differences between a Saint Bernard and a Chihuahua are, on many parameters, larger than the differences between a Chihuahua and a Siamese kitten. Nevertheless, the researchers at Yale and at Massachusetts General Hospital, using data similar to those used by the Israeli investigators, were able to classify 92 percent of brains as either male or female, even after controlling for overall size differences.[15] Another Israeli, Dr. Marek Glezerman, criticized the study on more fundamental grounds. The original study was just a study of brain *anatomy*, not a study of brain *function*. No conclusions about brain *function* can be drawn from a study of brain *anatomy*, Dr. Glezerman observed. Just because you and I both own Toyota Camrys doesn't mean that we drive the same. You may often drive recklessly, well over the speed limit, while I always drive cautiously, below the speed limit. No superficial examination of the *structure* of our cars will reveal the important differences in how we *use* the cars.[16]

But the most important shortcoming of the much-reported Israeli study was that it was based almost entirely on data from *adults*. The big differences between girls and boys are not in brain anatomy or brain function but in the pace and sequence of development. We now have very good evidence that relatively small differences in age can produce big differences in outcomes. For example, in one nationwide study of more than eleven thousand American students, the youngest kids in the classroom were, by eighth grade, roughly twice as likely to be diagnosed with ADHD compared with the oldest kids in the classroom, even though in that study the difference between the youngest kids and the oldest kids was typically less than twelve months.[17] But the difference in brain development between girls and boys is consistently greater than twelve months, on average. For example, in one large study of brain development, the average girl reached the inflection point—roughly the halfway point in brain development, indicated by the arrow in the graph on the next page—around age eleven, roughly four *years* before the average boy, as shown in the same graph.[18] Different studies have given different results, but every study of brain development in children shows that boys lag significantly behind girls in the pace of brain development.

In chapter 1 I related how—twenty years ago—I started seeing a wave of young boys flooding my office. Each boy's parent carried a note from somebody at the school (teacher, guidance counselor, reading specialist) suggesting that Justin or Brett or Carlos or Simon might have ADHD. I evaluated each of these kids to determine whether each one met the criteria for ADHD. Some kids did meet the criteria; others did not. I've already mentioned how some of the boys who were sent to my office with a presumed diagnosis of ADHD actually were normal boys who were sitting in the back of a class in which the teacher was a young woman who didn't talk very loudly.

Girls' Brains Develop Faster Than Boys' Brains

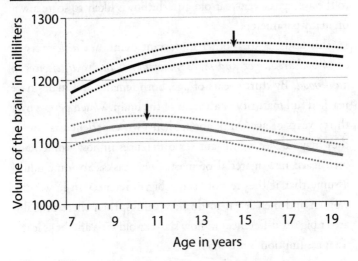

The darker line shows average volume of boys' brains, with 95% confidence intervals above and below. The lighter line shows average volume of girls' brains, with 95% confidence intervals above and below. The arrows indicate the inflection points, roughly the halfway point in brain development. Girls reach the inflection point roughly four years earlier than boys do.

Source: Rhoshel Lenroot and colleagues, "Sexual Dimorphism of Brain Developmental Trajectories During Childhood and Adolescence," Neuroimage, *volume 36, pp. 1065–1073, 2007, Figure 2(a).*

But there was another important difference that the school was overlooking. Girls and boys differ in the speed at which they mature. For example, researchers at Wellesley College found that three-and-a-half-year-old girls could interpret facial expressions as well as or better than five-year-old boys.[19] Comparing a five-year-old boy to a five-year-old girl may in some respects be similar to comparing a three-and-a-half-year-old girl to a five-year-old girl. The boy will appear less mature, less self-controlled, less able to concentrate and focus for sustained periods of time, compared to the girl. There are no differences between adult men and women in the ability to concentrate and focus. But children are not adults. When you compare the average five-year-old boy to the average five-year-old girl, or the average eleven-year-old boy to the average eleven-year-old girl, the boy is likely to score lower on many parameters.

This leads us to another important point. *Sex differences in childhood are larger and more important than sex differences in adulthood.* By thirty years of age, both females and males have reached full maturity of all areas of the brain. When people over thirty years of age think about their own experience as adults, they may not see significant sex differences in how women and men learn new material or master new tasks. So some adults assume that if they're not seeing big differences in how adult women and men learn to do new things, then there probably aren't big sex differences in how six-year-old girls and boys learn. That assumption is mistaken.

Acceleration

Thirty years ago, when kindergarten was all about finger-painting and singing together and playing duck-duck-goose, sex differences in brain maturation didn't matter as much. Thirty years ago, kindergartners weren't expected to sit in chairs and do pencil-and-paper exercises for much of the day. First graders might have to do that, but kindergarten was more about social-ization, about learning to get along with other kids.

Not anymore. Today educators throughout North America make no apologies for the academic character of the twenty-first-century kindergarten. The curriculum of kindergarten today is essentially the first-grade curriculum of thirty years ago.[20] The primary objective of most American kindergartens today is sim-ple: achieving literacy and numeracy. While that sounds good, there's a problem. Many five-year-old boys just don't have the patience to sit still for a sixty-minute lesson on diphthongs or the fine motor skills to write the letters of the alphabet as neatly as the girls do. In the jargon of educational psychology, the objectives of today's academically oriented kindergarten are not *developmentally appropriate* for many kindergarten boys.

The unspoken assumption behind the push to teach reading and writing in kindergarten is that earlier exposure will guarantee improved performance. But that assumption is valid only if what you're teaching is developmentally appropriate for your students. If you try to teach your seven-year-old kid to drive a car, you won't end up with a better driver. You may end up with a smashed fender and an injured child instead. Trying to teach kids to read before they're really ready to read can actually boomerang and turn them *off* to reading.

When I share this with kindergarten teachers, some respond, "Oh, we understand that! We understand that not every five-year-old is ready for reading, not ready for paper-and-pencil exercises and all that. We customize what we do to each child's individual needs."

That sounds nice. But what does it really mean in practice? What it actually means, sometimes, is that kindergarten is divided in two. Over here, with the teacher, are the kids who can handle the academic curriculum of today's accelerated kindergarten. These kids are sounding out words, writing short sentences, remembering to put a capital letter at the start of the sentence and a period at the end. This group is mostly girls with a few boys.

Over there are the kids who aren't ready to handle the accelerated academic curriculum. Those kids are playing with blocks or putting together puzzles—activities most of us recognize as traditional kindergarten activities from our own childhood.

A five-year-old boy may not be very good at fine motor skills such as writing the letters of the alphabet, and he may not be developmentally ready to learn about vowels and consonants. But there's one thing most five-year-old boys are very good at: figuring out that they've been put in the "dumb group." And they don't like it.

That's what happened to Matthew, the boy whose story opens chapter 1. Before starting kindergarten, Matthew had always been the star, the leading player in the drama of his life. "He was always ready to try anything," his mother told me. "Last July I suggested to my husband that we paddle a canoe across the Potomac, at White's Ferry. My husband didn't want to. But Matthew did, so we rented a canoe, just me and five-year-old Matthew, and we had a great time. The rental place gave him this little plastic paddle. He loved it. He talked about it for days afterward. But now it's different. It's like he's turned into a completely different kid. He never used to throw temper tantrums before, but he's throwing a tantrum almost every morning now, for no reason, refusing to get dressed, refusing to go to school. I have to carry him kicking and screaming into the car and then drag him from the car into the school. You'd think they were torturing him or doing something horrible. But they're not. I've sat in on his kindergarten and there's nothing wrong with it. The teacher is wonderful, in fact. She's very gentle, very patient. I've talked with her, and she's reassured me that this is nothing unusual. She keeps saying I shouldn't worry. But I'm still concerned. Matthew's starting to hate school."

While Matthew's reaction was extreme, many studies now have shown that when the main emphasis in kindergarten is on learning to read at the expense of other less structured and more developmentally appropriate activities, many boys tune out and turn off. Those boys develop negative feelings toward school that are likely to persist and color the child's entire academic career.[21] Deborah Stipek, who has served more than a decade as dean of the School of Education at Stanford University, has shown that kids who fail to do well in kindergarten develop "negative perceptions of competence," and those negative attitudes are "difficult to reverse as [they] progress through school."[22]

When Matthew's mother, Cindy, told me that her son was throwing a tantrum every morning, I advised her to take him out of kindergarten and put him back in preschool. Right now. One more month in that kindergarten and his whole attitude toward school might be irreparably damaged.

Cindy refused. She kept saying, "But he's bright. Who's ever heard of a bright child flunking out of kindergarten?"

He wasn't flunking out, I told her. This kindergarten was just not developmentally appropriate for him.

Cindy insisted on keeping Matthew in kindergarten. A month later she told me that the problem had been solved: Matthew wasn't throwing tantrums anymore. The teacher said that he was behaving better in class.

One year later Mom was back with Matthew, now in first grade. This time Cindy had one of those papers from the school. "Matthew is inattentive and easily distracted in class. . . . Would you please evaluate to determine whether Matthew might meet criteria for ADHD." And of course the teacher was absolutely right about Matthew not paying attention. Matthew *was* inattentive and easily distracted in class. He was now firmly convinced that school was just one big bore, an annoyance to be endured for a few hours each day until that wonderful moment when school let out and he could go home and do all the fun things he enjoyed. As far as Matthew was concerned, his life really began each day only when school ended.

"What's your favorite subject at school?" I asked.

"Recess," he said.

"What's your next-favorite subject?" I asked.

"Lunch," he said.

There are few good choices for parents at this point. "Retention in grade," holding Matthew back a year at the same school, won't solve the problem at this stage. You've already missed your best chance. There's a big difference between *delaying* a child's entry to kindergarten and his *repeating* first grade a year later. If you delay entry into kindergarten for a boy like Matthew so he starts at age six, he'll do better than if you start him in kindergarten at age five. But if you make him start kindergarten when he's not ready for it, and then you make him repeat first grade when the time comes, at the same school, he may do *worse* than if you didn't make him repeat.[23] The stigmatizing effect of having to repeat a year of school has a long-lasting effect that is not easily fixed. The boy labels himself as "dumb," and he believes that label, and no amount of talking on your part will change his mind.

In Matthew's case, the best intervention was to enroll him at a different school, in a different neighborhood with a new peer group, where he repeated first grade—but none of his peers knew that he was repeating first grade. He did well. He didn't have ADHD or any other psychiatric disorder. He just wasn't a good fit for the accelerated tempo of today's elementary education.

Matthew's story is all too common today. As I showed in my book *The Collapse of Parenting*, a child in the United States is now many times more likely to be on medication for ADHD compared with a child in the United Kingdom.[24] I have to wonder how many of these children, boys especially, are not paying attention in the classroom because they're trapped in a school that just is not geared to their needs, being taught at a tempo that's out of sync with their brain development.

The Medicalization of Misbehavior

Why are kids in the United States, especially boys, so much more likely to be on medication for ADHD compared with kids elsewhere? One part of the answer is what I call "the medicalization of misbehavior."[25] Instead of correcting our kids' misbehavior, we American parents today are more likely to medicate our kids, in hopes of fixing the behavior problem with a pill.

I'm not saying that boys are better behaved elsewhere. I have seen plenty of boys in Australia and New Zealand and the UK who are bouncing and making buzzing noises when they are supposed to be sitting still. But the teacher does not refer the boy for psychiatric evaluation. Instead the teacher tells the boy in a firm voice that she has had quite enough of that silliness, thank you, and that it is high time for it to stop.

Imagine an eight- or ten-year-old boy who misbehaves. He talks back to teachers. He is deliberately spiteful and vindictive. He doesn't listen. He once spit at the teacher. He seems to have little or no self-control. Thirty years ago, even twenty years ago, the school counselor or the principal might have said to the parent, *Your son is disrespectful. He is rude. He exhibits no self-control. You need to teach him some basic rules about civilized behavior if he is going to stay at this school.* Today it is much less common for an American school counselor or administrator to speak so bluntly to a parent. Instead, the counselor or administrator will suggest a consultation with a physician or a psychologist. And the physician or psychologist will look at the reports from the school and talk about Oppositional Defiant Disorder or Attention-Deficit/ Hyperactivity Disorder or Pediatric Bipolar Disorder.

What's the difference between saying *Your son is disrespectful* and saying *Your son may meet criteria for a psychiatric disorder*? There's a big difference. When I say *Your son is disrespectful*, the burden of responsibility is on you, the parent, and on your child. With that responsibility comes the authority to do something about the problem. But when I say *Your son may meet criteria for a psychiatric disorder*, then the burden of responsibility shifts away from the parent and the child to the prescribing physician and indeed to the whole burgeoning medical/psychiatric/counseling complex. And the reasonable next question from the parents is not *What should we do to change his behavior?* but rather *Should he begin taking a medication?*

The medications work. They do change the child's behavior. That's what I find so scary. These medications are being used in North America as a means of behavior modification to an extent that is almost unimaginable in other parts of the world.[26]

These are powerful medications. The most popular medications for ADHD are the prescription stimulants such as Adderall, Vyvanse, Concerta, Metadate, Focalin, Daytrana, Ritalin, and Quillivant. All these medications work in the same way: they increase the action of dopamine at synapses in the brain.[27] Dopamine is a key neurotransmitter in the nucleus accumbens, the brain's motivational center. More precisely, the nucleus accumbens is the part of the brain that is responsible for translating motivation into action. If a boy's nucleus accumbens is damaged, he may feel hungry but isn't likely to work to prepare a meal for himself. If you damage the nucleus accumbens, the result is likely to be less motivation, less engagement, less drive to achieve in the real world.

Many of the studies mentioned here are based on research in laboratory animals, not in humans. But researchers have recently documented that stimulant medications such as Adderall and Vyvanse prescribed for ADHD may actually shrink the nucleus accumbens and related structures in the *human* brain.[28] The smaller size of the nucleus accumbens in people treated with medication for ADHD can't be attributed to ADHD itself, because ADHD itself is associated with a slightly *larger*-than-average nucleus accumbens;[29] but after treatment, the nucleus accumbens is actually *smaller* than average. It appears, then, that stimulant medications for ADHD may shrink the nucleus accumbens in humans. That's especially disturbing in light of research that documents a nearly linear correlation between the nucleus accumbens and individual motivation. These studies suggest that the smaller the nucleus accumbens, the more likely that person is to be apathetic, lacking in drive.[30]

Today American parents are hungry for brain-based explanations, often overlooking common sense as a result. Consider the increasingly widespread problem of sleep deprivation in children. Instead of turning off the video games so their son can get a good night's sleep, many American parents are medicating their kids with Adderall or Concerta or Vyvanse or Metadate to compensate for the symptoms of sleep deprivation (such as inattention), often without any awareness that sleep deprivation is the underlying problem. Instead, the boy's failure to pay attention has been misdiagnosed as ADHD. Likewise: instead of acknowledging that their son misbehaves, many American parents would prefer that a doctor diagnose an imbalance in brain chemistry and prescribe Risperdal or Seroquel or Adderall or Concerta.

ADHD is real. But it is overdiagnosed. ADHD is primarily a cognitive disorder: kids who truly have ADHD *cannot* pay attention very well, even if they want to. But often kids are not paying attention in school not because they *can't* but because they *don't want to*. The question I asked Matthew—what's your favorite subject at school?—is useful in distinguishing the kid who truly has ADHD from the kid who just hates school. Ask: "What's your favorite *subject* at school?" Emphasize the word *subject*. If the answer is "recess" or "lunch," take a step back and reassess. This boy knows that recess is not a subject. If he says that his favorite subject at school is recess, he's telling me that he has no interest in school. He is disengaged. Maybe he hates school. Hating school is a major problem, but it is, by itself, not ADHD or any other psychiatric disorder. The appropriate intervention is not to put the child on powerful medications but to understand *why* the child hates school. Sometimes you will find that the problem is not in the child at all but in the school. Other times the problem is that the child has not been taught proper rules of behavior.

Don't give in to "the medicalization of misbehavior." Teach your son that a gentleman does not talk back to teachers, use bad language, spit, bite, kick, or otherwise disrupt the classroom. Regard medication not as a first resort but as a last resort when all other measures have been tried and have not worked.

Girls Are Shortchanged Too

So far in this chapter, I have shared my experience of the ways in which gender-blind education is harmful to boys. But girls are being shortchanged as well. Gender-blind education tends to perpetuate gender stereotypes, and as a result, fewer girls than boys are really excited about subjects such as physics, computer science, and advanced math. The long-term results are not good. In 1995 women constituted 37 percent of professionals working in computer science. Today women are just 24 percent of the computer science workforce, a number that is forecast to drop to 22 percent in 2025.[31] In 2015—the latest year for which data are available—78 percent of students who took the AP exam in computer science were boys, and only 22 percent were girls.[32] When teachers use girl-friendly instructional strategies for teaching computer science, the results can be dramatic: in one study, the use of girl-friendly instructional strategies more than tripled the proportion of sixth-grade girls who wanted to spend their free time working on their computer program, from 16 percent to 51 percent.[33] Gender-blind instruction disadvantages both girls and boys. (I realize that there are factors other than gender-blind instruction that discourage women from entering computer science, but the fact that girls are a minority of students studying computer science is certainly a major contributing factor.)

When I use the phrase "girl-friendly instructional strategies," some people cringe. They think I'm recommending that you bring in bunnies to teach biology to girls or that you try to teach physics to girls by talking about relationships. I cringe at that sort of thing too.

But my girl-friendly strategies are based on what really works in the classroom, not in stereotypes. When I lead workshops for teachers, I share what I have learned from my visits to more than four hundred schools over the past sixteen years. I have found that there is more than one way to teach the content. There are girl-friendly approaches and there are boy-friendly approaches. You can do both, even in the coed classroom, but you have to know what you are doing and how to do it.

In my workshops I go through each of the content areas—math, sciences, English, creative writing, expository writing, social studies, history, music, and visual arts—and I show how you can teach a particular content area in a girl-friendly way or in a boy-friendly way. The objective is to understand both approaches and to engage every student in the classroom: every girl and every boy. Allow me to give you a concrete example: number theory for middle-school kids.

As a rule, I have found that boys are more interested in number theory "for its own sake" at a much earlier age than girls are. You can fascinate a group of twelve-year-old boys by getting them to think about transcendental numbers such as Φ (pronounced "fie," not to be confused with π). Here's a good way to introduce Φ to twelve-year-old boys, which I first learned about from teachers at Fairfield Country Day School, a boys' school in western Connecticut:

I'm thinking of a number between 1 and 2.

The reciprocal of that number is equal to that same number minus 1.

Can you tell me what number I'm thinking of?

The teacher calls on a boy. "Uhh, one and a half?" the boy says. The teacher explains: Not quite. The reciprocal of 1½ is ⅔, and ⅔ does not equal ½ (which is 1½ minus 1). She calls on the next boy. He says, "Don't you have to write an equation?"

"Excellent," she says. "Won't you please come up to the board and write it?" With a little help, he writes the equation:

$$1/x = x - 1$$

With a little more help, another boy figures out that the equation above can be simplified if you multiply both sides by x, yielding

$$1 = x^2 - x$$

Subtracting 1 from both sides yields

$$x^2 - x - 1 = 0$$

You can then use the quadratic formula to solve for x:

$$x = (1 \pm \sqrt{5})/2$$

We're looking for a number between 1 and 2, so we choose the positive solution:

$$= (1 + \sqrt{5})/2$$
$$= 0.5 + 1.11803398874989\ldots$$
$$= 1.61803398874989\ldots$$

You can tell the boys that mathematicians refer to this number as Φ. Sure enough, this number Φ has the characteristic we were looking for: the reciprocal of this number exactly equals this number minus 1:

$$1/1.61803398874989\ldots = 0.61803398874989\ldots$$

None of the boys is especially excited about this. But now you change the subject (or appear to change the subject). You tell them about the Fibonacci series. A Fibonacci series is formed by adding two numbers to yield a third number and reiterating the process to form a sequence. The simplest Fibonacci sequence is

$$1 + 1 = 2$$

$$1 + 2 = 3$$

$$2 + 3 = 5$$

$$3 + 5 = 8$$

$$5 + 8 = 13$$

$$8 + 13 = 21$$

$$13 + 21 = 34$$

This yields the series 1, 1, 2, 3, 5, 8, 13, 21, 34, 55, 89, 144 . . .

Now ask your boys to take each number in the Fibonacci series and divide it by the number before it, starting with 3, and list their answers.

$$3/2 = 1.5$$

$$5/3 = 1.666 \ldots$$

$$8/5 = 1.6$$

$$13/8 = 1.625$$

$$21/13 = 1.61538 \ldots$$

$$34/21 = 1.61905 \ldots$$

$$55/34 = 1.61764 \ldots$$

$$89/55 = 1.61818 \ldots$$

$$144/89 = 1.617977 \ldots$$

$$233/144 = 1.61805 \ldots$$

Now you can point out to the boys (if they haven't noticed already) that this process seems to be converging on Φ. Why is that? you ask them.

While they're thinking about that, you show them a circle with a pentagon inside it, with a triangle inscribed inside the pentagon. Have them look at the triangle. Let them know that the side of the triangle is exactly equal to Φ times the length of the base. Why is that? Why does Φ keep popping up where you don't expect it?

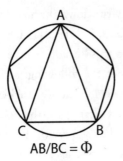

AB/BC = Φ

College women may be just as interested in number theory and transcendental numbers as college men are. As I said earlier, sex differences diminish as a function of age. But if you want twelve-year-old girls to be excited about the Fibonacci series, the strategy just presented is not effective. In order to get every twelve-year-old girl excited about number theory, you need to connect it with the real world. That's what I have observed in the classroom. At schools where the majority of twelve-year-old girls are really excited about number theory, they teach Φ and Fibonacci numbers, but they teach them differently. You begin by explaining how the Fibonacci series is formed:

1 + 1 = 2

1 + 2 = 3

2 + 3 = 5

3 + 5 = 8

5 + 8 = 13

8 + 13 = 21

13 + 21 = 34

And so forth. You write down the first twelve numbers in the Fibonacci series: 1, 1, 2, 3, 5, 8, 13, 21, 34, 55, 89, 144 . . .

In preparation for this session, you've already asked your girls to bring in any of the following: artichokes, sunflowers, pineapples, pinecones, delphiniums, black-eyed Susans, Shasta daisies, and field daisies. Start with the flowers. (Teachers have explained to me that they start with flowers not because flowers are "feminine" but because it's easier to count the number of petals on a daisy than it is to count the rows of bracts on a pinecone.) Count the number of petals. You'll find that the number of petals is almost always a number in the Fibonacci series: 8 petals for delphiniums, 13 for delphiniums, 21 for black-eyed Susans, and 34 for field daisies.[34]

Then you can move on to the artichokes, sunflowers, pinecones, and pineapples. These are more complicated. In these you're studying the number of rows, or bracts, rather than the number of petals. The number of rows counted vertically or obliquely will, again, be a number in the Fibonacci series. You can get more examples like these from the book *Fascinating Fibonaccis* by Trudi Hammel Garland. Older girls may enjoy *The Golden Ratio: The Story of PHI, the World's Most Astonishing Number* by Mario Livio. Or you might even let them read Dan Brown's novel *The Da Vinci Code* and challenge them to verify or invalidate each of the many claims made in that book about Φ and the Fibonacci series. Show them examples of natural phenomena that manifest Φ, such as a dying leaf or a spiral nebula. At this point you might also mention the fact that

$$\Phi - 1 = 1/\Phi$$

But don't expect the girls to ooh and aah over that fact the way the boys do. Twelve-year-old girls are likely to be more interested in the real-world applications of number theory than in remote abstractions. The girls are also more likely to be interested in the beliefs of the ancient Pythagoreans regarding the magical and mystical properties of Φ.

Now these girls will start asking questions. Why do numbers in the Fibonacci series keep showing up when you count the petals on a delphinium or the bracts on a pinecone? Why is it that a dying poinsettia leaf and a spiral nebula both manifest Φ? How can abstract number theory explain these similarities? And you will have accomplished something that is rare in North American classrooms: you've got twelve-year-old girls excited about number theory.

I like this example because it illustrates an important point: *There are few differences in what girls and boys can learn. But there are big differences in the best ways to teach them.* At the end of the day you will have taught both girls and boys about the properties of Φ, using the Fibonacci series as an introduction to number theory. But if you teach that material the way it's often taught (the way we taught it to the boys in my example above), then many of the girls will tune out and be bored.

When Is an A Not an A?

Remember Melanie, the gifted student who wanted to take physics her senior year? One of the things about Melanie that always impresses me is her willingness to try something new. She is supremely self-confident. In that respect Melanie is, unfortunately, not your typical girl.

Beth is another girl I know. Beth is every bit as smart as Melanie, but she doesn't have Melanie's self-confidence. Like Melanie,

Beth "aced" biology and was a favorite student of Ms. Griffith. But when Ms. Griffith suggested that Beth sign up for physics, Beth hesitated. "I just don't think I'm smart enough for physics," Beth said. "I've never done anything like that, and I don't want to risk getting a B or worse on my transcript." She ended up taking psychology in her senior year instead of physics.

Girls on average outperform boys in school (as measured by report card grades), in most subjects and in all age groups; and those differences are widening.[35] Because girls do better in school, one might imagine that girls would be more self-confident about their academic abilities and that they would have higher academic self-esteem. But that's not the case. Paradoxically, girls are more likely to be excessively critical in evaluating their own academic performance. Conversely, boys tend to have unrealistically high estimates of their own academic abilities and accomplishments.[36]

Those are some of the paradoxes teachers face: the girl like Beth who gets straight A's but has no real confidence in her own abilities; the boy who's getting B's and C's but thinks he's brilliant. That leads us to a basic difference in teaching style for girls versus boys. Many girls need encouragement. Some boys, on the other hand, need a reality check, a reminder that they're not as accomplished as they think they are.

A Blunder at Harvard

Gender differences made the headlines right around the time that the first edition of *Why Gender Matters* was published, owing to some unwise remarks made by the man who was then president of Harvard University: Larry Summers. On January 14, 2005, Dr. Summers offered several reasons why there are so few women professors in subjects like computer science and physics. President Summers began by acknowledging that sexism probably plays some role—but he did not consider sexism to be a major factor. Second, he asserted that women make different lifestyle choices than men do. In particular (according to Dr. Summers), women with small children at home might be less willing to put in long hours at work than men are.

If he had just stopped there, he might not have gotten into too much trouble. But Dr. Summers went on to say that a third factor must be at work specifically with regard to subjects like computer science and physics. The third factor, the esteemed professor said, has to do with innate differences in "intrinsic aptitude."[37] In other words—according to the president of Harvard University—women just don't have the brains to excel in physics.

When the president of Harvard University says that women are innately less capable in science, a firestorm is sure to erupt. On the conservative end of the spectrum, commentators such as Linda Chavez and Cathy Young sprang to Summers' defense. They suggested that because little boys prefer to play with trucks rather than dolls, boys are destined to be better at physics. They also invoked the idea that boys are more variable than girls: just as mental retardation is more common among boys than among girls, so too is genius more common among boys than among girls (according to these commentators).[38] At the other end of the spectrum, the majority of the Harvard faculty of arts and sciences rose in anger to denounce their president. One Harvard physics professor said it was "crazy" to suggest that there are any hardwired differences of any significance between girls and boys.[39] On March 15, 2005, the faculty voted no confidence in Summers' leadership.[40]

In fact, both sides of this debate got it wrong. The outraged liberals were demonstrably wrong on the facts when they asserted that there are no important hardwired differences between girls and boys: if you don't agree, please reread chapter 2 of this book. But Dr. Summers was wrong to suggest that *differences* imply an *order of rank*. A knife is different from a spoon. That doesn't mean that a knife is better or worse than a spoon. Girls and boys are different. That doesn't mean that boys are necessarily destined to be better physicists—unless physics is taught in a way that gives boys an advantage at the expense of girls.

In my book *Girls on the Edge* I shared some of what I learned from two visits to Korowa, a girls' school in Melbourne, Australia. At Korowa more than half the girls take the Australian equivalent of Advanced Placement physics. That's an extraordinary achievement. How do they do it? They teach physics differently.

At most high schools, physics instruction begins with that part of physics called *kinematics*: velocity, acceleration, and Newton's laws of motion. That means you're talking about race cars accelerating or soccer players colliding.

On both my visits to Korowa, I met with Jenn Alabaster, the lead physics instructor at the school. "Where is it written that physics instruction has to begin with kinematics?" she said to me. That's not where she starts the school year. She begins with the wave-particle duality of light: the fact that light sometimes behaves like a wave and sometimes like a particle, depending on how you test it. She has found that almost every girl is fascinated by the wave-particle duality of light—including the girly girl who has a photo of Kylie Jenner as the screen saver on her phone. Of course Ms. Alabaster teaches kinematics, but she teaches it toward the end of the school year. In most other schools I have visited, AP Physics *begins* with kinematics, and the wave-particle duality of light is pushed back into the final weeks of the school year, just before the AP test.[41]

So one aspect of girl-friendly physics may be as simple as the sequence in which the various curriculum items are taught. Beginning the school year with the wave-particle duality of light is a more girl-friendly approach than starting with kinematics and momentum transfer. It's not better. It's not worse. It's just different. Most schools teach physics using the boy-friendly sequence of topics, starting with football players colliding and bombs exploding. Then they wonder why more girls don't want to take the class. Girls may not sign up because they may not know how fascinating physics can be once you get past the collisions and the explosions. "If you're not aware of something that at some point might interest you, how can you choose it?" asks Karen Peterson, the principal investigator for a National Science Foundation–funded project that seeks to understand why girls and women are still underrepresented in subjects like physics.[42]

I don't think you have to have an all-girls classroom in order to engage girls in physics, although it might help. But you definitely need a teacher who understands and respects the differences between girl-friendly instruction and boy-friendly instruction. If you recall what we discussed in chapter 2 about sex differences in the visual system—how the boys' system is more geared for objects in motion and the girls' system is more geared for color and detail—then these sex differences in instructional strategies start to make sense in a larger context.

Some of what we're discovering regarding girl-friendly instruction may not be discovering so much as rediscovering. Historian Kim Tolley has shown that throughout the 1800s, girls routinely outperformed boys in subjects like physics and astronomy. During the same era, boys outperformed girls in foreign languages, especially Greek and Latin. The differences in performance were enormous. Girls routinely outscored the boys by wide margins—70 percent of girls passing compared with only

30 percent of boys—when girls and boys took the same physics exam. These differences were seen throughout the United States, in all social strata, from elite private schools to schools for orphans and Native Americans. The differences in performance were so universal—favoring girls in science and boys in classical languages—that educators in the 1800s had a saying, "Science for the ladies, classics for gentlemen."[43]

What was going on?

As for the boys, they may have done better than girls at learning Greek and Latin in that era for several reasons. First, the most popular ancient Greek and Latin texts that were taught, such as Homer's *Iliad* and Virgil's *Aeneid*, are texts whose main characters are men engaging in stereotypical masculine activities such as fighting and risk taking. Second, the instructional strategies employed in that era, such as rote learning, may be more boy friendly than girl friendly. Third, there seems to have been widespread acceptance of the stereotype that "girls can't learn Greek." Proficiency in Greek and Latin was a requirement for entry to the top colleges, such as the Ivy League, which accepted only men. Women's colleges in that era did not require knowledge of Greek or Latin as a condition for admission.

And why did girls in that era outperform the boys in subjects such as physics and astronomy?

One part of the answer is that subjects such as physics and astronomy were taught very differently in the 1800s, even when the actual facts, such as force diagrams and Newton's laws, were the same then as they are today. In the 1800s the emphasis was on *understanding* the big picture: How is the universe put together? What laws govern the movement of objects in space and on Earth? Learning physics was considered to be a way of understanding the mind of God and therefore was seen as a pious activity suitable for young women. (In the early 1800s, physics was often referred to as "natural theology.") One textbook from that era shows an engraving of a woman instructing a young girl in the use of a telescope. The implicit message of that picture, for a young woman of the time, was *You belong here. Physics is an appropriate subject for you to study.*

Contrast that picture with a typical photograph in a twenty-first-century physics textbook. I have seen the photo on the next page in a number of contemporary physics textbooks. If you show that photo to boys, the reaction is typically positive: "Way cool! That looks like fun! Can we do that? Shoot a rifle at an apple?" I showed this same photo to girls at Branksome Hall, a girls' school in Toronto. One of the girls raised her hand and asked, "Who had to clean up that mess?" Girls are less likely than boys to be excited at the prospect of firing a weapon at a defenseless fruit.

There is more than one way to present the content. Earlier in this chapter we considered various approaches to teaching Fibonacci numbers. Educational researchers Anat Zohar and David Sela found that the same is true of physics. Talking about bombs and bullets and collisions is a good way to teach physics to most boys. And that's the way it's often taught.

A quarterback is stationary. He is looking for a receiver. A cornerback blitzing from the blind side has a mass of 80 kilograms and is running at a speed of 8 meters per second. Assuming that the quarterback has a mass of 90 kilograms, and that the collision is perfectly inelastic with an incident angle of 30 degrees, calculate the motion of the cornerback and the quarterback immediately after the collision.

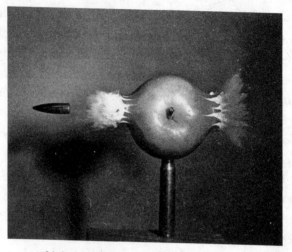

Boys are more likely than girls to get excited at the prospect of firing a weapon at a defenseless fruit. This photo is reproduced with permission of the Harold and Esther Edgerton Family Foundation.

That sort of question engages many boys. But it's less likely to be effective with girls. And not just because it's football. You can try the same thing with train cars colliding, and the girls will still be less excited than the boys, on average. Zohar and Sela found that simply plugging numbers into formulas was unsatisfying for most of the girls in the AP Physics classes they surveyed. The girls were more interested in knowing *why*.[44]

As one girl asked: Why is the gravitational force between two objects inversely proportional to the *square* of the distance between them? Why isn't it inversely proportional to the cube, or the fourth power? As it happens, we do have a set of introductory physics textbooks that focus on the *why*, written by the late Nobel laureate Richard Feynman. It's not watered down: it's rigorous and computational. But it's girl-friendly physics, because it always comes back to the question of *why*. Jenn Alabaster told me she always has a copy of *The Feynman Lectures on Physics* close at hand to share with a girl who wants to dig deeper into the question of *why*.

The great mission of education is to enable every child to fulfill their potential. But what a girl needs to achieve is often different from what a boy needs to achieve. Thirty years of gender-blind education have not ameliorated gender differences in important educational outcomes; in some cases, gender-blind education has exacerbated gender stereotypes by biasing prevailing teaching methods for a subject to appeal to one gender. Ignoring gender differences disadvantages both girls and boys.

CHAPTER 6

Sex

Tina and Jimmy

Tina Jimenez faced a potential triple whammy when she started ninth grade. Ninth grade at a new school isn't easy for anybody. Everybody's trying to figure out who's who and who's cool. Where do *I* fit in? But in addition to the challenge of a new school, Tina had the additional burden of having just moved to the area, not knowing anybody, and also of belonging to a minority group with almost no representation at her new school. Her family had just moved to suburban Maryland from Miami, Florida. Both her parents had immigrated to the United States in the 1970s from the Dominican Republic.

Being a dark-skinned Hispanic girl at Seneca Valley High—which is overwhelmingly white—might have been a major problem for some girls, but Tina made friends easily. Three weeks into the new school year she was off to a good start. Her soccer teammates were impressed by her fearlessness on the field. She was a skillful player, but she didn't make a big deal about it. The other girls on the team soon were including her in everything they did, adopting her as one of their own.

She and most of the other soccer girls were invited to a party the last Saturday in September at a large house in the upscale section of Germantown. Tina stayed close to her friend and soccer buddy Jennifer, a tenth grader. After they had been at the party for half an hour, Tina noticed an older boy staring at her. "Who's that?" she asked Jennifer.

"Who's what?" Jennifer shouted over the music.

"That blond guy over there, wearing the Redskins sweatshirt," Tina said.

"Oooh. That's Jimmy. Jimmy Mandeville. Senior. Football player. Not so great as a football player. But in other departments he's supposed to be a *monster*," Jennifer winked.

Tina rolled her eyes and shook her head. "I'm *totally* not interested," she said.

Jimmy came over to them, his eyes fixed on Tina. "Hi," he said. His breath smelled of beer—which was not surprising, as he was holding an open Budweiser can.

"Hi," both girls said.

Jimmy looked Tina up and down, his glassy eyes lingering on her chest. He was nodding his head in time to the beat of the music. "Wanna hook up?" he asked Tina point-blank.

Tina's eyes went wide.

"Hey, Jennifer!" Another boy appeared out of nowhere and grabbed Jennifer by the arm. "You gotta see this! Come on!" Jennifer gave Tina a sad look as if to say, *Sorry to leave you all by yourself.* And Jennifer was gone.

Please don't leave me, Jennifer, Tina thought. Her heart sank. Jimmy towered over her. The way he was nodding his head in time with the music began to irritate her. And she was worried that he might spill some of his beer on her blouse.

"Wanna hook up," he said again, more a statement than a question.

"What do you mean?" she asked, stalling for time. She knew what he meant. But she didn't know how to say no without offending him or sounding lame. And as a freshman talking to a popular senior, she didn't have the confidence to just turn her back and walk away.

He snorted in amazement, then burped. "Freshman girl. Come on, I'll show you." He grabbed her by the arm, tossed the half-empty beer can onto the carpet, and pulled her into a small study lit only by a tabletop lamp on a desk. Tina saw another couple already in a corner of the room, fondling each other. Before she could say anything, Jimmy pulled her down to the floor beside the desk.

Jimmy groped at her breasts with one hand while he fumbled with the snap on her pants with his other. Tina's mind was in a whirl. *This is crazy. How can this be happening?* She wanted to push him off, to scream . . . but what would happen next? The other kids would laugh at her. *Freshman girl. Prude. Dork.*

"Come *on*," Jimmy said. "What's your problem?"

"I—I don't know how . . ." Tina said.

"Seriously? I'll show you," Jimmy said. "Come on!" he snapped, standing up and pulling her to a kneeling position, facing him. He unzipped his fly.

Tina had never given a boy oral sex before. She had heard other girls talk about it, of course, but the idea repulsed her. Why would any girl want to have a boy's you-know-what in her *mouth*? Yuck. Now a total stranger, a boy she had never met, a boy she wasn't even attracted to . . .

Three minutes later it was over.

"Sweet. A little clumsy on your end, but sweet," Jimmy said. "With a little more experience, you could be dynamite, sister. See ya later." Zipping up his fly, he left the room without looking back.

"I couldn't see. Did you spit or swallow?" The question came from a skinny boy Tina had never seen before, who had apparently been watching from across the room. He giggled.

Tina thought she would vomit.

Hooking Up

Girls and boys face very different challenges when it comes to sex. Most young women enjoy physical intimacy more when it develops in the context of a loving relationship. Few women or girls really understand how different sex is for many men and for most boys. And the type of intimacy most common among teenagers today—hooking up—feeds into the worst kind of male sexuality. "Hooking up"—in case you didn't know—means being physically intimate with the understanding that *no* romantic relationship is implied and none is expected. It's sex without love, sex without the "bother" of a relationship.

"I can't tell you how many girls come in who are bereft about having had sex too soon," says New York psychologist Marsha Levy-Warren. She's seeing more and more teen and preteen girls whose emotional lives are in turmoil after some kind of sexual encounter. "They went to a party.... They hooked up and did what they assumed everyone was doing. Then they feel awful." Teachers and counselors are hearing about more and more sexual activity "of a detached, unemotional kind" among preteens and young teens. "I call it body-part sex," says Dr. Levy-Warren. "The kids don't even look at each other. It's mechanical, dehumanizing. The fallout is that later in life they have trouble forming relationships. They're jaded."[1]

"Oral sex is definitely a trend," says Professor Peter Leone of the University of North Carolina at Chapel Hill. "And it's happening in public because teenagers don't see it as a big deal." In some places "oral sex is taken so lightly that it's treated like a racy version of Truth or Dare or Spin the Bottle."[2] "A girl who did it for her boyfriend on a school bus was upset when she found a line of guys in school the next week wanting her to go down on them," says Tamara Kreinin, president of the Sexuality Information and Education Council. Another girl "went down on a bunch of guys at a party, and then the next week in sex ed, the other kids said, 'Amy was going down on guys at this party—she should teach the class.' The girl wasn't ready for that. I've had lots of kids tell me that they got this sick feeling in their stomachs the next day."[3]

Here's what one sixteen-year-old girl told me: "I was in a hookup with this guy Zachary. I tried to kiss him and he wouldn't let me. That was weird. I mean, we were doing stuff way beyond kissing, but he didn't want to kiss. I asked him why he didn't want to kiss me and he was like—'I don't kiss girls on the mouth because if I'm not in a relationship, why should I kiss?'"

Several boys have told me, in words similar to Zachary's, that they deliberately avoid kissing a girl when they're hooking up. These boys really believe that they're being virtuous—in a weird, twenty-first-century way—by *not* kissing the girl they're hooking up with. These boys believe that kissing a girl on the lips sends the message *I'm interested in having a romantic relationship with you.* They don't want to send that message. By keeping face-to-face interactions *out* of the encounter, by restricting their intimacy to oral sex or a groping "quick feel," these boys believe that they are at least being honest about their intentions—which are purely physical.

Another girl said: "I know it was just a hookup. But it felt so right, I was sure he would call. I just couldn't believe it when he never called. Then two weeks later, after I hadn't heard from him at all, I saw him at a party and he wanted to hook up again. It made me feel dirty. Like he just wanted to, like, *use* me, use my body. Like I wasn't really even there. Like he was just jerking off, using me instead of looking at porn."

In chapter 10 we will turn our attention to lesbian, gay, and bisexual individuals. Our focus in this chapter is on "straight" aka heterosexual girls and boys. But when I do presentations on the topic of girl/boy differences in sex and sexual motivation, somebody always raises their hand at this point with a question which is some variation on *This may be true for straight kids, but what about lesbian and gay kids?* The short answer is that gay boys are boys, and lesbian girls are girls. Young gay men, just like young straight men, are often interested in sex for the sake of sex and not necessarily as part of a romantic relationship. Young lesbian women, just like young straight women, are more likely to say that sex is more fulfilling in the context of a romantic relationship. Girl/boy differences are more profound and more fundamental than sexual orientation. I will flesh out this point at greater length in chapter 10.

Choosing Virginity?

The Centers for Disease Control has reported that the number of teenagers age fifteen to nineteen who have had sexual intercourse decreased significantly between 1988 and 2010.[4] The decrease was especially striking for boys. In 1988, 60 percent of never-married young men fifteen to nineteen years old reported that they had had sexual intercourse; by 2010 that figure had dropped

Fewer Teens Are Engaging in Sexual Intercourse

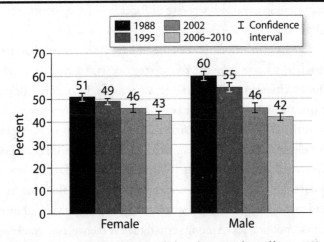

The proportion of teens ages 15 to 19 who have ever had sexual intercourse decreased between 1988 and 2010.
Source: *Centers for Disease Control and Prevention*

to just 42 percent. What happened? Are more boys saving themselves for marriage? Have they discovered religion? (In this chapter "sexual intercourse" means penile-vaginal intercourse; when I mean "oral sex," I will say "oral sex.")

Let's take a closer look at the CDC study. CDC investigators interviewed a demographically representative sample of 4,662 teens from across the country, asking each teen—in a structured one-on-one interview—whether she or he had ever had intercourse. Then the researchers compared those results with results from previous studies. In 1988, 51 percent of never-married young women fifteen to nineteen years of age reported that they had had intercourse at least once; by 2010 that was down to 43 percent. As noted, the decline for young men was even steeper (from 60 percent to 42 percent).

What happened? And why was the reduction among boys—a

reduction of 18 percent, from 60 percent to 42 percent—more than double the girls' decrease of 8 percent, from 51 percent to 43 percent?

As I have mentioned previously, I have visited more than four hundred schools over the past sixteen years. I have talked with kids in cities, in suburbs, and in rural areas. I can think of two reasons why fewer teens are having sexual intercourse compared with thirty years ago. The first reason is that oral sex is displacing old-fashioned penile-vaginal intercourse. The CDC report concerned only penile-vaginal intercourse. The CDC interviewers did not mention oral sex, except to make sure that each teen understood that the interviewer was asking about vaginal intercourse, not oral sex. Among sexually active teenagers in the 1980s and 1990s, vaginal intercourse was far more common than oral sex. Today oral sex is much more widespread than it was twenty or thirty years ago.

"Oral sex is the new second base," says Alexandra Hall, a journalist who spent weeks interviewing students at suburban high schools in the Boston area. "Things are very, very different in high school from the way they used to be. . . . [There has been a] profound shift in the culture of high-school dating and sex, with no-strings 'hooking-up' replacing dating."[5] "Kids don't date nowadays," agrees physician and bioethicist Leon Kass.[6] "Traditional dating is dead," concurs journalist and author Barbara Dafoe Whitehead.[7]

In the 1980s teenage sexual intimacy "had a different context. That context was called 'dating,'" says journalist Hall. "These days, something else is much more common. Single boys and girls go in a group to a friend's house (where the parents may or may not be home), drink or smoke pot, then pair off and engage in no-strings 'hook-ups.' A week later, when the same scenario happens again, they hook up with someone else." Michael Milburn, a professor at the University of Massachusetts, concurs that "the days of a boy showing up at a girl's front door and meeting her parents before he takes her on a date are almost obsolete. Dating has been replaced by house parties and a culture of 'hooking up.'"[8] I agree with Professor Milburn. The scenario of the boy meeting the girl's parents before taking the girl out on a date is indeed obsolete, along with the rotary-dial telephone. Whether it *ought* to be obsolete is a different question. Nobody disputes that the modern cordless house phone is a significant improvement over the old rotary-dial telephone. But the shift from the culture of dating to the culture of the hookup signifies a shift from romance to impersonal sex. That shift is not a cause for celebration, even if it has been associated with a decrease in the rates of penile-vaginal intercourse (and a corresponding decline in the rate of teenage pregnancy).

So: one big reason behind the decrease in vaginal intercourse is the greater prevalence of oral sex. A second major factor is the normalization of pornography and the growing tendency of some boys to prefer masturbation over actual sexual encounters with actual girls (see my comments on page 124 about John Mayer). Listening to teenage girls and boys, it seems that more and more of their experience is lived online or via a screen. If your top priority in life is getting ten thousand followers on Instagram or being the first in your group to finish all the missions in *Grand Theft Auto* or some other video game, then vaginal intercourse might take a backseat (no pun intended).

For many teenage boys, sex is an object in itself. The challenge for a teenage boy is to integrate the desires of the soul and spirit with the needs of the body, to weld his sexual drive to his desire for friendship and companionship. For many teenage boys (and for some adult men) that doesn't come easily. Some never reach that level of maturity. But there are some things a parent can do to help. First, though, we need to look more closely at basic differences between the sexuality of girls and women and the sexuality of boys and men.

Oxytocin Is Not Testosterone

What's the relation between love and sex? The neurochemical basis for both love and sex in females involves the hormone oxytocin, the same hormone released when a mother breast-feeds her newborn baby. "Oxytocin's effects on both [romantic] attachment and sexual behavior are estrogen dependent and gender specific," observes neuropsychologist Lisa Diamond, adding that there appear to be "more extensive oxytocin circuits in female than male brains."[9] In males, on the other hand, the hormone underlying sexual drive is not oxytocin but testosterone, the same hormone that mediates aggression in males.

Many researchers have used functional MRI to look at brain activity in women and men during sexual arousal. One consistent finding is that men show comparatively more activity in the older, more primitive areas of the brain such as the amygdala, thalamus, and hypothalamus, while women show proportionately more activity up in the cerebral cortex; that's true even when the women report feeling more sexually aroused than the men.[10] And these sex differences are apparently not affected by sexual orientation: reviewers found no significant differences in the patterns of brain activity of straight men compared with gay men but large differences between men and women, regardless of sexual orientation.[11]

These sex differences suggest that women's sexual experience is "happening" more in the cerebral cortex and is therefore more connected with the rest of what's going on in their mind. The sexual experience in men is less connected with the cortex, less connected with the outside world. One recent study actually showed that in young men sexual arousal decreases functional synchronization between cortical areas of the brain. That's a fancy way of saying that when a young man is sexually aroused, his brain literally comes unglued, and the different parts aren't talking with one another.[12]

The weight of the evidence strongly suggests that males and females experience sexual desire differently. As UCLA psychologist Anne Peplau observes, "women's sexuality tends to be strongly linked to a close relationship. For women, an important goal of sex is intimacy; the best context for pleasurable sex is a committed relationship. This is less true for men."[13]

You can say that again. For many boys and for some men, especially younger men, the sexual urge is closely tied to aggression. That's not surprising when you remember that in males both the sexual urge and the aggressive urge are mediated by testosterone. In one carefully designed study, a surprisingly high percentage—35 percent—of "normal" college men said that they not only fantasized about rape but would actually rape a woman if they had the chance and they were sure they wouldn't be caught.[14] In another study of "normal" college men, more than half said they would actually rape a woman if they were assured of not being punished.[15] Researchers have found that more than 80 percent of popular porn videos include some form of degrading violence against women: most often the woman is slapped or gagged or spanked or has her hair yanked.[16] But the men who watch these videos are not necessarily Neanderthals. In fact, researchers have found no association between a man's gender-role beliefs and the likelihood that he finds rape sexually appealing.

Some men who are strongly in favor of equal rights for women, who approve of women in leadership roles, and so on also say that they would rape a woman if they had the opportunity. In one recent study, men who watched pornography were actually somewhat more likely to endorse equal rights for women, compared with men who don't look at porn.[17] Nor is there any association, positive or negative, between a man's intelligence and the likelihood that he will be sexually aroused by depictions of rape.[18] Highly intelligent men are no less likely to fantasize about raping a woman than are men of below-average intelligence.[19]

Men and women experience sexuality differently. A significant number of men may feel tempted to engage in sexual assault, even if they are otherwise intelligent and believe in equal rights for women. Women are much less likely to feel a strong temptation to engage in sexual assault. These differences between women and men can be traced at least in part to biological causes, including the differences between testosterone and oxytocin. A sensible, commonsense approach to preventing sexual assault would begin by recognizing these hardwired differences. In chapter 12 I share what such an approach looks like.

Young men are much more likely than young women to find pornography satisfying and fulfilling. Few young women would use the word "fulfilling" to describe the experience of masturbating over pornography. But pornography has gone mainstream. The pop star John Mayer proudly told *Rolling Stone* magazine that he is "the new generation of masturbator": he would *rather* masturbate over pornography than have sex with actual women.[20] I haven't heard of any leading female celebrities who have boasted that they would rather masturbate over pornography than have sex with real people.

The motivation for sex is different for most teenage boys than for most teenage girls. Many teenage boys want to have sex to satisfy sexual desire. It's a gut-level, base-of-the-brain impulse not far removed from the need to have a bowel movement when you feel the urge. Many boys will tell you that the urge feels just that irresistible.

Not so for most girls. As psychologist Roy Baumeister has observed, "male desire aims at the sexual activity itself, whereas female desire aims beyond it toward other outcomes and consequences."[21]

Professor Joan Jacobs Brumberg, who has written two books about the psychosexual development of teenage girls, agrees. Sexual pleasure is usually not the motivating factor when teenage girls engage in sex, Brumberg finds. That's especially true for oral sex. Girls today provide far more oral sex for boys than did girls in previous generations, but Brumberg says that "they do so without pleasure."[22] It's just what you do, if you're an American girl today. It's part of your job description, especially if you want to be a popular girl. Deborah Tolman, a director at the Wellesley College Center for Research on Women, concurs that sex remains heavily weighted in favor of boys' needs and desires. With regard to oral sex, Tolman says, "The boys are getting it, the girls no. It's the heterosexual script that entitles boys and disables girls."[23] In her 2016 book *Girls and Sex*, Peggy Orenstein describes talking with girls who explained to her that giving oral sex to a boy doesn't feel particularly intimate or even personal. Orenstein drily observed, "I may be of a different generation, but, frankly, it's hard for me to consider a penis in my mouth as 'impersonal.' "[24]

When you ask teenage girls and boys why they're having sex, you'll hear very different answers from each gender. Boys usually answer that question with a snort. "Why *wouldn't* I have sex? As long as the girl wants it too—I mean, as long as she doesn't kick me or yell 'Fire!'—why shouldn't I?" Boys want to have sex because they feel sexually aroused. Simple.

It's different for most girls. In one major study, girls didn't even list sexual arousal as a reason for having sex.[25] Teenage girls often engage in sexual intimacy for reasons that are not related to sexual fulfillment. Girls may hope that having sex will earn them points in the popularity contest, or they may just want to please the boy they happen to be hooking up with, or they may feel pressured either by the boy or by other girls who *are* having sex.

One fundamental change that has occurred over the past thirty years is a change from the female paradigm to the male paradigm. Thirty years ago, a boy usually had at least to give lip service to the notion of being in love if he expected a young woman to be sexually intimate with him. No longer. That's the significance of the hookup replacing the romantic relationship as the primary sexual mode in teenage culture.

What's the result? Barbara Dafoe Whitehead concluded that the effect of today's "sex-drenched teen culture . . . is not to help young people learn how to choose a future life partner." At best, it helps them only to "manage their sex lives."[26] But a sex life without any emotional connection is not the best preparation for a lasting commitment to a romantic partner.

Sexual satisfaction may be another casualty of the switch to the hookup culture, at least for girls and young women. In one study of 24,000 students at twenty-one colleges, only about 40 percent of the women reported achieving an orgasm when the hookup involved vaginal intercourse, compared with 80 percent of the men. (And that's only for those hookups that involved vaginal intercourse.) By comparison, the same researchers found that about three quarters of women achieved an orgasm in their most recent episode of vaginal intercourse if that episode occurred in the context of a committed relationship.[27]

Dr. Drew Pinsky made an important observation about the

relation of alcohol to gender differences in hooking up. Both girls and boys are usually partly or totally drunk when they hook up. (Remember the sexual assault Jimmy perpetrated on Tina? He was drunk when he did that. Not an excuse, just a fact.) Dr. Pinsky found that girls and boys give completely different reasons *why* they get drunk before they hook up. Boys like to get drunk because it slows down their sexual response, allows them to relax, and decreases the likelihood of premature ejaculation. Girls like to get drunk because it numbs the experience for them, making it less embarrassing and less emotionally painful.[28] Among college students, more than half of hookups are preceded by alcohol use and/or drug use.[29]

Good or Bad?

In the first edition of this book, published back in 2005, I called attention to the fact that the hookup was displacing romantic relationships, and that oral sex was displacing vaginal intercourse. In my book *Girls on the Edge*, published in 2010, I made the same points even more emphatically, with an additional emphasis on the ways in which social media were contributing to the self-objectification of girls. Recently there has been a slew of books, such as *American Girls* by Nancy Jo Sales and the aforementioned *Girls and Sex* by Peggy Orenstein, making the same points. But a different tone has crept in to the public debate as well. Instead of lamenting the changes and trying to limit the damage, some writers are applauding the changes and minimizing the damage.

Hanna Rosin wrote a lengthy article for *The Atlantic* about the new reality of sexual intimacy, as told to her by young Americans. She challenged the notion, which she acknowledged to be widespread, that the new hookup culture is socially corrosive and ultimately toxic to women. Rosin instead asserted that hooking up is "an engine of female progress." Her argument essentially boiled down to this: *Girls and young women today are so busy. They have so much they want to accomplish. They don't have time for a relationship. Hooking up is more convenient and less demanding.* "Plenty of women enjoy having casual sex," one Yale woman told her.[30]

The anthropologist Peter Wood read Rosin's article, but he was not convinced. In answer to the Yale woman who said that plenty of women enjoy having casual sex, Wood observed

> If the cost of that view is not immediately apparent, it is still real. The woman who treats her sexuality as something detachable from strong mutual attachment to a single partner sooner or later discovers that men regard her as expendable. Rosin and her like-minded apologists for the hook-up culture shrug. What does it matter what men think? But the pretense that sex is just sex is never true. . . . There is no such thing as sex without consequences. Their experience is perhaps summed up in the line spoken by a female character in the 2001 movie *Vanilla Sky,* *"Don't you know that when you sleep with someone, your body makes a promise whether you do or not?"* Broken promises like that add up.

Wood concludes:

> The sexes are complementary. The distortion of women's sexuality plainly distorts men's sexuality as well, though in a more deferred way. Men, instead of learning how to be responsible, committed partners and eventually husbands

and fathers, learn that the pleasure-seeking dimension of their sexuality can be sustained with relative ease. As a result, the men shun social maturity. The women who are veterans of the hook-up culture find that, once they are in it, their options for getting out are reduced. . . . All of this distorts and diminishes the lives of those who are caught up in the pursuit of sex without attachment. They eventually become those for whom genuine attachment is far more difficult. . . . The [true] meaning of sex is that it leads somewhere—somewhere beyond orgasms and the excitements of strangers. An older generation called that "somewhere" marriage.[31]

The end result of multiple sexual encounters outside the context of a romantic relationship may be a lessening of the ability to form and sustain a healthy and lasting romantic relationship. And that may be true for both girls and boys, for both women and for men. We can't say for sure yet. We don't have a decades-long study in which girls and boys were randomly assigned to participate either in the hookup culture or in the dating culture. And I'm not holding my breath waiting for such a study. I wouldn't volunteer my daughter to participate. Would you volunteer yours?

I didn't think so.

Playing a Role

Many kids don't date anymore. Hooking up has become more common. As a result, scholars find, adolescent sexual intimacy is now often determined not by romantic attraction but by group affiliation. What does that mean?

To use the jargon employed by psychologists who study teenage dating: "Romantic pairs form most often on the basis of rank order in popularity rather than personal characteristics." Here's what that means: When fourteen-year-olds hook up, they do so less on the basis of romantic attraction and more on the basis of how popular the teenager is in the teenager's group. The most popular boy at the party hooks up with the most popular girl, the second-most-popular boy goes out with the second-most-popular girl, and on down the line.[32] And a primary determinant of popularity among teenagers is physical attractiveness.

Some years back, I was leading a conversation among high school students on the topic of sexual intimacy and romance. I asked the group what they thought about dating. "Only ugly people date," one boy said authoritatively. Startled, I asked the group to raise their hands if they agreed with the boy. The great majority of the kids raised their hands. "Now raise your hands if you do *not* agree," I said. Nobody raised their hands. This is how the high school students see it: If you're popular and good-looking, you won't have any trouble finding someone at the party who will hook up with you. If you're not attractive but you want some action, your best bet may be to find somebody who's as ugly as you are and date them.

For more than 150 years—beginning with British epidemiologist William Farr in 1858—researchers have consistently found that marriage has benefits for both men and women. In particular, both men and women who are married are healthier and are less likely to be depressed, on average, compared with unmarried men and women.[33] So it's tempting to speculate that the kids who are following a more old-fashioned social script might benefit from a commitment-focused style of dating.

But the same may not be true for teenage romantic relationships, with or without the sex. Teens who began a romantic relationship in the past year are more likely to report being depressed compared with teens who are not in a romantic relationship; and the effect is bigger for girls than for boys.[34] Likewise, teens who engage in sexual intimacy are more likely, subsequently, to become depressed; and that effect is *much* stronger for girls than for boys.[35] Hooking up—engaging in sexual intimacy outside of a romantic relationship—is more likely to lead to depression than is sexual intimacy in the context of a romantic relationship.[36] In one study young teen girls who had sex with boys were more likely subsequently to become depressed than were girls who didn't have sex, but young teen boys who had sex with girls were not at all more likely to become depressed.[37] In some studies young women who engage in sex are at increased risk for depression, but young men who engage in sex are actually at *decreased* risk for depression.[38]

Why is sexual intimacy in adolescence more likely to lead to depression in girls than in boys? Are girls just more fragile than boys?

I don't think so.

Researchers find that teen girls and boys often approach sexual intimacy with different scripts. Girls are more likely to be looking for a steady relationship, and they see sexual intimacy as an important stage in cementing that relationship. Boys know that script. A boy may play a role, deceiving the girl with a promise of a relationship that he may not fulfill. When the boy abandons the girl after a few episodes of sex, the girl is likely to become depressed, the boy not so much.[39] That also helps to explain why romantic relationships in adolescence are associated with a higher risk of depression, whereas marriage in adulthood is usually associated with a lower risk of depression. Many boys are faking it:

they are pretending to be lasting partners in a relationship when in fact they are not. A man who marries a woman is not, let us hope, faking it: he really intends (in most cases, at least at the beginning) to be a lasting partner in a relationship.

So the boy misleads the girl in order to get sex. But that's not always the story. I know a boy who was immensely committed to a girl who happened to be more popular and better-looking than he was. Such relationships tend to be unstable: adolescent romantic relationships last longer when they are a match between teens of roughly equal popularity and attractiveness. Anyhow, when the girl dumped him after about eight weeks, he was plunged into despair, convinced that his life was over. He started cutting himself with razor blades.

We all want our children to grow up to enjoy a loving, mutually supportive, and *lasting* relationship. Many parents imagine, reasonably enough, that romantic relationships in adolescence provide good "practice" for more serious relationships in adulthood. You can't run before you walk. Practice makes perfect.

Some psychologists who study romantic relationships in adolescence are coming to a different conclusion. Practice makes perfect only if you're practicing the right task. Most adolescents aren't. Psychologists Wyndol Furman and Elizabeth Wehner have studied adolescent romantic relationships over many years. For middle-school and even most high school students, they report that "adolescents are not very concerned with the fulfillment of attachment or caregiving needs. . . . Instead, their focus is on who they are, how attractive they are . . . and how it all looks to their peer group." Adolescents often develop bad habits in their dating relationships. A boy may get in the habit of regarding his girlfriend as a source of sexual gratification without really connecting with her as a human being. A girl may get in the habit of seeing her romantic partner as a "trophy boyfriend" without any idea of how to integrate him into her life. And both of them may get in the habit of dumping their current partner whenever a better-looking or more popular one becomes available. Over time, Furman and Wehner have found, "these individuals may become more skillful, but more skillful in developing the relationships they have come to expect."[40] By the time they reach adulthood and it's time to build a marriage that will last a lifetime, they have accumulated all sorts of bad habits that they need to break. They might be better off had they never had those teen relationships.

There are other reasons to be skeptical about the value of romantic relationships in early adolescence. According to one large survey, kids who become sexually active before fifteen years of age are three times more likely to be regular smokers, four times more likely to have tried marijuana, and six times more likely to drink alcohol once a week or more.[41]

Maybe we should regard sexual relationships in the same way we regard alcoholic beverages: as an adult pleasure to be enjoyed by adults only. Like alcoholic beverages, romantic relationships can be wonderful when responsible adults are partaking. But if unprepared teens use them, they can be deadly. Drunk driving kills. So can HIV/AIDS. And the boy who gets in the habit of exploiting his girlfriend sexually while ignoring her emotional needs is setting himself up for a lifetime of frustration and loneliness. Likewise, the girl who engages in sexual intimacy with one boy after another, month after month, year after year, without sustaining a serious romantic commitment, may find it more difficult to connect lasting romance with sexual intimacy—to remain satisfied with a single romantic partner—if she ever chooses to marry.

CHAPTER 7

Drugs and Alcohol

Caitlyn

Caitlyn never was a superstar. The youngest of three children, she always seemed content to hang back in the shadows while her two older brothers took the limelight. Alex, the oldest, was the smart one. He earned an A in every class without ever seeming to study and was accepted early to his first-choice school, the University of Pennsylvania.

Aaron, the middle child, was a jock. Soccer in the fall, basketball in the winter, lacrosse in the spring. Aaron was the first sophomore at our high school ever to be named a starter on the varsity soccer team. The following year he led his team in scoring. By December of his junior year he had received invitations to visit some NCAA Division I soccer programs, including Clemson and Virginia Tech.

Jill, their mother, was a full-time mom who attended every one of Aaron's games. Caitlyn seemed happy to tag along and cheer her brother on.

Because Caitlyn had always been withdrawn and shy, parents Jill and Harry were concerned she might have problems when she started middle school. Jill read *Odd Girl Out* and many of the other books parents of girls are supposed to read nowadays. On nights when Jill and her husband went to bed at the same time, Jill would read Harry excerpts from those parenting books. If Harry complained, she would say, "You need to be prepared. She's your daughter too."

Middle school is supposed to be a tough time for girls—but Caitlyn sailed through. In eighth grade she blossomed. Over a period of about ten months, she shed her baby fat and became a slender and attractive teenager.

When she started high school the following year, her popularity soared and her social calendar became crowded. Every weekend she received a barrage of invitations—to go shopping, to go to a party, or just to go to a friend's house to hang out. Nevertheless, her grades actually improved. She became obsessive about homework. By her sophomore year she was spending an average of three hours a night on homework. Her parents, especially Jill, marveled at her stamina, her discipline. "She's our late bloomer," Jill told her husband.

Caitlyn's weekends were filled with homework during the day, then parties or group trips to the movies Friday or Saturday night. Caitlyn begged her parents for more money to buy the latest fashions. Harry objected that Caitlyn's clothes budget was way out of line. "We're spending more on her clothes than we spent on Alex and Aaron *combined*," he said. "And what she's buying isn't so fabulous, if you don't mind my saying so. We're paying Neiman Marcus prices for Walmart clothes. One hundred dollars for a pair of faded blue jeans?"

"But she's a girl. Girls' clothes cost more. And girls care more about clothes," Jill said. "Boys can wear the same thing over and over again and nobody cares. If a girl wears the same outfit twice in a month, other girls notice." Secretly, though, Jill had to admit that Caitlyn's spending was excessive, and Caitlyn didn't show good judgment about prices. But Jill was so pleased to see her daughter finally coming into her own, finally taking center stage, that she couldn't bring herself to talk to Caitlyn about it. *She'll only be a teenager once,* Jill thought. Let her have this chance.

The college counselor said that Caitlyn was a shoo-in for the University of Maryland, but Caitlyn wanted to go out of state. As Caitlyn began her senior year, Jill and Harry's biggest concern was whether they would be able to afford tuition for an Ivy League school without cutting back on contributions to their own retirement plans.

In retrospect, all the telltale signs were there. But when the phone rang at 3:00 a.m. that Sunday morning early in November, Jill had no clue that Caitlyn had been hiding a secret.

Jill thought at first that the phone call must be a wrong number or a crank call. "Hello?" she mumbled into the phone.

"Hello, my name is Cathy. I'm a nurse at Shady Grove Hospital emergency room. Are you the mother of Caitlyn Morrison?" the nurse asked.

"Yes, of course," Jill answered.

"Caitlyn's friends brought her here about two hours ago," the nurse said. "Caitlyn is still unconscious. She tried to commit suicide."

"That's impossible," Jill said immediately, instantly wide awake. "How— what makes you say that?"

"We found empty bottles of Xanax and Vicodin in her purse," the nurse said matter-of-factly. "Her tox screen is positive for Xanax and Vicodin. And we found a suicide note."

"A suicide note? How— what does it say?" Jill asked. Then, before the nurse could answer, she said, "No, wait! How is she?

How is she?" *Please let her be all right*, Jill prayed. Suddenly she found it hard to breathe. Tears welled in her eyes. "Will she be okay?"

"Dr. Sorenson just told me that Caitlyn is stable enough to be transferred upstairs to the intensive care unit," the nurse said. "Normally we put teenagers in a special part of the peds ICU, but the peds ICU is completely filled, so she'll be in the regular ICU."

"Oh my God," Jill said, trying to grasp what was happening. Harry was still snoring.

"We've seen two other girls just in the past week, with the same story, exactly the same combination of drugs," the nurse said. "OD'd on Xanax and Vicodin. Those girls came in just like Caitlyn, and I can tell you both of them pulled through okay. So hopefully Caitlyn will pull through this fine too."

"I'll be right there," Jill said.

When Jill arrived at the hospital, Caitlyn was already in the intensive care unit. "I'm sorry, visiting hours don't start until eight a.m.," the unit clerk told her.

"But I'm her *mother*," Jill said impatiently.

"I understand," the clerk said. "If you'll just have a seat, I'll see whether the nurse can come out and speak with you now."

The nurse, a pleasant middle-aged woman named Rosemary, explained that ICU policy didn't allow visitors in the middle of the night, not even parents. "But don't worry. The moment Caitlyn starts waking up, I'll buzz you in, visiting hours or no," Rosemary said.

"She's still asleep?" Jill asked.

"She's unconscious," Rosemary said. "But Dr. Feingold expects her to regain consciousness by morning."

"Who's Dr. Feingold?" Jill asked.

"Dr. Feingold's the attending physician. He's an intensivist."

"What's an intensivist? Can't he do something to wake her up *now*?" Jill asked.

"I tell you what, Jill," Rosemary said patiently. "Don't worry about the details of your daughter's medical care. Leave that to us. Caitlyn is going to be just fine, medically speaking. You need to be focusing on other things."

"Like what?" Jill asked plaintively.

"Like what you're going to say to Caitlyn when you see her."

"I'll just tell her I love her. . . ." Jill said, and her voice trailed off. She realized that she still had no idea why her daughter had done this.

"Here's the suicide note they found on her," Rosemary said. "It was in her purse, on the top, where she knew we would find it." She held out a folded sheet of paper to Jill.

Jill nodded and took the paper without opening it. "Thank you," she said.

"Ask the clerk to buzz me if you have any questions," Rosemary said. "I'm working a twelve-hour, so I'll be here when visiting hours start."

Jill waited until Rosemary had gone before she looked at her daughter's note. After the first two paragraphs, she began to cry, so she stumbled to the women's restroom. Mercifully, no one else was there, giving Jill some privacy as she read her daughter's confession:

> *Dear Mom and Dad,*
> *I'm so sorry to be doing this. I know how much this will hurt you. But there just isn't any other choice for me.*
> *I guess you guys still don't know that I've been doing drugs for a long time now. I started in eighth grade. At first*

I just used Adderall, to lose weight. And it worked. I really thought I could get away with it. It was so easy to fool you guys, along with everybody else. Everybody just looked at the surface. People saw how thin I got, and everybody thought it was just great. They envied me. They never wondered: How did that fat girl get so thin?

Adderall was wonderful—except for the palpitations and the nausea and the headaches. But that seemed like a small price to pay. Then I started having panic attacks. So say hello to Xanax. Even with Xanax, though, I never could get really calm inside. Until I discovered Vicodin.

For a while I thought I could still pull it off. Especially because I knew other girls were doing it. I felt like I was juggling a dozen balls in the air all at once. Maybe I could just keep juggling forever. I had a routine: Adderall in the morning, Adderall and Xanax at lunch, Xanax after school, Xanax and Vicodin at bedtime. No problem.

Then the drugs stopped working. Not all at once. Gradually. I tried taking more. I increased the Vicodin to two a day. Then four. Then six. Then ten. The side effects got to be awful. I thought about stopping all the drugs, just going cold turkey. But that would mean going back to being fat and stupid. I could never get the grades I was getting without the boost from the drugs. And I couldn't stand the thought of being fat and ugly and stupid again. Once you've tasted the glory of being everybody's favorite girl, how can you give that up?

The truth is that the real me is an ugly, fat, stupid girl. I hate her. And I just can't go on pretending, taking drugs and trying to fool people. And I hate having to lie to you guys— about what I'm spending all the money on, about how I'm

*able to stay up all night studying, about how I lost all that
weight.*

*And I don't want to be the person I really am. I don't like
that person. She's ugly and stupid and fat.*

Please forgive me.

Love always,

Caitlyn

Different Drugs, Different Highs

Girls and boys turn to drugs for different reasons. For example, girls are far more likely than boys to use stimulant medications such as Adderall, Vyvanse, Concerta, and Metadate specifically for the purpose of losing weight.[1] Girls use drugs like Xanax and Vicodin to relieve stress, to calm down, and because their friends are doing it.

Most boys get involved with drugs for different reasons. Most boys who abuse drugs are looking for a thrill. And they want the excitement of doing something dangerous. Remember the chapter about risk, about boys' risk-taking behaviors? Boys are more likely to buy illegal drugs from strangers while girls are more likely to buy their drugs from people they know.[2]

What do teenagers themselves say about it? In a nationwide survey of 6,748 adolescents—selected to be geographically and ethnically representative of the entire United States—researchers found consistent gender differences in the reasons teenagers give for using drugs, alcohol, and cigarettes. Girls were sixteen times more likely than boys to say that they smoke in order to keep their weight down, for example. Boys were more than three times as likely as girls to say that they smoke in order to look cool.[3] Likewise for alcohol: teenage boys are more likely to drink because they want to feel intoxicated or because they want to impress their friends; teenage girls are more likely to drink as a way of coping with stress.[4]

Let's start by looking at some of the reasons why girls and boys use drugs and alcohol. Then we'll look at what you can do, as a parent, to keep your child from experimenting with drugs and alcohol in the first place or to get them to stop using if they've already started.

Risk Factors

Caitlyn's story illustrates some of the leading risk factors for drug use among girls: a negative self-concept coupled with anxiety and/or depression. By contrast, boys are more likely to use drugs—and to get drunk—because they're looking for a high, a thrill. (I have seen a few boys who use drugs and/or alcohol as a way of coping with stress, but that's less common among boys than among girls. Among adults, by contrast, I have seen a great many men who use drugs or alcohol as a way of coping with stress; but this is a book about children and teenagers, not adults.)

Caitlyn thought she was stupid and fat. She compared herself negatively with her brilliant brother Alex and her athletic brother Aaron. There was nothing about herself that she was proud of. Adderall helped her lose weight and gave her the energy to stay up late so she could do long hours of homework every night, night after night.

Girls who feel stressed and depressed are more likely to start using drugs and alcohol; but that's less true for boys.[5] Later in this chapter we'll explore some reasons for the difference.

Caitlyn's story also illustrates how academic stress can precipitate and perpetuate a girl's use of drugs. Don't underestimate the stress your twelve-year-old daughter is telling you about. From your perspective as an adult, whether she gets an A or a B in Spanish is not a matter of world-shaking importance. But in her world it may be.

The best way to protect a girl like Caitlyn from falling into the drug trap is to find ways to strengthen her self-confidence and self-concept and to de-stress her environment. Remember those heartbreaking words at the end of Caitlyn's suicide note: "*the real me is an ugly, fat, stupid girl. . . . I don't want to be the person I really am. I don't like that person. She's ugly and stupid and fat.*" Your job is to change the way Caitlyn evaluates herself, so that she's focusing not on how she *looks* but on who she *is*.

Good parenting requires knowledge, insight, and understanding. It's your job as a parent to know your child—not only to know who she is right now but also to sense who she could become, where her hidden strengths lie. You have to know your child better than she knows herself. And you have to resist the tendency to push your child in a direction that worked for you or for one of your other children.

In this case, Caitlyn's parents were "programmed," so to speak, by their two older children, Alex and Aaron. They had come to think that all kids were either jocks or brains. Caitlyn was neither, so—with all due respect to her parents, Jill and Harry—they assumed that Caitlyn didn't have any special talent of her own.

Were they right?

Rosemary, the nurse in the intensive care unit, was right about

Caitlyn's medical prognosis. Caitlyn regained consciousness the morning after she was admitted, just as Rosemary had predicted. Jill was at Caitlyn's bedside when she woke up. "I didn't die" were Caitlyn's first words to her mother. Jill couldn't tell whether Caitlyn was relieved or disappointed.

Two days later, Dr. Feingold cleared her for medical discharge, and Caitlyn was transferred to Potomac Ridge, an inpatient psychiatric facility. After two weeks of group therapy—as well as Wellbutrin and Lexapro (two antidepressant medications)—the doctor said that Caitlyn was ready to go home. "She's so much more relaxed now," Jill told me. "I don't know whether that calmness is just the medications, or whether that's what Caitlyn is really like when she's not taking Adderall. I wish she didn't have to take any medication at all."

The psychiatrist, Dr. Himmelfarb, insisted that Caitlyn would have to stay on the medications for at least six months, probably longer. Those were the same six months during which she was supposed to decide which college to go to. She had to take a grade of incomplete in two of her subjects that fall. Caitlyn was worried that her college applications would be in jeopardy because of those incompletes, but I sent letters to the colleges, saying that she'd been hospitalized for three weeks because of an (unspecified) illness. In the end, she was accepted at most of the colleges she applied to.

In the meantime, Caitlyn discovered something she enjoyed, something she was really good at. With Dr. Himmelfarb's approval, she started volunteering as an aide at Potomac Ridge. Because she had been an inpatient there herself, and because she was still a teenager, she had special credibility with the teenage inpatients.

One evening the aides on duty at Potomac Ridge were talking about Malia, a fourteen-year-old girl who had been put in the isolation room again after hitting an aide. Malia had been at Potomac Ridge for five days. This was her third time in isolation. "That girl's a bad number, a real mean one," said Sophie, one of the aides. "She's the sort who'd just as soon kill you as look at you." Two other aides, Taneesha and Ruthanne, nodded.

"Do you mind if I go in and talk with her?" Caitlyn said.

Sophie, Taneesha, and Ruthanne just stared at her. "You crazy? You want to die?" Sophie finally asked. "That girl will eat you alive and spit out your bones."

Caitlyn shrugged. "Do you mind if I try?" she repeated.

Sophie and Ruthanne watched through the small window of the locked room as Caitlyn sat down on the bed across from Malia. They couldn't hear what Caitlyn was saying, and at first it didn't seem to be having any effect. Malia remained sitting on the floor in a corner, huddled in a tight fetal ball with her head between her knees. But after Caitlyn had been talking for about a minute, Malia looked up. Sophie and Ruthanne were amazed to see an enchanting smile on Malia's face. "You know, that girl is almost pretty when she smiles," Sophie said.

Caitlyn stayed in the room with Malia for two hours. When she knocked on the door to be let out, Malia was by her side. "Malia's coming out with me," Caitlyn said, not a question but a statement. "She won't need to be in the locked room anymore."

Sophie looked suspiciously at Malia. Malia nodded. "I won't hit anybody," Malia said. "As long as I can talk with Caitlyn on the nights when she's here."

Caitlyn went to Potomac Ridge every evening for the next two weeks, spending an hour or more each night with Malia, mostly listening, sometimes talking. Nobody knew what they said to each other, but everybody could see that Malia had changed.

She wasn't violent anymore. She didn't shout or scream anymore. And she started sleeping at night.

"What do you girls talk about?" Dr. Osenick, the attending psychiatrist, asked Caitlyn just before Malia was discharged.

"Not much," Caitlyn said. "I tell her about myself a little. I tell her how bad I used to feel, how I used to hate my body, hate my life."

"You know," Dr. Osenick said, "if you ever become a professional therapist, one of the first things you'll learn is that you shouldn't tell your client too much about yourself. The focus of therapy should be on the patient, not on the therapist."

"Then I guess I won't ever be a professional therapist," Caitlyn said mildly.

Caitlyn was accepted to Cornell. She went to visit the campus in late April. She still hadn't decided which college she would go to, but Cornell was the only Ivy League school to which she had applied. She stayed overnight in one of the dorms.

"How'd you like it?" her mother asked her.

"It was scary," Caitlyn said. "All the kids seem so grown up. And some of the girls there are really skinny. And it's out in the middle of nowhere. I mean, Ithaca is like a gazillion miles from anywhere."

When Caitlyn said, "Some of the girls there are really skinny," a chill went through Jill's heart. Caitlyn had gained thirty pounds in the months since her suicide attempt. She was up to 140 pounds (at five feet four inches tall). Jill thought Caitlyn looked beautiful, but she was worried. On the other hand, what parent wouldn't want their child to go to an Ivy League college?

In May, Caitlyn decided to decline the offer from Cornell and go to Towson instead. "I need to stay close to home," she said. "And I want to keep volunteering at Potomac Ridge at least a few days a month. I'm going to be a therapist someday."

I think it's clear in retrospect that Caitlyn's talents lay in her ability to care about people. It's easy to be critical after the fact, but maybe Caitlyn wouldn't have started using drugs if her parents had tried harder earlier to find Caitlyn's areas of strength instead of just taking her along to watch Aaron play soccer and lacrosse. When Caitlyn was younger, she loved to be around animals. Suppose her parents had signed Caitlyn up to volunteer at the zoo or at an animal shelter in our town where no animal is ever euthanized. Empathic children like Caitlyn often love to care for animals. If her mother had driven Caitlyn to volunteer at the zoo, even if it meant missing some of Aaron's games, Caitlyn would have gotten the message that her interests mattered just as much as Aaron's triumphs on the field.

More generally: if Caitlyn's parents had made a higher priority of spending more time with Caitlyn, just for Caitlyn, she might not have felt like such a failure compared to her brothers. And specifically: if Caitlyn's parents had known more about what was going on in her life, including holding her accountable for the money they gave her—even something as simple as asking to see receipts for the clothes she bought—they would have discovered that she wasn't buying expensive clothes at all. She was using the cash to buy drugs, then picking up some old clothes cheap at Goodwill and claiming that she had spent the money on new clothes. In retrospect, her parents were astonished at their own gullibility in allowing themselves to be taken in by such a ploy.

I mentioned a moment ago how the stress of high expectations can lead girls to start using drugs. What can you do about that? You have to show your daughter that there are other ways to relax besides taking Xanax or getting drunk or smoking a joint. Join her for a long walk in the park, or introduce her to prayer or meditation. Share with her your own ways of coping. You can build a bond and hopefully decrease the risk that she will turn to drugs when she needs to relax. One mom I know likes to bake a cake when she's feeling stressed, and she's taught her two daughters to do the same. Maybe that's not the lowest-calorie way to relax, but it's a lot safer than illegal drugs. "Comfort cooking," she calls it.

These measures are less likely to work for boys, though. Boys are different.

Ethan

Mike and Uta adopted Ethan when Ethan was almost two years old. He had been born to a young woman who was incarcerated after being convicted of selling drugs. In addition to selling drugs, the woman admitted to using crack cocaine, heroin, and meth while she was pregnant. The woman had given Ethan up for adoption when he was born. He had been in a series of foster care placements from birth until the time Mike and Uta adopted him.

Mike was a research physicist at the National Institute of Standards and Technology. Mike had always been a geek. He'd met his German wife, Uta, while doing a three-year postdoctoral fellowship at the Max Planck Institute in Germany. Mike and Uta shared a love of the novels of Thomas Mann, the music of Gustav Mahler, and Mosel wine. They used to refer to themselves as the 3M Club: Mann, Mahler, and Mosel. Mike in particular was a great believer in the power of a good upbringing. He was confident that he would be able to raise his adopted son to share his tastes and his hobbies.

Wrong. Uta and Mike soon were getting a crash course in infantile masculinity. Ethan loved to smash things, throw food, collide into furniture head-on at full speed. Within a few weeks of Ethan's arrival in the home, Uta had packed everything breakable away in boxes, labeling the boxes carefully and then stacking them in the basement. Ethan found his way into the basement, tore open one of the boxes, and stomped on the china Uta had so carefully packed away. After that, they started calling Ethan "the little criminal," and they treated him like one too. They barricaded those parts of the house that were off limits to Ethan, and they kept him on a leash—literally—at the mall. Uta and Mike had originally planned to adopt two or three children, but after Ethan arrived, they decided one was enough.

I first met Ethan when he was fifteen years old, five feet ten inches tall, 180 pounds, and in ninth grade. He was already a star in basketball and football. We even heard a rumor that one of the big high schools down county was trying to steal him away to play for their teams. Ethan's grades had been mediocre all through middle school: C's and D's across the board, except for an A in physical education. But when grades came out for the first marking period of ninth grade, they were worse: he had failed English and Spanish, with D's in his other subjects. He still had his A in physical education, though. His father, Mike, decided that it was time to make a change.

"He can finish the football season," Mike said to me. "There are only two games left in the football season. But no basketball. Sports are taking up too much of his time. There's just no way he should be spending two or three hours a day on sports when he's failing English and Spanish. Don't you agree?"

I paused. "Honestly, I'm not sure I do," I said. "I'm not convinced that taking Ethan out of sports will improve his academic performance. In fact, it might backfire."

"Doctor, with all due respect," Mike said, "that makes no sense. The more time he spends on sports, the less time he has for school."

Mike and Uta pulled Ethan out of sports. "We want what is best for you," Uta told Ethan. "We want for you to be able to go to college."

"I don't want to go to college," Ethan said.

"Sometimes you have to do things you don't like, in order to get the things you want later," Mike chimed in.

"But what I want is to play basketball right *now*," Ethan complained. "How is taking me off the basketball team going to help me play basketball?"

Uta and Mike looked at each other, the same despairing glance they had exchanged so many times over the years. *Why can't Ethan understand?* was what the glance said.

When he started high school, Ethan had hung out with the jocks. But you can't hang with the jocks if you're not on the team—or it's hard, at any rate, especially if you're a freshman. One month into basketball season—the season that Ethan was not a part of—he was drifting. He was supposed to come straight home every day after school and work on his homework, but he wasn't. Instead, he was hanging out in the high school parking lot, catching rides to Rockville and the District of Columbia with the older boys, coming home late at night.

The first week of December, Uta smelled the sweet, pungent odor of marijuana on Ethan's clothes. She spoke with Mike that evening. They decided to confront Ethan. To their surprise, he didn't deny using pot.

"Yeah, I smoke pot. So?" he said.

"But you never smoked pot before," Mike said.

"That's because no *athlete*'s gonna smoke pot, because pot messes with your re*action* time," Ethan said, raising his voice. "Your re*action* time is what it's all about, see? But you made me quit basketball. So why the *HELL* shouldn't I smoke some pot?"

"Please don't swear, Ethan," Mike said.

"Right. No god*damn* swearing allowed in *this* house," Ethan said. "No *nothin'* allowed in this house."

"Ethan, we're just concerned for you, because pot damages your brain. You said it yourself. Pot slows your reaction time," Uta said.

"I don't need this shit," Ethan said, and walked out the door.

They didn't see him again for three days.

After Ethan had been missing for two days, they notified the police. "We need to report that our son is missing," Mike told the officer at the police station.

The officer listened to Mike's story. Then the officer said, "He's not missing. He's a runaway."

"What's the difference?" Mike asked.

"Missing means you don't know what happened to the person. Maybe they were abducted. You don't have any idea. Runaway means a juvenile under eighteen deliberately left home. Your son is a runaway."

"Runaway" seemed like the right word to describe the cascade of events over the next six months. Ethan began stealing money from his parents routinely, brazenly, once even taking money out of Uta's purse while Uta watched him do it. Uta and Mike bought a safe. They began locking their valuables in the safe at all times, even when they were at home.

Ethan flunked ninth grade. Mike and Uta consulted with a psychiatrist who specialized in adolescent drug addiction. The psychiatrist recommended that Mike and Uta allow Ethan to play football. "According to school rules, Ethan will be allowed on the team only if he can maintain his GPA above flunking. Right now Ethan's got no motivation to succeed," the psychiatrist told them. "At least being on the team will give him some motivation. And we'll get him in a random drug testing program. If he tests positive, he's off the team."

At six feet and two hundred pounds, Ethan towered over the other JV football players the following fall. But the coach kept him on JV just the same. "He needs to learn some discipline," the coach said. Sure enough, Ethan brought his grades up—to a C average. But rejoining the team didn't eliminate Ethan's drug habit. He wasn't stealing anymore, but he was still using drugs. Uta could smell pot on his clothes, and she found traces of pot or drug paraphernalia—mostly cigarette wrapping papers—in his clothes.

"Where is he getting the money?" Uta asked Mike one night as they lay in bed together. "And how is he able to pass the drug tests?"

"I don't want to know," Mike said, and turned on his side, away from his wife. "I'm going to sleep."

This Is Your Brain on Drugs

Remember what we talked about in the chapter on risk? Danger doesn't reliably deter boys. It may even spur some boys on. Educating boys about "the dangers of drugs" can be counterproductive. You may stimulate the behavior you're trying to discourage.

Did you ever see that old commercial where the man shows an intact egg and says, "This is your brain"? Then he cracks the egg and puts it in a frying pan, it sizzles, and he says, "This is your brain on drugs." That sort of commercial works reasonably well with girls. Girls watch the commercial and think, *Hmm, I don't want my brain to end up like an egg frying in a pan.*

Not so with boys—especially not with the sensation-seeking, risk-taking boys who are at greatest risk. Those boys see the frying egg, hear the narrator say, "This is your brain on drugs," and think: *Way cool! I totally want to fry my brain! Where can I get some of that stuff?* I know a teenage boy who wallpapered his room with the "This is your brain on drugs" poster and other posters like it, warning of the dangers of drugs. This boy uses drugs and he wants everybody to know it.

Mike and Uta meant well when they warned their son about the dangers of drugs. Uta, like most women, thought that telling her son about the dangers of drug use would decrease the likelihood that he would use drugs. After all, any sensible person would avoid using a substance that damages the brain, right?

Right. But many fifteen-year-old boys are not sensible people. They are fifteen-year-old boys.

What could Mike and Uta have done differently? I think they should have followed my advice in the first place as far as leaving Ethan on the team. Would that have prevented Ethan from using drugs? Maybe. Maybe not. Participation in competitive sports *has* been proven to be an effective strategy for decreasing the risk of drug use among teenage *girls*. But it's not been shown to have a reliable protective effect for boys.

Researchers have found that girls who participate in all-girls, school-sponsored sports are significantly less likely than other girls to use drugs and alcohol. But girls who participate in out-of-school sports are actually somewhat *more* likely to use drugs or alcohol, especially if the out-of-school sport is coed, such as surfing. By contrast, boys who participate in school-sponsored, male-dominated sports such as football are slightly *more* likely than other boys to use drugs or alcohol.[6]

Why the difference? Why might school-sponsored sports decrease girls' use of drugs and alcohol, while that's not true for boys? It goes back, I think, to issues of self-concept. Participation in extracurricular activities, and especially in competitive sports, raises girls' self-concept and self-efficacy: they come to feel that they are more in charge of their own destiny. Low self-concept is a major risk factor for drug and alcohol use among *girls*, so raising self-concept lowers the risk of drug and alcohol use among *girls*.

But boys are different. Many boys drink or use drugs because they're sensation seeking or because they want to look cool. Playing sports doesn't decrease their interest in sensation seeking or wanting to look cool. It may be the case that some boys who are the greatest risk takers are also the most likely to participate in competitive sports, in which case participation in sports may be a marker for boys who are at higher risk for drug and alcohol use— without being the *cause* of that increased risk.

On the other hand, I think Ethan had a point when he told his parents that an athlete wouldn't smoke pot. As Ethan said, if he is no longer an athlete, then he feels fewer reservations about smoking pot. Of course, there was more going on here than a cool calculation on Ethan's part of the pros and cons of smoking pot. He was angry at his parents. After talking with Ethan myself, I concluded that he was smoking pot for multiple reasons: in order to relax, in order to enjoy time with his friends, and also because he knew it would upset his parents. Ethan was smoking pot partly as a way of expressing his anger toward his parents. Many parents assume that their teenager is using drugs as a way of expressing rebellion against their parents. That's not true as often as parents think it is. And even when it is true, it's seldom the main motivation. But it can be a part of the story, as it was in Ethan's case.

Look in the Mirror

We've laid out some of the basic differences between girls and boys in terms of why they use drugs and alcohol, as well as a few of the risk factors and protective factors that increase or decrease the likelihood of their using drugs and alcohol. Now let's talk about concrete action you can take to decrease the likelihood that *your* daughter or son will use drugs or alcohol.

Look in the mirror. If you have a drinking problem, don't waste your time talking to your daughter or son about drugs or alcohol. Your word has no credibility. As I wrote in my book *The Collapse of Parenting*, you cannot teach your child a virtue that you yourself do not possess.

If you smoke cigarettes, you're stepping up to bat with two and a half strikes against you. "You smoke ten cigarettes a day. I smoke two joints a week. And smoking marijuana is legal in lots of states now. What gives you the right to tell me that what I'm doing is wrong?" That's what one teenage boy told his mother after she warned him about the dangers of smoking pot. Mom tried to answer that marijuana is more dangerous than tobacco. Her son responded with facts and figures purporting to show that tobacco is more dangerous than pot. Mom thought that her son was inventing most of the facts and figures, and maybe he was. But you don't want to get bogged down comparing the relative risks of marijuana and cigarettes.

If you've used drugs in the past, don't mention it unless you have no choice. Don't try saying, "I used pot when I was your age, so that's how I know how bad it is." Your teen has many good responses ready for that one, including:

- "Maybe it was bad for you. Maybe it wouldn't be so bad for me. You're not me."

- "Why shouldn't I be allowed to try something you did yourself?"

- "You turned out okay, didn't you? So it couldn't be that bad."

If your teen confronts you and demands to know whether you used pot, tell the truth. But don't boast or brag. Acknowledge your mistake, but don't try to use your prior experience for any advantage when you talk with your child.

Alcohol

When I was in school, back in the 1970s and 1980s, it was common to hear about boys getting drunk; girls, not so much. Today, across the English-speaking world, girls and boys are just about equally likely to use and abuse alcohol: the gender gap in alcohol use among teenagers has dwindled nearly to zero.[7] But the risks of alcohol use are greater for girls than for boys.[8]

Girls and young women appear to be more vulnerable to the toxic effects of alcohol than are boys and young men, even after adjusting for differences in height and weight.[9] Drinking too much alcohol damages girls' brains differently and more severely than the same degree of alcohol abuse affects same-age boys.[10] Studies looking at the brains of teenagers who drink alcohol have shown some really astonishing sex differences. For example: The prefrontal cortex is the part of the brain involved in decision making, balancing risk and benefits. Teenage girls who drink alcohol have significantly smaller prefrontal cortex volumes than teenage girls who don't drink alcohol; but teenage boys who drink alcohol actually have slightly *larger* prefrontal cortex volumes than teenage boys who don't drink.[11] More recent studies have confirmed and extended these findings: alcohol affects girls' brains differently from boys' brains.[12] In another study researchers followed teenagers who drank alcohol from age seventeen through age twenty-nine. They found that even if a girl stopped drinking completely in her twenties, that girl who had been a drinker at age seventeen was more likely than a boy who had been a drinker at age seventeen to have long-term issues with drug use, psychiatric problems, and poor adjustment to life in general.[13]

These sex differences are now well known among researchers who study alcoholism, but they are not well known to the rest of us. I have found that some people are uncomfortable with this information. To them it seems sexist to suggest that alcohol is more toxic to women than to men. But pretending that girls are no different from boys puts girls at risk. Nowhere is that clearer than when we are talking about alcohol abuse.

The Day Everything Changes

When you talk with your kids about drugs, stick to the facts. But keep in mind that which facts are relevant depends on whether you're talking to a daughter or a son.

Remember that girls get most of their drugs from friends and that the transaction usually takes place in a private home. Know where your daughter is. Know who her friends are. Talk to her friends' parents. Ask her to check in with you frequently throughout the day. Keep tabs on her. Make sure she knows that you will be checking up on her. And verify her statements, openly, with her cooperation. If she says that she's at Melissa's house, ask her to call you back using Melissa's home phone rather than the cell phone. Look at your caller ID: does the number match Melissa's home phone number? Make sure your daughter understands what you're doing and why. That knowledge will actually empower your daughter to refuse unsafe requests. If her friends invite her to go downtown to somebody else's home, she can tell them: "No, I can't, because my mom makes me call her from everybody's house and she'll see from her caller ID that I'm not where I told her I'd be." For thirteen- and fourteen- and fifteen-year-old girls, that technique really does work. "I wish *my* mom cared that much about *me*" is what one girl said after another girl I know explained her mom's requirements.

What about boys? My experience is that the approach I just outlined for girls is ineffective for most boys. First of all, the strategy of asking your teen to call you from the home of a friend is a nonstarter with many boys. Boys who "check in" with their parents will be ridiculed by other boys, as your son will quickly learn. Second, remember that boys are more likely to purchase drugs from a stranger, outdoors, in a park or on the street. So keeping track of which particular house your son is visiting is less relevant.

Regarding drug education: the evidence of the past thirty years suggests that educating boys about the dangers of drugs is a waste of time. On the contrary: emphasizing the harmful, mind-blowing, damaging effects of drugs can boomerang. That approach will pique the interest of thrill-seeking boys. Remember that these are the same boys who go snowboarding down a steep mountain without taking a lesson first.

So what works with boys? My recommendation is clear and consistent discipline. Tell your fourteen-year-old son, "If I catch you drinking or smoking or using any kind of drugs, we'll take the PlayStation and lock it away for the three months that you're grounded." Many teenage boys prize mobility and independence. Tell your fifteen-year-old son: "If I catch you using drugs, you won't be driving until you're eighteen, not sixteen." Tell your seventeen-year-old son: "If I catch you drinking or using drugs, you lose the car keys for six months. *Minimum* of six months." These measures may seem extreme, but they can also be life-saving. And these strategies work for boys.

Many parents don't think their kids are doing drugs. Other kids, maybe. But not *their* kid. Then comes the day when they find out. Mom discovers drug paraphernalia in her son's pants pocket. Or Dad finds an incriminating e-mail message on his daughter's computer.

What do you do now?

First: establish the prohibition. Second: offer alternatives.

Establish the prohibition. Whether you have a daughter or a son, you need to make clear that you absolutely prohibit the use of illegal drugs.

Offer healthier alternatives. But the right alternative may depend on whether we're talking about a girl or a boy. If your daughter is smoking in order to relax, you need to help her find other ways to loosen up. If your daughter is using a friend's Vyvanse to lose weight, you need to offer her safer ways to lose weight. Or better yet, help her to accept herself as she is, and shift the focus away from how she looks. (Take a look at my book *Girls on the Edge* for more strategies I've learned about working effectively with girls who are too concerned about their appearance.)

If you have a son who's a risk taker, a son who's using drugs because he's looking for a thrill, you need to help him explore safer, healthier ways to get that risk-taking tingle. You and he might look into snowboarding, skiing, mountain biking, moto-cross, mountain climbing, and bouldering.

Wait a second, you're thinking. You've just discovered your son is using cocaine. I'm telling you to buy your son a snowboard or a mountain bike. Am I saying that you should reward your son for using drugs?

I'm not saying that you can't discipline your son, or your daughter for that matter. But it's not enough just to take away your daughter's cell phone or your son's driving privileges. You have to offer alternatives. Positive alternatives that ease your daughter's anxiety or satisfy your son's desire for excitement.

The other objection I hear from parents of sons in this situation is that the alternatives I'm suggesting are risky. Your son could break his leg snowboarding. He could crack a rib mountain biking.

That's all true. But those risks are healthy risks. When your son allows a drug dealer to stick a needle in his arm, your son has entered a much darker world.

CHAPTER 8

Social Media and Video Games

Jason is sixteen. His sister Sonya is fourteen. They come from a stable home with two loving parents. Mom and Dad are concerned about Jason: He's not working hard at school and his grades are sliding. He spends most of his free time playing video games like *Grand Theft Auto* or *Call of Duty*, or surfing the Web for pictures of girls.

Both parents are actually quite proud of Sonya. She is a straight-A student and an athlete, and she has many friends. But when I meet with Sonya, she tells me that she isn't sleeping well. She wakes up in the middle of the night, feeling guilty about having eaten a whole slice of pizza at supper. She often has palpitations and shortness of breath. She has just started cutting herself with razor blades, secretly, on her upper inner thigh so her parents won't see. She hasn't told her parents any of this. On the surface she is the golden girl. Inside she feels that she is falling apart.

Her brother Jason, on the other hand, is happy as a clam. He can eat a whole pizza without the slightest remorse. He has no difficulty sleeping: in fact, his parents had to kick him out of bed at noon on a Saturday. He likes to spend his free time hanging with his two buddies who are just like him, playing video games and looking at pictures of girls online.

Jason and Sonya both spend much of their free time looking at screens in ways that were not possible twenty years ago. Jason is playing high-speed online video games and looking at high-resolution images of girls. Sonya is posting to Instagram and sending pics via Snapchat; neither of those apps existed before 2010. There has been a huge change in the lived experience of children and teenagers, it's happened really fast, and it has affected girls and boys differently.

Imagine a girl living in ancient times, by which I mean 1992. She's in her bedroom. She's writing in her diary, which is to say, she's writing with a pen in a bound volume of blank pages. She's writing about whom she doesn't like, why she doesn't like them, the kind of girl she really does like, the kind of woman she hopes to become. She might write five pages in an evening. She's not going to show those five pages to anybody. If she has a younger brother, she may even keep her diary under lock and key. But she's doing some important work. She's figuring out who she is and what she really wants.

Figuring out what you really want is not trivial. The American psychologist Dr. Abraham Maslow believed that many adults never figure it out. And they're miserable, because they're working hard at jobs they don't like, in pursuit of goals that are not meaningful to them. So this girl, living back in the 1990s, writing in her diary, is doing something meaningful. She is connecting with herself.

Now fast-forward to the modern era. It's unusual today to find any kids who are writing in a diary. When I meet with middle-school or high-school students, I often ask them, "Who here is on Instagram?" Almost all the hands go up. "Who here is on Snapchat?" All the hands go up. "Who here has a diary?" No hands. Then I say, "Let's expand the definition of a diary. It doesn't have to be a bound volume of blank pages. Let's define a diary as anything that you write in from time to time, even if it's just a file on your tablet, that is *private*. It's not for a school assignment. Nobody else will ever see it. Defining a diary that way, very broadly—anything that you write in from time to time, electronic or otherwise, that nobody else will ever see—who here has a diary?" Still no hands. Then, in an auditorium with three hundred kids, one girl raises her hand.[1] (Incidentally, I'm not saying that there is anything wrong with kids who write public blogs. But those blogs are not diaries. They serve a different function; they are still a kind of public performance, not a private self-exploration.)

Social media have displaced the diary in the lives of many girls. There's not time enough for both. Everybody's busy. And social media matters more, because other kids are watching.

Girls and boys use social media differently. A boy and a girl both go to a football game. They both take pictures at the football game. But the boy is more likely to take a picture of the game, or of the pretty cheerleader at the game. The girl is turning the phone on herself and taking dozens of selfies at the game. That evening, she goes through the selfies to find two or three where she's laughing and the kids around her are laughing, and that's what she posts on Instagram. *Here I am at the game. We had a great time.* If you don't like Jacob's photo of the pretty cheerleader, he may not care. But if you don't like Michelle's photo of Michelle, she's going to take it more personally. So Michelle is staying up until midnight, Photoshopping her picture for Instagram.

These differences are especially marked in the realm of sexuality. A girl is much more likely than a boy to post a photo of herself wearing a bikini; boys are more likely to post a selfie of themselves with a new trophy, or one where the emphasis is otherwise on something the boy has *done* rather than on how he *looks*. If you don't like Jake's selfie showing off his new fifty-five-inch flat screen, he may not care. But if you don't like Ashley's photo of herself wearing her new bikini, she's more likely to take it personally.

Girls increasingly are posting provocative photos of themselves on social media sites such as Instagram. And girls are much more likely than boys to post sexually appealing or sexually provocative photos of themselves.[2] A sexual double standard is now blatant on social media sites: girls feel pressure to present themselves sexually; boys don't.[3] In one recent study of Instagram selfies, teenage girls were much more likely to post sexualized poses (lying on their backs, etc.) while the boys were much more likely to post selfies of themselves lifting something heavy, showing off their muscles, etc. The girls were also much more likely than the boys to post photos of their bodies from the neck down, with no face at all. On Instagram, if you're a girl, it seems that what really matters is what's below your neck.[4] In some ways, social media create a lose-lose situation for girls. If a girl doesn't give in to the pressure and post suggestive photos, the boys may call her a prude. But if a girl does post sexualized photos of herself, recent studies suggest that other girls will perceive her as less appealing as a friend and less socially competent.[5]

Boys are more likely than girls to post a wide range of their lived experience on social media. Girls post a much narrower slice of their life. A boy and a girl both get sick. They both throw up. The boy posts a photo of his vomit on his Instagram. Girls almost never do that.

And there's yet another element that comes into play in understanding girl/boy differences in the consequences of using social media. Boys tend to overestimate how good-looking they are; they think they are better-looking than their peers rate them as being.[6] Girls are more likely to rate themselves *less* attractive than their peers rate them as being. As kids go through adolescence, girls become more dissatisfied with their bodies while boys become *more* satisfied with *their* bodies.[7] Girls are more likely than boys to notice their own mistakes and to remember them.[8] Boys are more likely than girls to overestimate how interesting their own lives are to other people.[9]

Now put all these findings together. Imagine a girl. Maybe she's eleven years old, or fourteen, or seventeen. She's sitting in her bedroom. All by herself. She's looking at what other girls have posted on Instagram or sent via Snapchat. There's Emily at the football game. There's Ashley at the party. There's Vanessa with her puppy; isn't it cute? And she thinks: *I'm just sitting here in my bedroom, not doing anything. My life sucks.* The more time you spend on social media, comparing yourself to other people, the more likely you are to become depressed. That's true for both girls and boys, but this effect is much larger for girls than it is for boys.[10]

When you look at all the research together, you can understand why social media are more likely to be toxic for girls than for boys. Girls are more likely than boys to post sexually provocative photos of themselves.[11] Women and girls are more invested in social media: they spend more time on social media, and more time texting, than do boys and men.[12] Boys are more likely to spend free time playing video games rather than filtering and cropping their selfie for Instagram.[13] (Video games have their own hazards, which we will get to in a moment.) And a boy, looking at Jacob's photo of his own vomit, is less likely to want to be Jacob; while a girl, looking at Vanessa's cute puppy and Emily's great selfie at the football game, may believe that Vanessa and Emily really are leading happier, more interesting lives than she is.

So what should you do about this if you have a daughter?

Begin by explaining to her that everybody's life is a mix of happy and sad, a mix of success and disappointment. And for most humans who have ever lived, there's been more sad than happy, more disappointment than success. Explain that that's true for almost everybody, even for Emily, who only posts fun and happy stuff on her Instagram. That's not a new insight. The First Noble Truth of Buddhism is that life is suffering. Socrates, facing his own imminent death, taught his students that true philosophy consists of the *cheerful* contemplation of one's own death.[14] Paul, writing to the Corinthians, told them that he had "reason to be sad, yet [was] always filled with joy" (2 Corinthians 6:10).

How can you do that? How can you be filled with joy when you have reason to be sad? You will experience many disappointments in life. You will watch your loved ones die. And then you will die. That's true for you. It's true for me. How, then, can any of us choose to walk through life joyfully? That, I think, is the first question of any serious philosophy or grown-up religion. But this girl, sitting in her bedroom looking at the other girls' Instagram and Snapchat feeds, will not take that first step on the road to maturity, because she still thinks that Vanessa and Emily are having a great time, that she's the only one who is bored. Frustrated. Lonely.

So one part of your strategy is to give the Talk, explaining that everybody's life is a mix of happy and sad, and not to be misled by the way girls represent themselves on social media. But the Talk, by itself, is not enough. You also must govern and guide your daughter's use of social media (and your son's use as well).

I encourage you to install apps and monitoring software such as Net Nanny or My Mobile Watchdog for this purpose. These programs make it easy for you to help your son or daughter to develop good habits and not to spend hours a day on social media. You can configure these apps to limit the amount of time your kid spends on any particular site or app such as Instagram or Snapchat. I suggest no more than twenty to thirty minutes a day.

Some parents prohibit access to these Web sites altogether. I understand their rationale, but I don't think that approach works for all families, or even for most. For many girls today, Instagram is a major means of communicating with friends. I get that. Twenty minutes a day is enough time to log on, get your messages, respond, and log off.

Parents have to take the lead in setting limits. It's not reasonable to put this burden in the lap of your fourteen-year-old daughter. What is she supposed to say when her friend says, *Hey, how come you didn't "like" the photo I posted on Instagram last night?* It's not reasonable to expect a fourteen-year-old to say something like *Researchers have found that the more time a girl spends on social media, the more likely the girl is to become depressed.* You have to allow her to say, *Hey, my evil parents have installed this app on my device that locks me out after twenty minutes. I'll like your photo when I log on again tonight, first thing, I promise.*

If you are uncomfortable governing and guiding your child's use of social media, then I encourage you to read my book *The Collapse of Parenting.* In that book I explore the arguments for and against authoritative parenting. I am not going to repeat those arguments here, except to say it's not your job to be your kid's best friend. There are lots of girls out there who can be your daughter's best friend. But a friend can't limit how much time your daughter spends on social media. You can, and you must.

In addition to limiting the amount of time your daughter or

son spends on social media, I also recommend that you "ban the bedroom." No screens in the bedroom. No devices in the bedroom. In the typical American household today, when kids go home, they usually go straight to their bedrooms and aren't seen again except perhaps for meals. That's crazy. A family can't be a family if the kids spend more time alone in their bedrooms than with their family members. Insist that your daughter or son do whatever they're doing online in a public space: in the kitchen or the living room. There should be nothing in the bedroom except a bed: no TV, no PlayStation, no Xbox, no screens. No electronics in the bedroom. That's not just my opinion. That's the official recommendation of the American Academy of Pediatrics.[15]

There are often unexpected benefits to banning the bedroom. I've heard from many parents who have told me that their daughter or son said that they had to stay up till midnight or later in order to finish all the homework that was assigned in school, and much of that homework had to be done on the computer, online. Once the computer is in the kitchen, with Dad answering his e-mails on his device across the kitchen table from his daughter, who is doing her homework on her device, she gets her homework done by 8:30 p.m. The daughter wasn't lying about staying up until midnight: she just didn't realize how many hours she was spending on social media, or shopping online. But when Dad is in the same room, a few feet away, she gets online, gets the homework done, and is ready for bed.

Video Games

We have seen that girls are more susceptible than boys to the toxic effects of social media. Conversely, boys may be more vulnerable than girls to the bad effects of video games. To begin with, the average boy spends significantly more time playing video games than does the average girl.[16] Boys are more likely than girls to sacrifice real-world social activities in order to play video games, and more likely to skip doing homework in order to play video games.[17] Boys are twice as likely as girls to play *violent* video games.[18] And even when girls and boys spend the same amount of time playing the same video games, different areas of the brain "light up" in boys compared with girls, leading researchers to conclude that video games may be more rewarding to boys, more likely to give boys a thrill, compared with girls.[19]

If you haven't played video games in the past ten years, you may not understand how addictive some of them can be, owing to advances in technology. A boy can now play a video game in which he climbs into a tank, feels the rumble from three-hundred-watt subwoofers as his tank treads crush the rubble of a demolished house, and fires off depleted uranium rounds at enemy outposts as he enjoys the thrill of victory—or the agony of defeat when three enemy tanks blast him almost simultaneously. But the agony of defeat is lessened by the knowledge that he can just hit "restart" and play it all over again.[20]

Today any boy with a high-speed Internet connection can play in real time against another gamer across town or on the other side of the planet. Sophisticated headsets allow boys to engage in simulated online combat in teams, arranging coordinated ambushes of enemy fighters using high-tech virtual weaponry. After your son has spent two hours leading a squad of fighters in a raid on terrorist headquarters, issuing commands through his headset-mounted microphone to his online comrades, and raced through a hail of virtual bullets to destroy the enemy power generator, well, studying Spanish grammar from a textbook can seem pretty dull. The virtual world is fast moving, interactive, collaborative. And fun.

And it is *heroic*. For years Sony's lead advertising line for its PS4 video game console was "Greatness Awaits." The official Sony commercial offers some insight. The actor, a young man looking directly into the camera as special effects explode around him, says, "Who are you to be ordinary? Who are you to be anonymous? You—whose name should be spoken in reverent tones, or in terrified whispers!"[21] In the real world maybe you're just an ordinary, anonymous kid who's not doing very well in school. But in the world of the video game, you can be great. You can be a hero.

I had the honor of giving a keynote presentation at a statewide conference for juvenile-justice professionals in New Mexico. The topic was "boys adrift"—boys who aren't doing well in the real world, boys who aren't doing their best, boys who are disengaged. (The title of my second book was *Boys Adrift*.) After my presentation, there was a panel discussion. One of the panelists was Judge John Romero, who is the Presiding Judge of the juvenile court in Albuquerque. At that time, Judge Romero also presided over a therapeutic program for boys on probation. Judge Romero talked about how many teenage boys he met who had been convicted of a violent crime, often gang-related violence. He shared how he talked with these boys in the less formal setting of the therapeutic program, without the robe and the trappings of court. Judge Romero asked the boys: *Why are you doing this? You seem to be a smart kid. Don't you understand that joining a gang and engaging in gang-related violence greatly increases the chance that you're going to get killed or go to jail? And greatly decreases the likelihood that you will graduate from high school or get a good job?* Judge Romero acknowledged that it took him some time, more than a year of listening to the boys, before he understood what they were saying to him. He told us that *these boys want to be seen as heroes in the eyes of their peers, and in their own eyes.* The gang understands that. The gang gives the boy a gun and a mission: to kill the leader of the rival gang. If the boy succeeds, he's a hero. If he is killed trying, he's still a hero. If he is arrested by the police and sent to jail, he's still a hero. If he chickens out, he's a wuss. That's a challenge the boy can understand.

We all nodded. But then Judge Romero looked straight at the audience. "Most of you here don't live in the barrio," he said, referring to the low-income Spanish-speaking neighborhoods where most of the Albuquerque gangs are based. "Many of you may be thinking, *I'm so glad this doesn't apply to me. My son spends his evenings upstairs in his bedroom.* But the differences between your son in the suburbs and these boys in the barrio are not as big as you might think. The biggest difference may be that the boy in the barrio is engaging in actual violence with a real gun. Your son, upstairs playing *Grand Theft Auto* or *Call of Duty*, is engaging in pretend violence with a pretend gun. But the underlying dynamic is the same. In both cases the boy is less concerned about achievement in the real world, at school, and more concerned about carrying out his mission—in the video game or in the world of the gang—and impressing his comrades. In both cases the boy is trying to prove to his friends, and to himself, that he is a real man."

Boys want to become men and to see themselves as men. If we don't give them better guidance about how to do that in a constructive way, they will look to their peers. The result may be gang-related violence for boys who find themselves living in the barrio. In more affluent settings the result may be boys who spend many hours a week playing violent video games. In the final chapter I will have more to say about what we can do, individually and as a society, to help boys become good men.

The Ruling of the Court

We have already seen that boys are at least twice as likely as girls to play *violent* video games. And there is now evidence that violent video games such as *Grand Theft Auto* and *Call of Duty* have effects that are qualitatively different from those of nonviolent games such as *Zuma* and *Tetris*.[22] Young people who play violent video games change their brains, becoming desensitized to violence, in ways not seen in young people who play nonviolent video games.[23] The more realistic the violence, the bigger the effects.[24] Playing violent video games over a period of months and years appears to cause more aggressive behavior and more aggressive thoughts and feelings, as well as decreased empathy; that's not true for playing nonviolent video games.[25]

Boys who spend many hours each week playing violent video games are at increased risk of disengaging from the real world. One of the most highly regarded researchers in this field, Professor Craig Anderson, has pointed out that the strength of the evidence linking violent video games to antisocial behaviors is every bit as strong as the evidence linking secondhand smoke to lung cancer or lead poisoning in infancy to lower IQ scores. Professor Anderson also notes that the controversy now surrounding video games is reminiscent of the controversy surrounding cigarette smoking in the 1960s or lead poisoning in the 1970s. After all, many smokers will never get lung cancer. And some people who get lung cancer are not smokers and have never been exposed to cigarette smoke. Likewise, not all boys who play video games twenty hours a week will disengage from real life, and not all boys who disengage from real life are video game players. But Professor Anderson insists that we not ignore the significant risks that video games create.[26]

. . .

Legislators in California heard about this research. They were especially concerned by the studies showing that playing the most violent video games can change personality in children and teenagers, causing kids to become less caring and more hostile. They thought: *There ought to be a law.* So they wrote a law, making it a civil offense—punishable by a fine of up to one thousand dollars—for stores to sell the most violent video games directly to children under eighteen. Parents, if they chose, could still purchase violent games and give them to their children to play, but the law would prohibit a kid from walking into a store and buying the most violent games without his parents' knowledge. Governor Arnold Schwarzenegger signed the statute into law.

But it never took effect. The video game industry, supported by the American Civil Liberties Union (ACLU), promptly brought suit. The industry and the ACLU claimed that the California law violated the video game companies' First Amendment right of free speech. The case went to the United States Supreme Court. In a decision written by the late Justice Antonin Scalia, the court ruled in favor of the video game industry, rendering the California statute null and void.

In a concurring opinion Justice Samuel Alito expressed his concerns about violent video games. He agreed with the California state legislators that "the experience of playing video games (and the effects on minors of playing violent video games) may be very different from anything that we have seen before." He expressed his horror at video games in which "victims by the dozens are killed with every imaginable implement, including machine guns, shotguns, clubs, hammers, axes, swords, and chainsaws. Victims are dismembered, decapitated, disemboweled, set on fire, and chopped into little pieces. They cry out in agony and beg for mercy. Blood gushes, splatters, and pools. Severed body parts and gobs of human remains are graphically shown. In some games, points are awarded based, not only on the number of victims killed, but on the killing technique employed."[27]

Justice Alito understood the concerns of the legislators and of the parents who had campaigned for the bill. But he joined Justice Scalia in ruling that deciding what games children will play is not the job of the California State Assembly. It's the job of the parents.

There is no law prohibiting any child from buying any video game, no matter how violent or vicious the game may encourage the player to be. There can't be such a law, not in the United States, as a result of the Supreme Court's ruling.

No one else can do this job for you. *You must know what games your child is playing.* There should be no expectation of privacy when your son is playing a video game. You should be looking over his shoulder to make sure that the game meets safe criteria (we will talk about those criteria in just a moment). If your son is going to a friend's house, you must ask whether they will be playing video games, and if so, then you must find out whether the parents share your concerns about violent video games. If the parents have no idea what you are talking about, or if they won't even be home, then you must tell your son, *No, you are not allowed to go to that friend's house.*

And what about preparing for the real world? The demands of real life require skills quite different from the skills required to master video games. Imagine a young father, in his twenties, let's say, trying to comfort his crying baby daughter. There are no buttons to push, no photon torpedoes to fire. The right thing to do may be simply to rock the baby and hum a lullaby. The chief virtue required may not be lightning virtuosity with a game controller but merely . . . patience. If you need to get along with a belligerent coworker, the chief virtue you need may not be blazing speed, but ... patience. In most video games the best way to deal with difficult people is to vaporize them with rocket-propelled grenades. In the real world, what you need most is not high-tech lethal weaponry but patience.

The stereotypical pastimes of boys and men in previous generations were pretty good at teaching skills like patience. Thirty years ago, and even more so fifty years ago, it was more common for boys and men to go hunting and fishing together. Boys who go fishing with an experienced fisherman soon learn that a good fisherman has to be able to wait patiently. That sort of patience might serve a young father well. But video games do not teach that kind of patience.

So what rules should you lay down for your son? Professor Anderson has provided some practical guidelines based on the published research.[28] He recommends first of all that you either play the game yourself or watch it being played. Then ask yourself these questions:

- Does the game involve some characters trying to harm others?

- Does this happen frequently, more than once or twice in thirty minutes?

- Is the harm rewarded in any way?

- Is the harm portrayed as humorous?

- Are nonviolent solutions absent or less "fun" than the violent ones?

- Are realistic consequences of violence absent from the game?

If you answer yes to two or more of these questions, then Professor Anderson suggests that your son should not be allowed to play the game. The first consideration should not be how many hours per day or per week your son is allowed to play these games. The first question should be what kind of video games he is allowed to play at all. Violent video games that reward antisocial aggression—games such as *Grand Theft Auto*—should not be permitted in the house. Period. "Antisocial aggression" means aggression such as killing police officers or prostitutes, aggression that runs counter to all acceptable social behavior.

Another consideration that I mentioned earlier is what activities are displaced by playing video games. If your son is neglecting his friendships with nongamer friends to spend more time playing video games, then he's spending too much time playing video games. If he refuses to sit down to dinner with the family because he's in the middle of a video game, that's not acceptable. He needs some help from you getting his priorities straight.

And what about teenage boys having relationships with girls? Surprisingly, especially to those of us over thirty, many boys today seem to prefer playing video games to being with girls. Mr. Welsh, a teacher at T. C. Williams High School in Alexandria, Virginia, has heard any number of stories along these lines. Girls at his school have told him that at parties they "are often totally ignored as the guys gather around TV screens, entranced by one video game or another. 'Girls sit around watching the guys play until they get fed up and drive off looking for something else to do,' says junior Sarah Kell, for whom the games range from 'stupid and boring' to 'disgusting.' 'We try to tell them they're wasting their time, but they just keep going. Some guys stay up playing until three in the morning on school nights, and then they try to do their homework.'"[29]

Boys prefer video games over girls? A reporter for *The New*

York Times spoke with students at a number of college campuses. She discovered many young men who seemed more interested in playing their video games than in being with their girlfriends. The reporter interviewed one young woman in college who had broken off her relationship with a young man, "in part out of frustration over his playing video games four hours a day. 'He said he was thinking of trying to cut back to fifteen hours a week,' she said. 'I said, "Fifteen hours is what I spend on my internship, and I get paid $1,300 a month." That's my litmus test now: I won't date anyone who plays video games. It means they're choosing to do something that wastes their time and sucks the life out of them.'"[30]

A young man in college today has unprecedented sexual opportunities. Unlike his father or grandfather, he is likely to be attending a school where men are outnumbered by women. Even boys who are not the best-looking or particularly popular now have an excellent chance of finding young women who will accept their advances. Nevertheless, as *The New York Times* reported in a front-page story, college administrators are reporting that more and more young men show no interest in meeting young women (or meeting other men, for that matter). They don't want to meet anybody. They just want "to stay in their rooms, talk to no one, [and] play video games into the wee hours. . . . [Some] miss classes until they withdraw or flunk out."[31]

Here are guidelines for the appropriate use of video games, based especially on the work of Professor Craig Anderson cited previously:

- **Content:** You should not allow your son to play video games in which the player is rewarded for killing police officers or noncombatant civilians. The video game industry itself provides a rating system for games, assigning a rating of M for "mature" to this kind of antisocial violence. M games are not supposed to be sold to or used by anyone under eighteen years of age. But just because a game is rated T for "teen" doesn't guarantee that it's appropriate for your son. Familiarize yourself with the T-rated games. Even games rated E for "everyone" cannot be assumed to be safe. In fact, Professor Anderson's team has found that some of the E-rated games were more violent—and engendered more violent behaviors—than some games rated T.[32]

- **Time:** No more than forty minutes a night on school nights, and no more than one hour a day on other days—and that's only after homework and household chores have been completed. And your minutes do not roll over. If your son goes three weeks without playing any video games at all, that doesn't mean that he's allowed to spend eight hours on a Saturday playing video games. That's binge gaming, analogous to binge drinking, and it's unhealthy.

- **Activities displaced:** Make sure your son knows where his priorities should be. Family comes first; schoolwork and household chores come second; friends come third; video games are somewhere further down the list. If your family is one in which most family members still sit down to share a common evening meal, then sitting down to dinner with the family should be more important than playing a video game, more important than talking on the phone with a friend, more important even than finishing a homework assignment. Homework is more important than talking with friends or playing a video game. Taking a phone call from a friend should be a higher priority than playing out a video game, though.

"I'm Not Quitting"

Governing and guiding your son's use of video games is a good idea, but it's only half the challenge. You want to help find a constructive alternative. In some cases, competitive sports might provide such an outlet. What kind of free-time activities and hobbies would be the best choice for this kind of boy? How can this particular boy best satisfy his desire to be tested and to triumph?

Let me share with you the experience of one of my own patients. At age twelve Aaron Grossman was an avid video game player. His behavior bordered on addiction. One key characteristic of addiction, incidentally, is *loss of control*: the boy knows that he shouldn't be spending so much time playing video games, he may not even want to play that much, but he feels that he just can't help it. So Aaron was spending three or four hours a day playing video games, mostly sports games like Madden NFL. When his parents asked him whether he'd like to try playing real football, though, he said no. He wasn't interested.

His mom and dad, Jennifer and David, decided to sign Aaron up for football anyway, Pop Warner football. They didn't ask Aaron. They just told him that he was going to play. I've found that parents can do this kind of compulsory sign-up for a boy only up to about age twelve or maybe age thirteen but generally no later. If you drive a sixteen-year-old boy to an activity he doesn't want to attend, he may simply get out of the car and walk away. But Aaron's parents judged correctly that their son was still young enough to go to the practice on their say-so.

Once Aaron was surrounded by other boys who were doing their best to run, kick, throw, and catch, he joined in. After all, the format of the first day of Pop Warner football isn't much different from gym class at school. It's familiar.

On the drive back home that first day, Jennifer wisely did not ask whether Aaron had a good time. Asking whether Aaron had a good time would have been very nearly equivalent to asking him to admit he was wrong and his parents were right. Instead she just said, "Practice tomorrow starts at eleven a.m., right?"

He nodded.

The practices were every day, Monday through Friday, sometimes lasting several hours. It was hot. The second week, the boys put on their equipment: helmets, shoulder pads, the whole deal. Mom gasped the first time she saw another boy knock Aaron to the ground. But Aaron got up immediately and trotted back to where the coach was explaining the next drill.

The next day was the first scrimmage. Aaron was knocked down several times, one time pretty hard. It was a hot, muggy August day. On the ride home, Aaron was visibly flushed and tired. After driving in silence for several minutes, his mom finally said, "Aaron, if you want to quit, it's okay. Dad and I appreciate your making an effort."

Aaron shook his head. "Coach can kick me off the team if he wants to," he said, "but I'm not quitting."

The words were so corny, so reminiscent of Richard Gere's line to Louis Gossett Jr. in *An Officer and a Gentleman* that Mom almost laughed. But then she realized that her son had probably never seen *An Officer and a Gentleman*. He was serious.

Aaron stopped playing video games altogether during football season. When the season ended in November and his team didn't make the play-offs, he said, "Maybe next year."

He started playing Madden NFL again, on and off, after the season ended, but seldom more than thirty minutes a day. "It's nothing like the real thing," he told his mom spontaneously one day. That's the closest he ever came to thanking his parents for signing him up for real-world football.

Insight, or Not

When psychologists say that a client has good *insight*, they mean that the client understands the situation, and has a good grasp of what needs to be done. Some boys have insight into their video game predicament. Others do not.

Jacob did not. Jacob Stolzfus was twenty-two years old when his parents brought him to see me in the office. Although he had above-average intelligence, he had been a mediocre student in high school. He barely managed to graduate. He now worked a few hours a week assisting his father, who worked as an independent contractor doing home remodeling. His parents were concerned by Jacob's complete lack of ambition. He had no job except for the occasional work provided by his father; no education beyond high school and no interest in further education, vocational or otherwise; and no plans for the future. His parents were also concerned about his lack of any social life. He had no girlfriend, indeed no friends at all.

The four of us met together: Jacob, his parents, and me. His parents spoke first. "I've been researching it online, and I'm worried," his mom said. "He has no ambition. No friends. And no *concern* about any of it. I looked it up online and more than one site mentioned the possibility of schizophrenia."

I nodded, although schizophrenia seemed unlikely. After listening to the parents for a few more minutes, I turned to Jacob. "What's your favorite thing to do in your free time?" I asked him.

He snorted. "What do *you* think?" he said.

"I don't know. That's why I asked you," I said.

"Well, it depends," he said. "Jerking off is number one if I haven't done it in a day or two. But you can't jerk off all day long. Believe me, I've tried to, more than once. So when I'm not jerking off, I play video games." (For readers outside of North America: "jerking off" is slang for "masturbating.")

"How many hours a day do you spend playing video games?" I asked.

Another snort. "As many as possible," he said.

"How about in the past seven days?" I asked. The four of us then worked through the past seven days, going over what Jacob had done each day as near as they could recall. We concluded that he had spent at least forty hours in the past seven days playing video games. It was the equivalent of a full-time job. His favorite games were violent games such as *Halo*, *World of Warcraft*, *Grand Theft Auto*, and *Assassin's Creed*.

"Do you see a problem there?" I asked Jacob.

"None whatsoever," he said with a charming smile.

"Who are your best friends?" I asked.

"I have dozens. Where do you want me to start?" he answered.

"Just tell me the first names of three of your best friends."

"Their names, or their gamer handles?"

"Preferably a real name," I said.

"Well, there's Jonathan," he said.

"When did you last see Jonathan?" I asked.

"I've never seen Jonathan," Jacob said. "He lives in Singapore. He's in my *World of Warcraft* guild."

"When's the last time you had a friend over at your house?" I asked.

"Yeah, I see what you're getting at. The virtual world isn't as good as the real world, right? That's what you think, right?" Jacob said.

"Yes, that's fair," I said. "I do think real-world relationships are more important than relationships which exist only online or in a virtual world. So when's the last time you had a friend over at your house?"

No response from Jacob. "It's been a long time," his mom said after a pause.

"Years," his father said.

After another forty minutes of evaluation, I was ready to make a recommendation. "I don't see any evidence that Jacob has schizophrenia or any other major psychiatric disorder," I said. "And he doesn't appear to be either anxious or depressed. I think that the time he spends playing video games and other online activities has displaced his real-world activities. He's spending too much time in front of an electronic screen."

"That's what I think too," his father said. "But what can we do about it?"

"If Jacob were younger, if he were ten years old instead of twenty-two years old, then it might be reasonable to impose some limits. If he were ten years old, you could allow him to play video games for maybe thirty or forty minutes a day. But that won't work at this age, in my experience."

"Why not?" Mom asked.

I turned to Jacob. "If your parents were to limit your video games to forty minutes a day, would you turn off the game after forty minutes?"

Another snort. "No way," he said. "I'm just getting started after forty minutes."

"That's what I thought," I said. "And if you try to turn off the game in the middle of a game, a man twenty-two years of age can get upset."

"That's an understatement," Jacob said, and for the first time all three of them—Jacob and his parents—laughed.

"Right," I said. "The only effective intervention in this context, with a man twenty-two years of age who is spending more than forty hours a week playing video games, is complete abstinence. You have to eliminate all access to video games."

Jacob's face froze.

"You mean we have to remove the Xbox?" his mother asked.

"Remove the Xbox from the house. Destroy it or give it away. Eliminate all access to video games, including the cell phone."

Jacob's face unfroze, changing into an angry grimace. "That's totally unacceptable," he said. "I'm an adult. I'm over eighteen. You can't tell me what to do. My parents can't tell me what to do."

"That's true," I said. "You are an adult. You are free to walk out of your parents' house and make your own way in the world. But if you leave"—and now I turned to the parents—"if you leave, your parents are not to support you. You are on your own. Right now you are living in your parents' home, but you're not paying your way. You don't pay rent. They pay for your food. They pay for your Internet access. If you are going to stay in their house, then you have to abide by their rules."

With my encouragement, the parents followed my instructions. They donated the Xbox, and all the video games they could find in the house, to Goodwill. They took away their son's cell phone. They removed the computer from his room. They password-protected their own computer and refused their son access to their computer except under supervision.

Four weeks later, they were back, as I had requested.

"It's unbelievable, the difference," Dad said.

"What's different?" I asked.

"Everything is different," Dad said. "At work, for example. It used to be pulling teeth to get Jacob to help me at all, and I had to check everything he did. But now he's showing initiative. And to be blunt: he's a lot smarter than I thought he was."

"How do you mean?" I asked.

"Well, take this past week, for example," Dad said. "We were doing an upscale remodeling job. The homeowner wanted us to install this high-tech shower unit with massage jets, body jets, everything, all voice controlled by computer. I didn't want to tell the owner the truth, which is that I had never done anything like it. I was struggling. Jacob stepped right in, showed me how to do it, and did most of the wiring himself. He figured it out just by reading the instructions. The unit worked perfectly. It was impressive."

Jacob was staring down at the floor, but I thought I saw a hint of a smile on his face.

"It wasn't easy," his mom said. "Not at first. Jacob didn't talk to us at all for the first week. He would make his own meals and take them into his room. But then, after about a week, he started joining us for supper. And he just seemed to *wake up*. It was as though he had been in a fog all those years he was playing video games. Maybe he just wasn't getting enough sleep. Now he actually talks at suppertime."

"He just seems smarter now. He understands better. He's got a better attention span. He's got more patience," Dad said.

"What do you think?" I asked Jacob. "Do you agree?"

"No, I don't," Jacob said. "I don't feel any different. Not any smarter, that's for sure."

"If it were up to you, would you start playing video games again tomorrow?" I asked.

"Absolutely," Jacob said.

His parents sighed.

Jacob showed no *insight*. No awareness of how his video games had displaced real-world activities.

Jacob starting playing video games regularly when he was five years old. His parents were impressed by his skill and manual dexterity playing the games. They were misled. Researchers find that the younger the age when boys start playing video games, the more likely they are to become addicted, to sacrifice real-world activities in order to play their game.[33] As you consider how to implement the guidelines I have shared in this chapter, you also need to take into consideration the *age* of your child. The younger the child, the less time they should spend in front of a screen and the more time they should spend in the real world. That's equally true for girls and for boys.

Don't wait for your son to show insight into his situation. I have seen many parents who expect their eleven- or fifteen- or twenty-four-year-old son to act logically on the basis of the evidence. The parents will say: *Look how much time video games are sucking out of your life. See how your friendships have withered since you started spending twenty hours a week in front of a screen. See how tired you are all the time, except when you are playing the game.*

Parents consider these points compelling. They expect their son to have *insight* and to act based on the evidence.

Don't wait. You may be waiting months, years. If your son is one of the millions of boys and young men who have allowed video games to displace real life, you must intervene. Remove the device, if necessary. Limit screen time.

If you don't, who will?

Gender Nonconforming

Martin

Sally first realized she was pregnant while sitting in the office of her divorce lawyer. She'd been married for four years, and she was at the end of her rope. Even though she worked longer hours than Mark and brought home more money, Mark still expected her to be the housekeeper, picking up his clothes, cleaning house, cooking all the meals. He even had the nerve to complain when supper was late, when he'd been home all afternoon watching TV while she worked her tail off at the bank. She'd suggested marriage counseling; Mark refused. He didn't have the slightest clue how badly the marriage was broken and apparently had no interest in fixing it.

A friend at work gave her the name of a good divorce lawyer. At the first visit, the lawyer was going through a checklist of questions.

"Any children?" the lawyer asked.

"No," Sally answered.

"Any possibility that you might be pregnant at this time?"

Sally was about to answer, "No, of course not," but then she paused. When had she had her last period? For that matter, when was the last time she and Mark . . . ? Then she remembered that Saturday night more than a month ago, when she had thought that just *maybe* this marriage could still be saved. That moment in the attorney's office was the first time she realized that her period was late. "I don't think so," Sally answered at last.

"You don't *think* so?" the attorney repeated quizzically.

Eight months later, she gave birth to Martin. In the meantime, Mark had moved to Los Angeles and Sally was contemplating life as a single mother.

Many parents imagine that their children are above average, but Sally was *sure* that Martin was precocious. And she was right. By one year of age, Martin had a vocabulary of about twenty words, including "zebra." By age two he was talking in full sentences. By age four he was sounding out words in the phonics workbook. When he started kindergarten, the teacher immediately put him in the accelerated reading group. Martin was the only boy in that group of six children.

From the beginning, Martin loved school. He always sat in the front row, raised his hand to answer every question, was always polite. His teachers adored him. "If all boys were like Martin, life would be a joy," said Mrs. Messner, his first-grade teacher, wistfully. "I just wish he would go outside at recess."

"Martin doesn't go outside at recess?" Sally asked.

"Lately, no," Mrs. Messner said. "He begged me. He said, 'Mrs. Messner, why should I waste time going outside and just standing around? Why can't I just stay inside and read?' He just doesn't like recess. All the other boys are running around like wild animals, and Martin stays close by me or one of the other teachers."

"I was like that too," Sally said. "I never liked recess."

By the end of third grade, Martin was reading at the sixth-grade level. He started writing poetry, taking great care in the arrangement of words on the page. His favorite font on the computer was *French Script*. His handwriting flowered into an elaborate cursive, and he began making little circles for the dots over *i* and *j*.

Sally's friends warned her that Martin was becoming a bookworm. She should sign him up for some sports, they said.

That sounded like a good idea. "What would you like to play?" she asked her son. "Soccer? Basketball? Football?"

"I don't like any of those," he said. Pause. "But I do like bowling with Karen and Samantha," he added at last.

"Bowling's not a sport," Sally said.

"Yes it is," Martin said. "They have tournaments on TV."

Finally Martin agreed to take some tennis lessons, but his heart wasn't in it. "My schedule is too busy," nine-year-old Martin announced to Sally one day a few weeks after the tennis lessons began. "I need more time to practice piano. The tennis lessons are a waste of time and money." Martin could be very firm, especially when negotiating with his mother.

"All right," Sally said. No more tennis lessons. What was the point of spending money on something that Martin didn't even like?

At least he has friends, Sally thought. She and Martin agreed on eight children to invite over for his tenth birthday party: seven girls and one boy, as it happened. Martin wanted the party to have a *Lord of the Rings* theme. Martin claimed that all of his friends liked *The Lord of the Rings*. Sally asked her son which character he liked the most.

"Frodo, of course," Martin said.

"Really? Why 'of course'?" Sally asked. "Why not Gandalf? Or Legolas? Or Aragorn?"

"Aragorn is a very unrealistic character," Martin said dismissively. "Frodo is much more believable."

"But Aragorn at least is a human being," Sally answered, determined to win one of these debates for once. "Frodo is a four-foot-tall hobbit. How can you say Frodo is more realistic than Aragorn?"

"Because Aragorn is so strong, so great at everything. It's just not believable. He's always fighting off somebody evil—orcs or Uruk-hai or Nazgûl, whatever—and he always wins against ridiculously long odds," her son said. "It's just not plausible. Frodo is weak. He's small. He doesn't fight anybody—except Gollum at the very end, and Gollum is even smaller and weaker than Frodo is, and anyhow Frodo basically lost that fight. Gollum bit the Ring off his hand."

Sally wanted to compliment her not-quite-ten-year-old son on using the word "plausible" correctly in a sentence, but she paused as she considered the implications of what Martin had just said. Being strong and talented was unrealistic, according to Martin. Winning against long odds was unrealistic. Being *weak* was realistic. She needed to sort this out.

The court had granted sole physical custody of Martin to Sally. Nevertheless, Sally made a point of inviting her ex-husband, Martin's father, to spend time with Martin, especially over the summer months. Mark had mellowed and matured in the years since the divorce. He'd had two children by his second wife, and he seemed to be a good father to them. (Sally suppressed the urge to ask Mark's second wife, Jennifer, whether he had gotten any better at helping around the house.) Mark called from California one evening to ask Sally whether Martin could join him and his six-year-old son, Jared, on a fishing trip. "My company is chartering a forty-foot boat. About a dozen people are going. We'll sail to Catalina Island, do some fishing out there, then that night we'll be at sea on the open ocean. There's nothing like it, Sally. The stars are so bright, it's like they're just ten feet over your head."

"It sounds like fun," Sally said sincerely.

But Martin refused. "There's nothing more stupid than fishing," he said authoritatively. "You sit on a boat waiting for some poor fish to chomp down on your hook, then you viciously yank on the hook, which is stuck in the fish's mouth, and then you drag the fish up on the boat and cut out its guts. What fun. I don't *think* so. No, thank you."

"But Martin—" Sally began.

"Besides, I'm supposed to be at my music camp then," Martin said. "You're not asking me to give up my music camp, are you?"

Sally and Mark continued to talk after Martin got off the phone. "Martin doesn't want to do *any* regular guy things," Mark said. "He says fishing is stupid, even though he's never tried it. He wouldn't go to a football game with me, even when I had those tickets for a Redskins game when I visited you guys last November. He doesn't want to play soccer. Jeez, he wouldn't even play video games with me when we went to the video arcade."

"So what difference does any of that make?" Sally said defensively. "He's getting straight A's. He has friends. He's happy."

"But what does he do for fun?" Mark asked.

"He plays piano. He writes poetry. He reads."

"You call that fun?" Mark asked incredulously.

"For Martin those things *are* fun. Martin is very intellectual. That's just who he is. Besides, where is it written that every boy has to like football? Or video games? Or fishing?"

"So what's this music camp he's going to?" Mark asked.

"It's a very good music camp. Martin really wants to work on piano over the summer."

"What kind of piano music does he play?" Mark asked.

"Lots of different kinds," Sally said.

"Oh yeah? Can he play jazz? Fats Waller? Keith Jarrett?"

"No, of course not," Sally said. "He only plays classical. Beethoven. Clementi. Debussy. You should hear him play 'Clair de Lune.'"

"Jeez. Give me a break," Mark said.

The other boys didn't really start picking on Martin until middle school. That's when Sally began getting phone calls from the guidance counselor. Somebody had stuffed tampons into Martin's locker with a note attached saying "You need these." Then a week later somebody spray-painted the word "fag" on his locker. The following month two boys bumped into Martin in the hallway, pretending it was an accident, and knocked him over. Sally was horrified by the bruise on Martin's cheek where his face had hit the floor.

"Doesn't it bother you that the other boys pick on you?" she asked her son.

"Not really," he said with a shrug. "They don't understand me. All they understand is video games and sports. They're afraid of what they don't understand, and they respond the only way they know how. With violence. I just need to be careful, stay away from them, that's all."

"But why don't any of your friends stand up for you?" Mom asked.

"I don't have any friends," Martin said matter-of-factly.

"How can you say that? What about Karen? What about Samantha?" Mom asked.

"They're not my friends anymore. Ever since the boys starting picking on me. Karen and Samantha are friends with those boys now. Especially Karen. She's always hanging out with them. When she saw how the boys hate me, she started avoiding me."

"That must hurt. You must feel terrible," Mom said.

"No, I don't. It doesn't bother me. Besides, I do have friends."

"Really?" Mom said eagerly. "Who?"

"I'd say my best friends right now are Isaac Asimov and Robert Heinlein," Martin said calmly.

Mom had to pause for a moment, searching her memory to recognize the names. "But Isaac Asimov and Robert Heinlein . . . They're both dead," she said. A chill ran down her spine. "They were both science fiction writers."

"Right," Martin said. "Isaac Asimov wrote the *Foundation* trilogy. It's about a mutant who's more powerful than all the normal people. He looks small and weak, but he's actually stronger than anybody because of his special powers. Robert Heinlein wrote *Stranger in a Strange Land.*"

"But you can't go out to lunch with them. You can't talk to them. You need friends you can talk to," Mom said.

"Not true," Martin said. "They're my best friends. I have tons in common with them."

The Anomalous Male

There is plenty of variation *within* the sexes. Beyoncé, Angelina Jolie, Serena Williams, Martha Stewart, and Hillary Clinton don't seem to have much in common with one another. Nor, for that matter, do Pee-wee Herman, Sylvester Stallone, Lil Wayne, Justin Bieber, and the late Michael Jackson. But how significant are the differences? How do those differences affect what we've discussed earlier in this book?

Let's begin with a study published by scientists at NASA who were studying astronauts on the space shuttle some years back. One of the less-well-known facts about spaceflight is that women who fly in the space shuttle are typically very dizzy after they return to Earth. Their blood pressure tends to be lower than it should be for several days after the flight. If they stand up too suddenly, they get dizzy, because their blood pressure is too low. The same phenomenon has been reported in male astronauts, but much less often. Wendy Waters and Janice Meck at the Johnson Space Center in Houston wanted to study this phenomenon. So they tested female and male astronauts right after the astronauts returned from a mission on the space shuttle—thirty-five astronauts in all.

Their findings confirmed what many previous reports had suggested. Every female astronaut they tested was extremely prone to dizziness after the flight. Few of the men were. The stress of spaceflight had very different effects on most of the men compared with all of the women.

The extraordinary finding in this study concerned those few men who *were* dizzy after spaceflight, men who showed the female-typical drop in blood pressure after space flight. These men were less often pilots by training, more often mission specialists: biologists, physicists, or computer geeks with no background in aviation, men who were on board just to run a particular experiment. Among the "real" astronauts, the men who *fly* the shuttle, the anomalous female-typical pattern was rare. But one in four male mission specialists showed the female-typical pattern.[1]

None of the females showed the male-typical pattern. Very few of the "tough guys" showed the female-typical pattern. But among the geeks, one out of four men showed the female-typical pattern. What's going on?

There's growing evidence that a small subset of boys (and men) have some characteristics that are more typical of girls and women. That doesn't mean they're "transgender"—we'll get to transgender in chapter 11. And it also doesn't mean they're gay. Different researchers have used different terms for these boys and different criteria to define them, so it's hard to consolidate the findings across the various studies. But there's reason to believe that these boys have a lot in common.

Harvard professor Jerome Kagan spent many years studying these boys, whom I'll call "anomalous males."[2] Kagan began by analyzing baby boys who were only a few weeks old. He would simply touch the babies gently and see how they responded. Most baby boys don't mind being touched, but a few react intensely. When touched, those boys begin crying and thrashing their arms and legs. Kagan followed these boys for years, from infancy through childhood and into adolescence: he studied some of these kids for more than three decades. He found, first of all, that about half of these boys never outgrow their dislike of novelty. As teenagers, these boys shy away from strangers and new adventures, just as they did when they were babies.

Even more striking, Kagan found that these boys have other characteristics in common. Specifically, these "anomalous males" are

- more likely to have allergies, asthma, or eczema than other boys;[3]

- more likely to have a narrow face, i.e., a facial width-to-height ratio less than 0.55[4] (a narrow face in males, but not in females, is associated with lower dominance and more fearfulness;[5] young men with narrow faces are less aggressive and less likely to be successful in martial arts compared with men with broader faces, even after controlling for physical size[6]);

- less willing to engage in rough-and-tumble play.[7]

Sociologist Patricia Cayo Sexton also studied such boys. She found other characteristics in addition to those identified by Kagan. According to Sexton, these boys also typically

- are precocious, particularly with respect to language skills;

- are often loners with few close friends;

- may enjoy sports but typically prefer noncontact sports such as tennis, track, bowling, and golf (they don't like to hit or be hit, so they're not playing football or soccer).[8]

I would add one more characteristic to those listed above, based on my observations over the past twenty years: if you give one of these boys a blank piece of paper and a box of crayons, that boy will almost always draw a person or a pet or a tree. In other words, he draws the same sort of picture that the girls draw. He doesn't draw a scene of action at a moment of dynamic change, as most other boys do. (Reread chapter 2 if you don't see the significance of this.)

A word about terminology. In the first edition of this book, published in 2005, I noted that these boys were sometimes referred to as "sissies." I didn't like that term then, and I don't like it now. It's derogatory. In this book we are trying to *understand* kids, not mock them or make fun of them. I preferred the term "anomalous male" over "sissy" because "anomalous" just describes the facts: these boys are not typical boys.

In recent years, however, a new term has become the preferred term in the field, and that term is "gender-nonconforming." While I agree that we don't want to use the term "sissy," I see problems with the term "gender-nonconforming." In modern American culture, being a conformist is a bad thing. Being a nonconformist is a good thing. Saying that one group of kids are "nonconformists" and another group of kids are "conformists" is derogatory to the "conformists." The fact that the conformists are in the majority doesn't make it any less unfair to put a derogatory label on them.

This point is not trivial. We will come back to it in the next two chapters. A subtle but pervasive bias has infiltrated gender studies over the past decade: a bias that allows saying unkind things about the majority under the guise of being kind to the minority. But I think: bias is bias. The fact that someone is biased in favor of a minority—in this case, the anomalous male—doesn't excuse the bias. It's still unfair. Throughout this chapter, I will continue to use the term "anomalous male" to refer to the boy who draws people, pets, flowers, and trees; who has a narrow face; who doesn't like rough-and-tumble play, etc. I prefer this term over the currently politically correct term "gender-nonconforming" because "anomalous" just describes the reality, whereas "gender-nonconforming" subtly implies that the nonconformist is better than the conformist. I don't think one kind of boy is intrinsically better than another. I am just trying to understand the differences.

The anomalous male, then, appears to represent a distinct physiological type and is a real challenge to parents—who often don't even recognize the kinds of problems their son may face. On the contrary, many parents, especially mothers, react the way Sally and Mrs. Messner did. Martin was quiet and well behaved and never got into trouble. What's not to like?

Many parents don't recognize that their anomalous son is heading for a special kind of trouble . . . until middle school begins. When the tidal wave of puberty hits, the neatly arranged life that seemed so stable and peaceful in elementary school is often washed away. For many of these boys, their closest friends during the elementary school years were girls. When puberty arrives in middle school, hanging out with the cool kids becomes intensely important to many girls, and the anomalous male is not a cool guy to hang with. So the girls are gone.

Sexton found that these boys often become anxious about sex around this time. Some begin using pornography. Others become depressed. The "geek" may become a loner, finding solace in his books and his fantasies. "I am a rock, I am an island," are the words of the disturbing Paul Simon song that so accurately portrays such a boy:

> *I have my books and my poetry to protect me.*
> *I am shielded in my armor.*
> *Hiding in my room, safe within my womb,*
> *I touch no one and no one touches me.*[9]

Let's follow the anomalous boy into high school. His grades are good; his social life, not so much. I've seen plenty of these boys over the past thirty years. All too often they've developed a smooth façade that hides the hurt they feel inside. After all, they have the approval of the adult world. Why should they care if other kids make fun of them or spray-paint nasty words on their locker? As Sexton observed, these boys are "reluctant to acknowledge the connection between school honors and feminization, or to inquire into whether their success can be attributed more to acceptance of female norms than to brilliance or superior intellectual endowments. . . . Few feel victimized; they feel more like heroes and victors."[10] By the time such a boy is in high school, I don't know whether anybody could change him or broaden his horizons, or even whether they should try, as long as this boy is not feeling anxious or lonely. He may grow up to be a mission specialist on the space shuttle, after all. He probably won't be the pilot, but that's okay with him: he'd probably prefer to be the mission specialist.

Throughout this book, I've tried to share my perspective that gender is important, gender is complicated, and gender is meaningful. Know your child and celebrate the kind of boy or girl that your child is becoming. How to apply that perspective in the case of the gender-atypical boy?

The answer I give to parents is that you don't want your child's gender issues to lead to distress, if it can be avoided. The gender-atypical boy can easily become anxious, lonely, and withdrawn. But Jerome Kagan and his Harvard colleagues presented evidence that parents who intervene early can pull their anomalous son out of the tendency to withdraw. Kagan suggested that *parenting style* is a critical factor in determining whether a boy outgrows his fearful, withdrawn tendencies or whether he remains stuck in that mode. The sons of protective parents who are "sensitive" to their child's preferences are the boys who have the *worst* outcomes. Baby boys who are fearful and withdrawn become more fearful and withdrawn if their parents shield them from minor stresses and injuries. Such parents, Kagan found, "made it more, rather than less, difficult for the child to control an initial urge to retreat from strangers and unfamiliar events. The equally accepting mothers who made age-appropriate demands [for their sons to mix and mingle] helped their highly reactive infants tame their timidity. . . . Mothers who protect their [timid] infants from frustration and anxiety in the hope of effecting a benevolent outcome seem to exacerbate the infant's uncertainty and produce the opposite effect."[11] In Kagan's research, when parents who had timid children also believed in being "sensitive to a child's needs" *in every case*, the timid baby boy grew up to be a timid, fearful child.[12]

The Boy in the Mirror

When I was writing the first edition of this book, back in 2003 and 2004, I had a bit of a shock as I read the work of Jerome Kagan, Patricia Cayo Sexton, and others who described the anomalous male. I realized that I was reading about . . . me. I was an anomalous male. As a child, I drew pictures of stationary people and stationary dogs, rather than scenes of action. I taught myself to do macramé. I didn't like to hit other people. I attended a sleep-away summer music camp—Interlochen, near Traverse City, Michigan—for three summers at ages eleven, twelve, and thirteen. By the end of my third summer at Interlochen, I knew many Gilbert and Sullivan operetta songs by heart. I had lots of friends in elementary school—mostly girls. In middle school the mean boys started calling me "Len the Fem." I was precocious in English and creative writing. I was a loner in high school: one of my favorite songs was Paul Simon's "I Am a Rock." My mother divorced my father three months after I was born and she never remarried, so there was no adult male in the household.

Many years later, when my patient told me about her son Martin and his desire not to miss his summer music camp, I knew exactly how he felt. And as a clinician, I also understood Martin's mother's wish to push Martin out of the shell he was constructing for himself.

Sexton believed that anomalous males are made, not born. She wrote that these boys' problems come "from overprotective parents and can best be remedied through association with a normal adult male."[13] Later in this chapter, we will consider new evidence that Sexton may have been wrong. The differences between the anomalous male and gender-typical males may be genetically programmed, at least in part. Nevertheless, I have seen in my own clinical experience how these boys can become more comfortable with typical male activities if they get a little push from their parents—or from themselves.[14] And as a result, new horizons open up.

Amy

Amy was the firstborn of two daughters. Her parents, Barbara and Howard, didn't realize what a tomboy Amy was until their second child, Zoe, was born. "Amy and Zoe were like night and day," Barbara told me one day in the office. "When Amy was six months old, if a stranger came into the room, Amy would crawl across the floor and tug on the stranger's shoelace," Barbara continued. "Zoe was so different. When Zoe was six months old, if a stranger came into the room, Zoe would just start crying and crying until I picked her up. Then she'd just bury her face in my chest."

"And as they grew older?" I asked.

"Amy was your classic tomboy," Barbara said. "She was always playing with the boys, building forts, throwing snowballs, climbing trees. She loved building forts."

"And Zoe?" I asked.

"Zoe was into girly things. Dolls and dress-up and baking cakes. My husband and I were big believers in going against gender stereotypes, you know—"

"Sure," I said. "I know exactly what you mean."

"So when Zoe was three years old, we bought her a set of toy earthmoving equipment: a little dump truck, a backhoe, a front-end loader. Amy loved that sort of stuff, so we bought three brand-new toys like that for Zoe."

"Did she like them?" I asked.

"She loved them," Mom said. "But she didn't use them the way they're meant to be used. First she put all three vehicles in a little circle, facing each other, and then she put little ribbons on the dump truck. 'That's not quite how the dump truck is supposed to work, sweetie,' I remember telling her. 'But it's the dump truck's *birthday*,' Zoe explained to me very patiently. 'And here are its two *best friends*,' she said, pointing to the backhoe and the front-end loader. Later that afternoon I came into her room and she very loudly told me, 'Shush! They're sleeping!' She had carefully laid the dump truck, the backhoe, and the front-end loader in her bed, and drawn the covers up over them so you could just see the headlights of each of them."

"That's cute," I said. "What about Amy?"

"Right. Well, you know," Mom said, "Amy was talented in sports. Competitive sports. We signed her up for MSI [the local soccer league]. She was really brave, even when she was just six or seven years old. She was never afraid of the ball. Most of the other girls were, but not Amy. She didn't mind getting bumped or bruised. And you know, she's built more *solidly* than Zoe. She has a stockier build. Zoe is more delicate."

"Maybe that's a result of the differences in their interests," I suggested. "Maybe if Amy played with dolls while Zoe ran around on the soccer field, then Zoe would be the stocky one."

"Maybe," Barbara said doubtfully.

Zoe is often anxious. Amy is not. Amy has her act together. She knows what she wants—in school, from her friends, and from the boys in her life. She makes whatever arrangements are necessary to secure her objectives. She's an honor-roll student, she's captain of the girls' soccer team, she has a variety of hobbies—including, curiously enough, cross-stitch and macramé—and she is popular with the athletic crowd at her school, both girls and boys. But she's not your typical girl.

Differences

A handful of scholars have compared gender-atypical boys like Martin with gender-atypical girls like Amy. An important contribution was made, again, by Patricia Cayo Sexton, who found that while the anomalous boys

> were noncompetitive, non-athletic and fearful, the [anomalous] girls were fearless, independent, and competitive. Girls who were bold and daring from ages ten to fourteen became the most intellectual women as adults. . . . Among girls, strangely, high intelligence was associated with both greater masculinity and greater femininity. Bright girls were more likely than other girls to be dominant and striving and at the same time have more feminine qualities.[15]

Boys with many feminine characteristics tend to be less popular and at higher risk for anxiety and depression, especially in middle school and high school. By contrast, the anomalous girl appears *more* likely than her peers to be popular and well adjusted. The girl who is the captain of the lacrosse team is more likely to be a top student than the girl who plays no sports. The tomboy—the girl who prefers some male-typical activities—should be encouraged to pursue those gender-atypical activities. Girls who show some male-typical characteristics—such as a willingness to confront others openly—generally do *better* than average socially. On the other hand, boys who show female-typical characteristics such as a reluctance to engage in rough-and-tumble play are more likely to have more problems socially.

Anomalous girls have an advantage in school and in life; their social horizons are likely to be broader than those of other girls. Anomalous boys have an advantage in school, but they pay a steep price for that advantage, and their social horizons are likely to be narrower than those of other boys.

Is It Blue or Is It Periwinkle?

Back in chapter 2 we considered differences in the visual systems of girls and boys. I mentioned there that girls may have more resources in the visual system that are devoted to color and detail, while boys may have more resources in the visual system that are devoted to detecting speed and direction of movement. (I provide more information about this topic in the Extra Stuff on vision at the end of the book.) But do those differences apply to gender-anomalous girls and boys? Would they apply to a girl like Amy or a boy like Martin?

One study that bears on this question was conducted by researchers at Auburn University. They began by asking college women to complete a fifty-nine-item "femininity questionnaire." Do you enjoy putting on makeup? How often do you read women's magazines like *Glamour* and *Cosmopolitan*? Some of the young women scored high: they were the "girly girls." Other women had low scores on femininity: let's call them the "tomboys." The researchers then showed college students, one by one, a series of colors: say, a swath of lime green. They then asked the college students to match the color to the correct word or phrase: lime green, mint green, jade, or emerald. Many of the young men struggled with this task. But the girly girls aced it: they got nearly all the challenges correct.

How about the tomboys? Did they score as well as the girly

girls? Did they score like the boys? Or were they somewhere in between?

When I give presentations and I pose this question and ask for a show of hands, most people guess that the tomboys scored in between the young men and the young women. But that's not correct. The tomboys did just as well as the girly girls.

If you read through the material at the end of the book in the section titled Extra Stuff: Sex Differences in Vision, then this result won't be surprising. For girls the difference between lime green and emerald green is obvious—and that's true whether the girl is a tomboy or a girly girl. Boys can learn the difference between lime green and emerald green, but the distinction is less obvious for the average boy than for the average girl.[16] On this parameter tomboys have more in common with girly girls than they have in common with boys.

We have seen that gender-atypical boys share many traits in common with one another that they do not share with gender-typical boys: gender-atypical boys are less likely to enjoy playing contact sports like football; they are more likely to have a narrow face; they are more likely to have allergies or asthma; and they are more likely to draw people, pets, or plants, compared with gender-typical boys. No such distinctions apply to gender-atypical girls. If you give a blank piece of paper and a box of crayons to a tomboy, as I have done on many occasions, she will usually draw a person or a pet. The person she draws may be a soccer player, but (unless she has had formal training as an artist) that soccer player is standing still, holding the ball, and not engaged in action. The tomboy girl uses just as many crayons, or nearly as many, as the girly girl. The tomboy chooses to draw an athlete, while the girly girl chooses to draw a ballerina. So *what* they draw is different, but *how* they draw is very similar. On this parameter, and others, the distinctions between the tomboy girl and the girly girl seem fairly superficial. By contrast, the distinctions between the gender-typical boy and the gender-anomalous boy are profound: not only do they draw completely different things, but they draw them differently. The gender-typical boy is drawing a rocket smashing into a planet or a warrior killing an alien with a laser. The gender-anomalous boy is drawing a person or a pet, stationary, not engaged in action.

And the differences go deeper still. The gender-atypical boy— who hates playing football and who draws pictures of people with eyes, mouth, hair, and clothes, rather than stick figures— seldom transforms in a month or a year into a football player who draws stick figures engaging in combat. There may be exceptions to this rule.[17] But the exceptions are rare, most likely fewer than one boy in a hundred.

With girls it's different. The tomboy who likes to play football with the boys may next week be a girly girl who wants to dress up for the prom. Next week? Maybe even tonight. In my first-hand experience, it's not rare for the same girl to be *both* a tomboy who likes to play contact sports *and* a girly girl who loves to wear makeup and get dressed up for the prom. It's not the norm, but it's not rare. And in my experience, such girls—who are *both* girly girls *and* tomboys—are becoming more common.

Gender-atypical girls may always have been more common than gender-atypical boys. The proportion of girls who want to play soccer or climb trees is usually higher than the proportion of boys who want to sew or learn to do ballet. And the proportion of gender-atypical girls appears to be rising, so much so that it's no longer unusual for a girl to play soccer or basketball, which was not true forty or fifty years ago. But it's still unusual to find boys who want to sew or learn ballet.

Why might that be the case? I will suggest in a moment that

gender-atypical girls and boys are the way they are because that characteristic is hardwired; indeed, the tendency toward gender nonconformity may be genetically programmed. I have also hinted above that the trait of gender nonconformity in boys is different from, and more hardwired than, the trait of gender nonconformity in girls. (More evidence on this point in just a moment.)

But like many genetically programmed traits, the expression of these traits is susceptible to cultural influences. Over the past thirty years, and especially in the decade since the publication of the first edition of *Why Gender Matters*, there has been a growing cultural bias in favor of kids being gender-atypical—at least for girls. Today girls are encouraged to play contact sports, to play in the mud and get dirty, to engage in rough-and-tumble sports, to an extent that would have amazed our parents. Yet it's still rare to find boys receiving much encouragement to knit or do macramé or learn ballet. That may explain, in part, why girly girls who are also tomboys may be more common today than they were forty or fifty years ago, whereas boys who knit samplers and also play football are no more common today than they were in the past.

But there is more to this story. Genetic factors play a larger role in boys than in girls.

The Androgen Receptor

Androgens are hormones, such as testosterone, that are found in much higher concentrations in men than in women. Male sex characteristics such as facial hair, a large Adam's apple, deeper voice, greater muscularity, and greater aggressiveness have all been linked to androgens such as testosterone.

But how do androgens work? The answer begins with the

androgen receptor. Androgens such as testosterone and dihydrotestosterone bind to the androgen receptor, which becomes activated. The activated androgen receptor then binds to certain genes and turns them on, resulting in masculinization.

That process begins in the womb. The male fetus produces testosterone, which masculinizes the male brain.[18] The biggest sex differences in the expression of genes in the human brain occurs not in adulthood, nor in puberty, but in the prenatal period before the baby is even born.[19]

So far so good. Girls and boys are different. But some of the most startling discoveries of recent years have helped scientists to understand variations *among* girls and *among* boys better than before. Researchers now understand that the gene for the androgen receptor varies from one boy to the next. Every gene is made up of units called *codons*; each codon normally codes for one amino acid in the protein that gene is programmed to make. One end of the androgen receptor gene has a series of codons called CAG codons because the codons are a repeating string of cytosine (C), adenine (A), and guanine (G). These codons used to be called "nonsense" codons because they don't directly code for amino acids. But nobody calls them nonsense codons anymore, because scientists now recognize that these CAG codons help determine how active the androgen receptor will be.

The number of CAG codon repeats in the androgen receptor gene varies from one person to the next, from a low of eight repeats to a high of thirty-one repeats. Many research teams have now discovered that if you're a boy and your androgen receptor gene has a low number of CAG repeats, then your androgen receptor is very active and you will tend to be more masculine. If you're a boy and your androgen receptor gene has a high number of CAG repeats, then your androgen receptor is less active and you will tend to be less masculine.[20] This new research helps to explain much of the noise in earlier research on testosterone levels. Two young men may have exactly the same testosterone level, yet one young man is very masculine—he plays football, he is aggressive, he is muscular—and the other young man hates football, is timid, and is not muscular. The same testosterone molecule may cause lots of activity via the androgen receptor in the first young man and much less activity via the androgen receptor in the second young man.

In recent years there has been substantial research linking variation in CAG repeats with behavioral outcomes such as aggressiveness, impulsiveness, and depression. That research helps to broaden and deepen earlier research on testosterone levels and various behavioral outcomes. For example: what's the relationship between testosterone levels and depression in adult men? It turns out that the answer depends critically on the number of CAG repeats in the androgen receptor gene. If you're a man and you have a low number of CAG repeats—which means that you are likely a very masculine man—then your mood depends on testosterone. In one study, among men with a low number of CAG repeats, depression was more than *five times* as common among men with low testosterone than among men with high testosterone. But among men with a high number of CAG repeats—men who will be, on average, less masculine men—there was no difference in the frequency of depression between men with low testosterone levels and those with high testosterone levels.[21]

Researchers have now documented many links between the number of CAG repeats in the androgen receptor and outcomes related to behavior and personality. For example, young men with a low number of CAG repeats have been found to be more impulsive than young men with a high number of CAG repeats.[22] And several studies have suggested that men with a smaller number of CAG repeats are more likely to be aggressive and to engage in criminal violence, independent of their testosterone levels.[23] Incidentally, this link between the number of CAG repeats and aggressiveness may not be confined to humans. In dogs as well, a low number of CAG repeats has been associated with higher aggressiveness.[24]

For me, the take-home message of all this research on the impact of the number of CAG repeats on behavioral traits associated with masculinity is simple: the tendency for a boy to be a rough-and-tumble boy is hardwired to a significant extent. That also means that the tendency for another boy *not* to be a rough-and-tumble boy is also hardwired. Trying to get a timid boy who doesn't like to hit or be hit to sign up to play defensive tackle in football is not likely to be a productive effort.

How can I reconcile that statement with my earlier citation of Jerome Kagan's work, in which Kagan commended parents who intervened to push their timid son to be bolder? The age of the boy makes a big difference. Kagan was looking at parents of young children, some of whom were just toddlers. I have found that parents who push their two-year-old son to come out of the corner and play with the big doggie are often successful in their efforts, especially if the dog isn't too rough. But parents who try to get their bookish fourteen-year-old to sign up for football are less likely to be successful.

There are exceptions. I did know one family where the parents were able to get their fourteen-year-old son to try out for football by contacting the coach and asking whether he could just try out for the placekicker position. The coach agreed (he didn't have a placekicker). The son made the team. Nobody would ever mistake him for a jock. But he did make two or three friends on the team. And his social standing rose, because he was now a football player. And he told me that he became more comfortable around guys. "I used to get nervous going past a bunch of jocks, because of the way they treated me back in seventh grade," he said. "But then after I started being the placekicker and I was pretty good at it, everything changed. The same guys who used to pick on me were now clapping me on the back after I kicked the extra point." He seemed to grow in self-confidence as well.

If your son is a gender-atypical boy who draws people, pets, and trees; who doesn't like to play rough-and-tumble sports; who has mostly girls and few boys for friends; then maybe a gentle push is in order. Maybe not football. But help him to be comfortable with all-male or mostly male activities. The vacation activity proposed by Martin's father—an overnight fishing trip—is a great idea. Camping or skiing in a mostly male group, ideally with a grown man whom you trust to look after your son, also works.

After I wrote the first edition of this book, I received some critical e-mails from readers who challenged me on this point. They took me to task because I encouraged parents to nudge their gender-atypical son to engage in gender-typical, mostly male activities, but I didn't advise parents to push their tomboy daughter to engage in gender-typical, mostly girl activities. It doesn't seem fair.

I agree. It doesn't seem fair. But it does make sense. As I have explained, boys who are gender anomalous and who remain gender anomalous are at significantly higher risk of loneliness, anxiety, and depression as they move through adolescence. But girls who are gender anomalous are not at higher risk for any bad outcomes. Furthermore, girls don't seem to need much help becoming more girly, if they want to. I've seen tomboys who adopt girly-girl personas in a matter of days, or even a matter of hours, for example during prom season. And then they take off the prom dress and easily slip back into the tomboy role, wearing jeans and T-shirts and beating the boys at the boys' own game.

I've already shared how the mean boys in middle school called me "Len the Fem" and "fag." Martin's mother told me that the boys teased her son relentlessly, claiming that he was gay. Likewise, gender-anomalous girls and women have told me that some people believe, or hint, that they are lesbian, especially if they don't care to participate in gender-typical activities, don't use makeup, and don't like to gossip with the girls. What's the reality? Are gender-anomalous boys and girls more likely than gender-typical boys and girls to be gay or lesbian? How about bisexual? Those are some of the topics we turn to next.

CHAPTER 10

Lesbian, Gay, Bisexual

Daniel

You know how TV reporters interview the neighbors after some guy does something terrible? "We never would have expected this from him," the neighbors say. "He always seemed like such a *normal* guy."

I felt as though I were trapped in one of those interviews, listening to Wendy and Paul describing their son Daniel, who had just started eleventh grade. "Daniel was a perfectly normal little boy," Wendy was telling me. "I mean, he was all boy. He loved his trucks and his trains. He played football, T-ball, soccer, everything little boys love, you know? There wasn't anything sissy about him."

"Right now he's playing on the varsity football team. He plays linebacker on defense, tight end on offense," Paul added. "Coach told me last week he's got a shot at playing college ball if he kicks his game up a notch."

"And then we found *this*," Wendy said, handing me a sheaf of pages.

Daniel's parents had printed out about a dozen pages of Daniel's e-mails. I read them carefully:

> If you jerk off over a picture of a guy, does that mean you're gay? I try jerking off over pictures of chicks, but I keep imagining it's a guy. I look at the girl's neck and I pretend it's a guy's neck. I keep wishing it were a guy in the picture instead of a chick. I can't help it.

I flipped to the next page:

> If I really am gay, I'll kill myself. I'll drive my car off the Bay Bridge. I think it could be really cool, actually. I could rent a convertible and just soar through the air, right off the bridge and into the sky. I'll get high right before I do it. One super rush and then you die.
>
> I'm just worried I won't die. I might just get brain damaged or paralyzed or something. I'll end up just hooked up to tubes and things. If I'm gonna kill myself I have to make sure I do it right the first time cause I might not get a second chance. You got any ideas?

Daniel's correspondent had typed back:

> Shoot yourself in the head while the car is in the air. Just to make sure you die.

That's helpful, I thought. "Who is Daniel sending these messages to?" I asked.

"We don't know. 'Skibum678@hotmail.com.' We don't know who 'Skibum678' is," Paul said.

"Does Daniel know that you're reading his e-mail, that you've seen these messages?"

Wendy and Paul both shook their heads.

"What led you to search his e-mail messages in the first place?" I asked.

"I was looking through the photo galleries on his phone while he was at school, and I found porn," Wendy said. "Porn for gay men. I showed it to Paul, and—"[1]

"Wendy asked me whether boys normally go through a phase where they look at gay porn. I said *hell no!* I've never seen anything like this stuff. I didn't even know this kind of stuff existed," Paul said.

"We have some questions for you," Wendy said, glancing at the list she had prepared. "Our first question is *Do you think Daniel really is gay, or is it just a phase?* Our second question is *If Daniel is gay, what should we do about it?* Our third question is *How did this happen?* What did we do, or not do, that might have led to his becoming gay?" Wendy was reading quickly; she was close to tears. "Will he outgrow it? We went online to research this, but there are so many different Web sites. We didn't know which ones we could trust, you know? So we thought we'd start by asking you."

"There's no way he's gay," Paul said before I could respond. "I mean, look at the girls he's taken out! He's dated some really good-looking girls. What about that girl he took out last month. I think her name was Ingrid something. She was gorgeous."

"Ingrid Rasmussen. She's a lovely girl," Wendy added.

"Why would a boy who's gay go out on a date with a pretty girl?" Paul asked.

"Plenty of reasons," I said. "Here's one: Many gay boys who are Daniel's age aren't yet a hundred percent sure that they're really gay. They're still wondering whether they might be bisexual, or even straight. They may think that if they can find just the right girl, a girl who can get them sexually aroused, then they'll be straight and everything will be fine."

"Daniel and Ingrid only went out that one time," Wendy said. "I asked Danny how it went, and he said, 'Fine.' I asked him whether he would ask her out again, and he just shrugged his shoulders and said, 'Maybe, maybe not.'"

"Even if a boy knows he's gay, he may still ask a girl out on dates, because he doesn't want *other* people to know," I continued. "He may even be physically intimate with a girl, even have sex with a girl, to quell any rumors about his sexual orientation."

"How can a gay guy have sex with a girl?" Paul asked.

"Easy," I said. "He just imagines that he's having sex with another guy."

"That's sick," Paul said.

"It's the same way heterosexual men in prison have sex with other men," I said. "They imagine they're having sex with a woman. Sexual arousal is more about what's going on in your head than what's going on between your thighs."

Paul and Wendy took a moment to ponder this.

"Many teenage boys are just not ready to 'come out' as gay," I continued. "Even today, many don't want their sexual orientation to become public knowledge. At the same time, they're desperate for someone to talk to, someone they can trust. And, like almost all teenage boys, they're experiencing strong sexual feelings. They're looking for an outlet."

"Maybe he's just bisexual, not a hundred percent gay," Wendy said hopefully.

"Men who are truly bisexual are uncommon," I said. "Some teenage boys who call themselves bisexual are actually gay but they aren't ready to acknowledge their sexual orientation, even to themselves. Some boys perceive less social stigma to being bi than to being gay."

"What about my other question? Will he outgrow it? Could it be just a phase?" Wendy asked.

"Here's one way to think about homosexuality," I said. "The difference between a gay man and a straight man is something like the difference between a left-handed person and a right-handed person. Being left-handed isn't just a phase. A left-handed person won't someday magically turn into a right-handed person."

"Some people are in between," Wendy said hopefully. "Some people are ambidextrous."

"Some people *are* in between," I agreed.

"And you're saying it's not our fault," Wendy said. "It's not something we did wrong raising him. I suppose that's a relief. But what do we do now? What about that e-mail? He's thinking about suicide! Are we supposed to ignore that?"

"Of course not," I said. "Your first priority should be to make sure your son knows that you will always love him, no matter what, gay or straight. Next I suggest you contact one of the local support groups for gay teenagers. I can give you some phone numbers. Talk with one of their counselors first. They can give you some guidance about how to proceed, and they can advise you about how to put Daniel in touch with their people."

"I can't believe you seriously want to send our son to some gay clinic," Paul muttered. "He might catch AIDS or something."

I ignored Paul's remark. "Let me give you those phone numbers. Or if you're shy about making the phone call, I'll call myself, right now, while we're all here together."

Right and Left Versus Right and Wrong

In the United States today, and indeed around the world, discussions of homosexuality can easily become politically charged.[2] It's not hard to see why. As recently as 2003, homosexual behavior was a criminal offense in thirteen states in the United States: two adult men could be sent to jail for having a consensual sexual encounter with each other.[3] As I write this chapter, homosexual sexual contact is illegal in seventy-four countries around the world.[4] When I share research on lesbian/gay/bisexual topics, people on the conservative end of the spectrum sometimes think I am defending homosexuals. People on the other end of the spectrum sometimes think I am being too timid or too conservative.

I have learned (the hard way) that we have to start at the beginning: with a discussion of what's normal, what's a normal variation, what is pathological, and what is morally wrong; and who decides. These are different categories. You and I must be certain that we understand each other.

I have found that it's useful to begin the conversation with a discussion not of homosexuality but of left-handedness. One hundred years ago, left-handedness was considered *pathological*: an abnormal condition requiring intervention to change the individual from left-handed to right-handed. The belief that left-handedness was abnormal was not unique to that era: on the contrary, that belief has been shared by many cultures in many eras, often with an added connotation linking left-handedness with evil or weakness. The Latin word for "left," *sinistra*, is also the source of our word "sinister." The Old English word *lyft*, from which we get our word "left," meant "weak" or "weakness." The French word *gauche* means both "left" and "clumsy" or "inept."

One century ago it was common for teachers to "correct" left-handed children, forcing them to write with their right hand instead of their left. President Harry Truman recalled being forced to write with his right hand as a child instead of his left.[5] All that began to change around the middle of the twentieth century, in part due to recognition that left-handedness is *common* and that left-handedness is *innate*. It's now generally recognized that between 7 percent and 10 percent of the population is left-handed. And it's equally well recognized today that left-handedness is innate, even though left-handedness sometimes is not clearly manifest until early or middle childhood. As a result, left-handedness has come to be recognized as a *normal variation*: it's not as common as right-handedness, but it is within the range of normal.

Let's now contrast left-handedness with familial hypercholesterolemia (FH). FH is a genetic condition that causes very high cholesterol levels even if you eat only healthy foods. It's not a choice. Nobody chooses to have FH. Like left-handedness, FH is innate: you are born with it, or you aren't. But unlike left-handedness, FH can lead to stroke, heart attack, and early death unless it is treated aggressively and early with medications to lower cholesterol. For that reason, FH is considered *pathological*. It's not a normal variation. As a general rule, **conditions that require medical intervention are not normal variations**; they are outside the range of normal. Conversely, conditions that do not require medical intervention are more likely to be normal variations.

The trajectory of homosexuality has closely followed the arc of left-handedness over the previous century. One century ago, homosexuality was believed to be both rare and pathological.

Throughout the early and middle twentieth century, it was common for doctors to recommend "conversion therapy" to cure men of homosexuality. Many of the treatments that were widely employed as late as the midtwentieth century are now seen as barbaric. Consider the case of Alan Turing.

Today Alan Turing is widely regarded as one of the greatest mathematicians of the past five hundred years. He helped develop the machine that broke the German Enigma code during World War II. He wrote some of the key early papers on artificial intelligence, before modern computers had even been invented. But his genius was not widely recognized in January 1952, when he was arrested on charges of homosexual behavior, charges that he did not contest. He was given a choice between imprisonment and chemical castration: injections of female hormone intended to eliminate male libido. He chose the injections. On June 7, 1954, he died of cyanide poisoning. His death was ruled a suicide.

Today most researchers agree that homosexuality is a normal variation, just as being left-handed is a normal variation. And the moment I say that, when I'm doing a presentation on this topic, is when somebody—or several people—raise their hands to voice their objections.

Two Objections

When I do this presentation, this is the point where somebody will raise their hand—or sometimes just interrupt. "Dr. Sax, homosexuality is morally wrong," one person said. "Who are you, Dr. Sax, to say that homosexuality is normal? Or 'a normal variation'?"

My answer: whether a behavior is morally right or morally wrong is a question that is completely separate from the question of whether a particular condition is within the range of normal. A behavior can be normal and still be considered morally wrong. For example, drinking and enjoying alcohol in moderation is a normal behavior, but in many cultures and religions—from Islam to Mormonism—it is considered immoral and wrong. I am not praising or criticizing Islam or Mormonism. I'm just explaining that a behavior can be perfectly *normal* while nevertheless being unequivocally *wrong* in certain belief systems. It's unproductive for advocates of any particular morality or religion to claim that everything that they consider wrong is necessarily abnormal, to equate "wrong" with "abnormal" as though those two words mean the same thing. They *don't* mean the same thing. Something can be normal from a medical perspective but still be wrong from your perspective: for example, if you're Mormon and we're talking about drinking beer.

When I lead my workshop on lesbian/gay/bisexual/transgender issues, I ask: What causes someone to be homosexual rather than heterosexual? Is it innate or acquired? And that's when somebody else will raise their hand. "Dr. Sax, I think your question is offensive," one attendee said. "By asking, 'What causes homosexuality?' you are implying that there is something wrong with being homosexual."

But that's not true. We can reasonably ask, "What causes left-handedness?" without implying that there is something wrong with left-handed people. Left-handedness is less common than right-handedness, so it is not inappropriate to ask what causes left-handedness. Likewise, people who identify as homosexual are less common than people who identify as heterosexual, so it's perfectly reasonable to ask what causes some people to be homosexual.

To sort out innate factors in homosexuality, or left-handedness, or any other condition, it's helpful to do a *twin study*. Identical twins share 100 percent of their DNA. Fraternal twins share, on average, about 50 percent of their DNA, the same as any pair of siblings with the same parents. If a condition is more commonly shared by identical twins than by fraternal twins, that's good evidence that the condition is genetically programmed, at least in part.

Dr. J. Michael Bailey and his colleagues at Northwestern University conducted a large study in which they asked homosexual men who were twins whether their twin brothers also were homosexual. Among homosexual men who had an *identical* twin brother, 52 percent of the identical twins were also homosexual. Among homosexual men who had a *fraternal* twin brother, only 22 percent were also homosexual. And among homosexual men who had an *adopted* brother, only 11 percent were also homosexual. The high concordance among identical twins provides strong evidence that homosexuality, at least in men, has a strong genetic component. It is, to some degree, hardwired.[6]

Subsequently, Professor Bailey and his colleagues conducted a larger twin study using the Australian national database of twins. This time they looked not only at gay men but also at lesbian women. Again they found substantial concordance among identical twin men: if one man was homosexual, there was an increased likelihood that his identical twin was also homosexual. The concordance was lower for men who were fraternal twins rather than identical twins. But for women the pattern was different: if a lesbian woman had an identical twin sister, that identical twin was only slightly more likely to be lesbian than was a fraternal twin sister.[7] Similar findings have been reported more recently for a large study involving twins in Sweden.[8] The evidence from the twin studies suggests that genes play a bigger role in male homosexuality than in female homosexuality.

Bailey and his colleagues recently reviewed all published twin studies of sexual orientation. They found that, on average, the identical twin of a homosexual person had a 25 percent chance of also being homosexual, compared with a 13 percent chance for the fraternal twin of a homosexual person.[9] These results are consistent with some genetic influence, but they also show that environment matters. (Otherwise all identical twins of homosexual persons would be homosexual.) But Bailey's group clarifies that "environment" is broader than the "social environment"—the ways that parents and peers treat us—and includes biological factors too.

One biological factor that is not strictly genetic is older siblings. How many older siblings do you have? And if you have older siblings, are they sisters or brothers? The answers to these questions offer more evidence that the basis for male homosexuality is different from the basis for female homosexuality. More than two decades ago, psychologist Ray Blanchard noticed that men with older brothers were more likely to be homosexual than were men with no older brothers; and the more older brothers a man has, the more likely he is to become homosexual.[10] Older sisters have no effect on the likelihood that a man will become homosexual; neither do younger brothers or sisters. More recent research shows that this effect holds only if the older brothers are *biological* older brothers, sharing the same mother; adoptive older brothers, or step-brothers with different mothers, have no effect on the likelihood of a boy growing up to be a homosexual man.[11] But Blanchard and his colleagues found that this effect did not hold at all for homosexuality in women. Older sisters, older brothers, younger sisters, younger brothers: none of them systematically increased or decreased the likelihood that a girl will grow up to be a lesbian woman.[12] These findings led Blanchard to suggest that the immune system plays a role in the development of homosexuality in men, but not women. Specifically, Blanchard suggested that each male child a woman bears might trigger the development of antibodies in the woman's body against portions of the Y chromosome. With each successive male child, she makes more antibodies against the Y chromosome, and those antibodies may increase the likelihood that the male fetus will grow up to be homosexual.[13] That finding is now called the "fraternal birth order" (FBO) effect. Evidence from twin studies, as well as the studies of the FBO effect, provide good evidence that homosexuality has a biological basis, and that the basis of homosexuality in men is different from the basis of homosexuality in women.

Lipstick Lesbians and Other Variations

There's now substantial evidence that both gay men and lesbian women come in at least two varieties, which we might call hard and soft, or masculine and feminine. Some gay men project a masculine or even hypermasculine persona: think of the muscleman in leather on a motorcycle. Other gay men are openly effeminate. Likewise, lesbian women will tell you about "femme" and "butch." The femme lesbian, also known as the "lipstick lesbian," is likely to dress in traditionally feminine attire and is more likely to engage in traditionally feminine pastimes and mannerisms, such as wearing makeup. The butch lesbian is more likely to wear her hair short and she may have less interest in makeup. Among both gay men and lesbian women, it is common for opposites to attract: a butch lesbian will partner with a lipstick lesbian, for example. Google "Ellen DeGeneres and Portia de Rossi wedding" for a sense of how this looks. However, while this is common, it is by no means universal. I have met butch lesbians who have part-nered with other butch lesbians, effeminate gay men who have partnered with other effeminate gay men, and masculine gay men who have partnered with other masculine gay men.

These differences are often apparent early in life, and they have consequences. Professor Bailey reports that very feminine gay boys tend to figure out that they are gay earlier than masculine gay boys do.[14] The boy who likes to wear girls' dresses and play with dolls is likely to be teased by other kids, who will call him "gay." When he asks a grown-up what "gay" means and thinks about the answer, that boy may start to wonder about his own sexual orientation. But the boy who loves to play football is much less likely to be teased. He hangs out with other boys. He may take much longer to realize that girls do not turn him on. Con-versely, butch girls who like to wrestle hogs may be more likely to figure out that they are lesbian earlier than the girly girl who likes to wear makeup.

In my own experience as a clinician, I have seen gay men who are masculine, gay men who are feminine, and gay men who are indistinguishable from straight men on every parameter. It's a continuum. Likewise, I have seen lesbian women who wear com-bat boots, lesbian women who wear lipstick and makeup, and lesbian women who are indistinguishable from straight women.

Among gay men the divide between masculine and feminine varies somewhat across cultures. In our own culture, by which I mean mainstream English-speaking culture in the twenty-first century, the effeminate stereotype of the gay man predominates. Back in the summer of 2003, Bravo launched *Queer Eye for the Straight Guy*, a weekly TV show that *Entertainment Weekly* de-clared the summer's breakout hit.[15] Each week the "Fab Five"—a squad of five gay men—would swoop in on an unfashionable straight man and make him over into a suave, debonair hunk. The makeover took about three days. The straight man was portrayed as clueless, initially, in matters of taste. The gay men bought him new clothes, redecorated his apartment, even taught him how to shave, and so on. It was a funny show. But how accurate was its message—that gay men are naturally more competent—and more "feminine"—than straight men in matters of fashion and personal appearance?

Louis Bayard, a gay man and a self-described slob, wrote an op-ed piece for *The Washington Post* in which he described how the show had become "a major problem for some of us in the gay community. . . . [The] show is placing enormous pressure on me and on the great silent majority of gay men who really aren't that fab." Bayard then proceeded to give a detailed account of just what a slob he is. Spiderwebs and insect carcasses are everywhere in his apartment. The cat litter hasn't been changed "at any time in the last decade." He burns bacon to a shriveled black crisp that sets off the fire alarm . . . and then he eats it. He wears a red T-shirt with blue and white plaid shorts. He hasn't shined his shoes in years. And so forth. "Slovenliness knows no sexuality," he wrote.[16]

How does this tie back into the previous chapter? In chapter 9 we considered boys who are gender-atypical, boys who don't like to hit or be hit, boys who are more likely to enjoy pastimes stereotypically associated with girls. Are those gender-atypical boys more likely to be gay?

Yes, they are. Gender-atypical boys are *somewhat* more likely than gender-typical boys to be homosexual.[17] And many gay men recall being gender-atypical in childhood.[18] For example, in one study researchers compared about one thousand gay men and lesbian women with about five hundred heterosexual men and women. They found that gay men were more likely than straight men to report gender-atypical behavior and preferences. For example, gay men were more likely than straight men to say that they hadn't liked sports when they were boys and that they had enjoyed hopscotch or playing house. But even in that study, fewer than half of the gay men said that they had enjoyed gender-atypical activities such as playing house or hopscotch. The majority of the gay men were gender-typical.[19]

So I think it's important to stress that many gay men were not effeminate as boys and are not effeminate now. I have heard from many gay men who tell me how frustrated they are when people say, "But you don't *look* gay!" after the man shares his sexual orientation. Apparently, quite a few people still expect gay men to look and act effeminate. Many gay men don't fit that stereotype. Many of the gay men I've known over my thirty years as a medical doctor are roughly as gender-typical as straight men are. They'd rather watch football than figure-skating. They hate talking about their feelings. Some gay men are gender-atypical. But the fact that a man happens to be gay doesn't necessarily mean that he is gender-atypical. Conversely, a gender-atypical boy won't necessarily grow up to be a gay man.

When we look at the evidence regarding lesbian women, the relationship between gender-atypical behavior in childhood and sexual orientation in adulthood is weaker than it is for gay men. Some researchers have even argued that for women there is *no* relationship between a girl's behavior in childhood, gender-conforming or not, and her adult sexual orientation: those researchers claim that women are lesbian or straight for reasons that have nothing to do with, and can't be predicted based on, any facet of childhood behavior.[20] That claim may be too strong. There is good evidence that a girl's behavior in childhood does predict, to some extent, that girl's sexual orientation in adulthood. For example, in one study researchers invited lesbian women and straight women to share videos from their childhood. Lesbian women were more likely than straight women to have engaged in boy-typical activities like, say, pretend sword fighting.[21]

Sexual Orientation/ Gender Identity

On a superficial level, the lipstick lesbian putting on makeup might seem to have more in common with the "flaming gay" man putting on makeup than she has in common with her partner, a butch lesbian. But biological sex—male or female—seems to run deeper than sexual orientation—gay or straight. Gay men, whether masculine or feminine, have more in common with straight men than they have in common with women. For example, when asked to describe an ideal sexual partner, a thirty-year-old straight man will typically choose a young woman, roughly eighteen to twenty-two years of age. By contrast, when a thirty-year-old straight woman is asked to describe her ideal sexual partner, she is likely to choose a man a few years older than she is; and the same is true of lesbian women. On this parameter, gay men are indistinguishable from straight men and quite different from women, whether gay or straight: they prefer partners who are significantly younger than they are. Gay men and straight men are also more likely to agree that the physical attractiveness of an ideal sexual partner is of paramount importance; straight women and lesbian women are more likely to say that physical attractiveness, while nice, is not the most important thing even in an ideal partner.[22]

Likewise with regard to interest in casual sex. Straight men and gay men both commonly say that they would welcome a one-night stand with an attractive stranger; straight women and lesbian women report much less interest in a sexual encounter outside of an ongoing romantic relationship. In chapter 6 we talked about how most girls, and most women, are looking first and foremost for a *relationship*. Most boys, and more than a few men, are interested first and foremost in *sex*. Many teenage boys and young men—both gay and straight—masturbate over pornography, and some hire prostitutes (male or female, as the case may be). Masturbating over pornography and hiring prostitutes are activities that are far removed from having a mutual, ongoing relationship. You can't have a relationship with a picture on a screen. Girls and women (whether lesbian or straight) are much less likely to hire prostitutes or masturbate over pornography, although some do. Girls and women, whether lesbian or straight, are more likely to be looking for a meaningful relationship rather than a one-night stand.

In their study of homosexuality, William Masters and Virginia Johnson found that many gay men are "hypermasculine" in the sense that they often engage in sex for its own sake rather than in the context of a relationship.[23] Masters and Johnson interviewed hundreds of gay men over many years. Many gay men told them about having dozens or even hundreds of sex partners, sometimes more than one partner in a single evening. Some gay men described having anonymous sex with men they didn't even know. Masters and Johnson found that lesbian women, by contrast, seldom have sex with women they don't know.

Some researchers have suggested that the greater numbers of

sexual encounters of gay men compared with straight men might reflect the "hypermasculinity" of gay men. But other researchers believe that this difference between straight men and gay men arises simply because straight men have to contend with the reluctance of women to engage in casual sex. As the evolutionary anthropologist Donald Symons has written, "heterosexual men would be as likely as homosexual men to have sex . . . with strangers . . . and to stop off in public restrooms for five minutes of fellatio on the way home from work if women were interested in these activities. But women are not interested."[24] Men—whether straight or gay—are much more likely than women (whether straight or lesbian) to express interest in a casual sexual encounter with an attractive stranger.

What About Bisexuality?

Straight women can be sexually aroused by attractive men, and lesbian women can be aroused by attractive women, right? So presumably a woman who is aroused by *both* women and men would be unusual, would be bisexual, right?

Maybe not.

When researchers ask women about their preferred sexual partner, the majority of women say that they prefer men; a minority of women say that they prefer women; and a separate minority of women say that they have no preference between women and men; they go both ways. Straight women are women who prefer to have sex with men. But when researchers show straight women videos of men having sex with women, women having sex with women, and men having sex with men, there is *no difference* in the objective arousal exhibited by straight women. Based on objective measures of arousal, straight women are equally aroused by all three videos, including the video of gay men having sex with other gay men.[25]

But when researchers *ask* straight women which video is most arousing, the straight women say that the video of a man and woman having sex is the most arousing, followed by the video of the two women having sex, followed by the video of the two men having sex. There is a disconnect between what the straight women *say* is sexually arousing and what's happening down below.[26]

Researchers have long recognized that what somebody *tells* you turns them on sexually may not truly *be* what turns them on. For example, a gay teenage boy who has not come to terms with his own homosexuality may claim that he is aroused by pictures of pretty girls and not aroused by pictures of handsome boys. He may truly believe that he is telling the truth. Researchers developed a device that measures whether a man's penis is becoming erect: it's called a *penile plethysmograph*. That gay young man's penis will respond to the picture of the attractive man but not to the picture of the pretty girl. The objective measures, which are based on blood flow, give an accurate picture of what's really going on, whereas the subjective measures—what a woman or man tells you—can be influenced by what the woman or man wants you to think of her or him, and by what the woman or man wants to think of herself or himself.

In the example I just gave, where straight women were shown various videos, it's likely that the straight women thought of themselves as straight women. They probably believed that straight women would be more aroused by a man and woman having sex than by two women having sex, so that's what they told the investigators they felt, and maybe that's what they thought they really did feel. There is a long history of research demonstrating that when you ask a question, most people will give you the response that fits best with their self-concept of themselves. To do otherwise risks an unpleasant situation that psychologists call *cognitive dissonance*. But in fact, objective measures of genital arousal showed that the straight women were equally aroused by two women having sex as by a man and a woman having sex. That pattern was slightly less true, but only slightly less true, for lesbian women. Lesbian women did show more genital arousal to two women having sex than they showed to a man and a woman having sex; but it was a small difference.

That's different from what researchers find with men. Straight men are aroused by women, and gay men are aroused by men. Actually, the average straight man is more aroused by videos of women having sex with women than by a video of a man having sex with a woman. The presence of a man in the video, even if it's just a man having sex with a woman, results in less sexual arousal for the average man. Gay men showed a completely different pattern of arousal: they were totally aroused by videos of gay men having sex, not at all aroused by videos of women having sex with other women, and only slightly aroused by videos of men having sex with women.[27]

The differences between straight men and straight women were dramatic. Straight men were aroused by women and not by men; but straight women—in terms of genital arousal—were equally aroused by all three scenarios: women having sex with women, women having sex with men, and men having sex with men. This difference led Dr. Bailey to ask, *Do* straight women even *have* a sexual orientation?[28] Professor Bailey notes that a big part of this question has to do with how we define "sexual orientation." If sexual orientation means the kind of sex that causes the genitals to become sexually aroused, then you can see Dr. Bailey's point: straight women are equally aroused by all three scenarios, so maybe straight women don't have a strong sexual orientation in the way that men (both gay and straight) do. Dr. Bailey reintroduced the old-fashioned term "sexual *preference*." I'm old enough to remember the era, thirty years ago, when "sexual orientation" and "sexual preference" were synonyms. The term "sexual preference" has fallen out of use over the past three decades. For men the term doesn't make much sense. To say that a gay man has a homosexual "sexual preference" is sometimes not accurate. One reason I began this chapter by sharing a conversation with the parents of a certain young man I knew, whom I called Daniel, is because that young man did *not* prefer to be gay. He would have preferred to be straight. But he didn't have a choice. His sexual *orientation* was not, at that time, his sexual *preference*. (In later years Daniel did come to accept and even to celebrate being gay.)

But Dr. Bailey thinks maybe we should consider using the term "sexual preference" in a meaningful way, at least regarding straight women. For women, both straight and lesbian, sexual satisfaction is about more than genital arousal and sexual climax. It's first and foremost about a loving relationship. We explored that difference in chapter 6. A straight woman may say that she prefers to have sex with a man, *and that matters*, because she is more likely to feel fulfilled and loved in that context. The fact that she shows genital arousal to a depiction of lesbian sex does not mean that she is "really" lesbian or bisexual. It just means that there is more to a woman's sexual experience than genital arousal. It might mean that genital arousal is not the most important part of sexual intimacy, at least for some women.

This section is about bisexual people, but I haven't even mentioned bisexual people yet. I had to begin by explaining the distinction between subjective and objective sexual arousal, as well as the difference between sexual preference and sexual orientation, in order for the research on bisexual people to make sense.

Nobody has ever disputed the reality that some women are bisexual. Nowadays we are immersed in a flood of women who want us to know that they go both ways. For example, the singer Ke$ha told an interviewer, "I don't love just men. I love people."[29] Not to be outdone, entertainer Miley Cyrus boasts of being "pansexual." As she told one reporter, "I am literally open to every single thing that is consenting and doesn't involve an animal and everyone is of age."[30] Drew Barrymore, Lady Gaga, Angelina Jolie, Lindsay Lohan, Nicki Minaj, Anna Paquin, Katy Perry, and Rihanna are all celebrity women (listed here in alphabetical order) who have publicly stated that they are bisexual. There is no corresponding stampede of young male celebrities who want you to know that *they* are bisexual.

Indeed, there has been dispute regarding the existence of men who are truly bisexual—and much of that dispute has been fueled by comments from gay men. "You're either straight, gay, or lying" is an old aphorism among gay men.[31] That saying reflects the trend of men who were gay but claimed to be bisexual because there was—in earlier eras, at least—less social stigma attached to being bisexual than to being gay. And there is good evidence that at least some men who identify as bisexual in their teens will, a few years down the road, identify themselves as gay.[32]

So Professor Bailey and his colleagues recruited thirty straight men, thirty-three bisexual men, and thirty-eight gay men for a study. In this study the men's sexual orientation was determined by asking questions about their desired sexual partner, as well as by their self-identification as gay, straight, or bisexual. They then showed each man a video of two gay men having sex with each other or a video of two lesbian women having sex with each other. Most of the gay men were much more aroused, subjectively and objectively, by the video of the gay men than by that of the women. Most of the straight men were much more aroused, subjectively and objectively, by the video of the lesbian women than they were by the video of the gay men.

What about the bisexual men? If bisexual men are "truly" bisexual, then at least some of the men should have been equally aroused, or almost equally aroused, by the two videos. But analysis of the data "did not show even a hint of the expected effect," according to Bailey and his colleagues. "Both homosexual and heterosexual men had much higher arousal to one sex than to the other, and this was equally true of bisexual men."[33] About three quarters of the bisexual men showed a pattern of arousal that was indistinguishable from that of gay men; and about one quarter of the bisexual men showed a pattern of arousal that was indistinguishable from that of straight men.

Professor Bailey's study garnered lots of press. National Public Radio even aired a short interview with Professor Bailey. The host began by saying, "Men who say that they're bisexual may not be telling the truth."[34] More recently, Dr. Bailey conducted another study, making more of an effort to find men who were, indeed, truly bisexual. This time the researchers didn't just ask men whether they were bisexual. In order to participate in the subject as a bisexual man, a man had to report having had at least two sexual encounters with a man and at least two sexual encounters with a woman. He also had to report having been in a romantic relationship with a woman lasting at least three months, and also having been in a romantic relationship with a man lasting at least three months. The subjects were not aware of the inclusion criteria in advance: they were just asked, "Have you ever been in a romantic relationship with a man? If so, for how long?" The researchers also recognized that some teenage boys identify themselves as bisexual but then "come out" as gay in their early twenties. So every man had to be at least twenty-five years old in order to participate.

This time, Professor Bailey and his colleagues *did* find men who "truly" were bisexual: they were equally aroused by men and by women, both subjectively and objectively. Dr. Bailey and his team acknowledge that such men may be uncommon.[35] But they do exist. However, this more recent report did not attract a flurry of attention in the mainstream media; there were no interviews on National Public Radio.[36]

Bisexual women are common. Bisexual men are less common, but they do exist.

Lesbian

As we've discussed, women and men experience sexuality differently, regardless of whether they are gay or straight. Like Professor Bailey, Professor Lisa Diamond has questioned whether the categories "gay" and "straight" have the same meanings for women that they do for men. Professor Diamond spent five years talking with women who were in a sexual relationship with another woman. In many cases a woman had become romantically and sexually involved with another woman not so much because she was consciously seeking a lesbian relationship but simply because she loved the woman so much that sexual intimacy seemed a natural next step.[37] Some of these women reject the labels of "lesbian" or "straight" or "bisexual." They insist that they relate to each person as an individual. If they love that person in a romantic way, if they want to be close to them and hold them and kiss them, then sexual intimacy may just come naturally.

What's the connection between sex and love? We touched on this topic in chapter 6, but Professor Diamond has explored how this question relates to the issue of lesbian and straight. Most people, and even most psychologists, have assumed that romantic love usually arises in the context of sexual desire. In fact, for most of the twentieth century psychologists believed that romantic love was little more than a sublimation of the urge to have sex. "What's Love Got to Do with It?" was the name of a hit song back in 1984. "What's love but a second-hand emotion?" That notion, which seemed so modern and cutting edge in 1984, may not be accurate, at least for women. Diamond and other psychologists now suggest that romantic love may derive from completely different sources than sexual desire—at least in women, at least in *some* women. These psychologists point out that long-term romantic relationships share some characteristics with the relationship between a parent and child.[38] Maybe it's no accident that lovers sometimes address each other as "baby." Maybe love and affection come from a different part of the brain than sexual desire does (at least in some women). Maybe romantic relationships derive from the same part of the brain that parent-child love comes from. This notion is related to an area of psychology known as *attachment theory*.

If the attachment-theory explanation is correct regarding the basis for romantic love in (some) women, then we might have to rethink some of our assumptions about same-sex relationships. "Infants do not become selectively attached to other-gender versus same-gender caregivers," Diamond points out.[39] Parent-child attachment isn't programmed for opposite-sex attachment. Mothers don't naturally bond better with sons, and fathers don't naturally bond better with daughters. But if parent-child attachment isn't weighted in favor of the opposite sex, and if parent-child attachment forms at least part of the basis for romantic attachments in adulthood, at least for (some) women, then it might be possible even for a "straight" woman to experience romantic feelings for another woman without necessarily wanting to be sexually intimate with her.

Professor Diamond has found that lesbian relationships often do arise out of friendship. Two women may form a passionate friendship, may want to spend lots of time together, may even cuddle together. But if those women label themselves as "straight," it might not occur to either of them to explore the option of sexual intimacy. Still, their relationship with each other might be more spiritually intimate and more emotionally fulfilling than the *sexual* relationships they have with their boyfriends or husbands. How meaningful is it, then, to classify those women as lesbian or as straight? "What does sexual orientation orient?" Diamond asks. She suggests that maybe our rigid categories of gay versus straight get a little blurred when talking about women.

Where to draw the line between gay and straight? Does that line have the same meaning for all women? You will recognize that Dr. Diamond's argument overlaps somewhat with Dr. Bailey's suggestion that straight women don't have a sexual orientation. The implication of Dr. Diamond's work is that many women who consider themselves heterosexual might actually be bisexual if the right woman came into their lives. And if that's true, then it might be equally true that some women who consider themselves lesbian might also be bisexual if the right *man* came along. Not all. Not most. But some.

What You Need to Know If . . .

This is a book intended primarily for parents, for teachers, and for others who work with kids. The material I've presented so far in this chapter is only a foundation for the most important stuff: what you need to know, and do, if your daughter or your son comes to you and tells you that she or he is not straight.

You need to know: Girls and boys who are not straight are at increased risk of depression, compared with straight kids.[40] In one study more than 20 percent of teens who are not straight reported attempting suicide in the past twelve months.[41] And kids who are not straight are nearly three times more likely than straight kids to use drugs and alcohol.[42] But there's nothing inevitable about this. Lesbian girls and gay boys who report strong support from their parents are much less likely to have these problems.[43]

What does "strong support" mean?

It means that you tell your child, "I will always love you, no matter whether you are straight or gay."

It means that when your daughter brings her girlfriend over to the house to meet you, you greet the girlfriend as warmly as you would greet a boyfriend.

It means that you talk with the school counselor and make sure that the school has strong programs and policies in place to prevent your nonstraight child from being bullied. There has been real progress on this parameter over the past thirty years. When I was a young doctor, back in the 1980s, I recall a gay boy being bullied at the high school. The parents contacted the school to inform them what was going on. They were met with a shrug of the shoulders and a comment along the lines of "What do you expect? He's a homosexual." Today that sort of reaction would be very rare. It still happens—you can find stories online—but such incidents are much, much less common than they were twenty or thirty years ago.

The most common question I hear from parents of girls and boys who are not straight is *Will they grow out of it?* The answer to that question varies, depending whether you're talking about a girl or a boy. If your son tells you that he is gay, then the answer is No, he almost certainly will not grow out of it. Almost all gay boys become gay men who remain gay men.

If your daughter tells you that she is lesbian, or that she is in love with another girl and wants to be intimate with her, the answer is trickier. No one story predominates. There are lesbian women who will tell you, "I always knew I was lesbian," just as there are gay men who will tell you, "I always knew I was gay." But I knew a girl—let's call her Vanessa—who at age fifteen was madly in love with a seventeen-year-old boy—let's call him Caleb—and dated him for several months before Caleb broke off the relationship. Then, one year later, she fell in love with a girl. "I always thought I was straight—until I met Gretchen," Vanessa told me. Gretchen was Vanessa's best friend. They snuggled together under a blanket to watch movies at home. They hugged. Gretchen had been in a romantic relationship with one girl before, but Vanessa had not. Then one day Gretchen touched Vanessa in a different way. Vanessa was going to push Gretchen's hand away, but Gretchen said, "Don't you like it when I do that?" Vanessa told me that she had to think for a moment before she realized she *did* like it.

A few weeks later, Vanessa told her mom that she was lesbian. Mom said, "But what about Caleb? You said you were in love with Caleb!" Mom tried to convince Vanessa that Vanessa was really bisexual, or mistaken somehow about her sexuality. **That's**

a mistake. I understand where Mom is coming from, of course. And it's possible that Vanessa is indeed bisexual. Professor Diamond has found some women who can be in a loving relationship with a woman one year and a man the next. When the woman is in the relationship with a woman, she may conceptualize herself as lesbian. When the same woman is in a relationship with a man, she may conceptualize herself as straight. Nothing is gained by arguing with her about what term to apply. And in most cases, nothing is gained by arguing with your daughter about what word to use, either.

But here's a word of advice: if you have a daughter like Vanessa, and a year down the road she breaks up with Gretchen and starts dating a young man, do *not* say, "I always knew that lesbian thing was just a phase." That's another big mistake, for many reasons. First of all, it wasn't "just a phase." Second, you are showing disrespect for your daughter and for her relationships. If you have a daughter like Vanessa, there's a good chance that she is bisexual. She may be with a young man this year and a young woman the next. If you disparage her same-sex relationships, you are not decreasing the odds of her having more same-sex relationships: you are just increasing the odds that she won't *tell* you about her same-sex relationships. And the distance between you and your daughter will grow. A few years down the road, when she announces that she is marrying a woman, you will be the last to know.

You don't want that. You want to remain an important part of your daughter's life, as you should. And you don't accomplish that objective by pretending that your daughter is somebody she's not.

One question I hear less often today than twenty or thirty years ago is *Are there any programs that can change my son/my daughter?* The answer to that question is: No. There is no program that has been proven to be effective in changing anybody's sexual orientation in any direction. There are many programs that have *claimed* that they can change someone's sexual orientation. But those claims have generally turned out to be untrue or unsubstantiated. Indeed several states, such as California and New Jersey, have outlawed "reparative therapy" programs claiming to change a child's or a teen's sexual orientation.[44]

There are still many unanswered questions about sexual orientation, some of which seem (to me) to be urgently in need of answer. For example: Researchers in the Netherlands found that a gay man who is in a relationship with a gay man is eight times more likely to commit suicide than is a straight man who is married to a woman; by contrast, a lesbian woman in a relationship with a lesbian woman is no more likely to commit suicide than is a straight woman who is married to a man. The researchers point out that the Netherlands is one of the most tolerant and accepting countries in the world for gay men and has become even more tolerant and accepting; but in this study the younger men were at the same high risk as the older men.[45] There has been very little research directed to understanding the reasons behind this finding. I think it's important that we figure out why this is so and what, if anything, we can do about it.

The majority of parents, like the majority of adults, are straight. If you are a straight parent and your daughter or son tells you that she or he is gay, it's okay to be flummoxed. It's okay to be confused. It's even okay to be upset, but I advise you not to let your son see you crying yourself to sleep. It's hard for your son to reconcile "I love you even if you are gay" with the image of you sobbing hysterically. Your son may reasonably wonder whether your words are sincere.

It's okay to seek help. Not necessarily professional help: there is nothing wrong with you or with your child (unless your child is anxious or depressed or has another psychiatric disorder). But it's a good idea to talk with people who are experienced at guiding straight parents through this time: other parents, families, and friends of lesbians and gays. In fact, that was the name of a group I know and recommend: Parents, Families, and Friends of Lesbians and Gays. That name was a bit of a mouthful, so in 2014 they changed their name to PFLAG. If you go to www.pflag.org and click on "find a chapter," you can connect with a local office in every one of the fifty states, the District of Columbia, and Puerto Rico. If you are in Canada, go to www.pflagcanada.ca. In the United Kingdom, go to www.pflag.co.uk. In Australia, go to www.pflagaustralia.org.au. (I have no affiliation, commercial or otherwise, with PFLAG.)

Lesbian girls face special challenges, as we have seen, and so do gay boys. But at the end of the day, a lesbian girl is still a girl, and a gay boy is still a boy. What about the boy who says that he's really a girl trapped in the body of a boy—or a girl who says she's really a boy trapped in the body of a girl? That's our next topic.

CHAPTER 11

Intersex and Transgender

Intersex

Here's what's normal in our species: The mother contributes the egg, which has an X chromosome. The father contributes a sperm, which has either an X chromosome or a Y chromosome. If the egg is fertilized by a sperm with an X chromosome, the result is a female with XX chromosomes, and the baby is born with a vagina and two ovaries. If the egg is fertilized by a sperm with a Y chromosome, the result is a male with XY chromosomes, and the baby is born with a penis and two testicles. That's true for straight girls and straight boys. It's equally true for lesbian girls and gay boys.

But sometimes it doesn't happen that way.

For example: sometimes, very rarely, two different sperm—one carrying an X chromosome and one carrying a Y chromosome—reach the egg at exactly the same moment, and both sperm fertilize the same egg. That's called *double fertilization*, and the result may be an individual who has both XX cells (female) and

XY cells (male). Scientists refer to this individual as an XX/XY *mosaic*.[1] Such individuals may have both an ovary and a testicle. Such an individual is said to be *intersex*. The term "intersex" refers to individuals who are both female and male.[2] (A very old-fashioned term for such individuals is "hermaphrodite.")

Intersex is rare. I reviewed the scholarly literature on intersex for a peer-reviewed article that I published in the *Journal of Sex Research*. Adding up the estimates of prevalence for all intersex conditions, I came up with the result that two out of every ten thousand live births are intersex.[3] If you are a teacher and you work with one hundred students a year, you would have to work for thirty-five years to have a better than fifty-fifty chance of encountering one intersex child.

Although the term "intersex" is still widely used, the term "disorders of sex development" or "DSD" has become the preferred term among doctors who work with these individuals. That's due in part to the fact that some individuals who have problems characteristic of intersex individuals may not actually be intersex. One example is cloacal exstrophy.

Disorders of sex development, like intersex conditions, are very rare, and cloacal exstrophy is no exception. Only about one baby in every 400,000 live births has cloacal exstrophy. Cloacal exstrophy is a birth defect in which the bladder and the large intestine are both malformed and get tangled together. In XY males with cloacal exstrophy, the penis is typically either small and malformed or absent altogether.

What should parents be advised to do if their son is born with cloacal exstrophy?

John Money was regarded as one of the leading scientists in the field of gender studies back in the 1960s and 1970s. He championed the idea—which was novel at the time—that gender is just a social construct. Kids aren't *born* girls and boys, Money believed; they *become* girls and boys because of the way their parents raise them. When a boy accidentally had his penis burned off in a botched circumcision, the boy's parents traveled from Manitoba to Johns Hopkins University in Baltimore to get Dr. Money's advice. Dr. Money advised the parents to raise their son as a girl. After all, if gender is just a social construct, something that society simply invents, then you can put a dress on a boy and raise him as a girl and everything will be fine. Dr. Money also recommended that the parents have their son castrated (removing the testicles) and begin female hormone supplements around the age of puberty. Gender is just an invention of society, Dr. Money said, but a penis—now *that's* something you truly can't do without if you're going to call yourself a boy!

Dr. Money published reports of "the boy who was raised as a girl." According to Dr. Money, the child was growing up happily in the female role, delighting to play with dolls and help Mom in the kitchen. Meanwhile, the child's identical twin—yes, there was an identical twin, who was not circumcised—was all boy: he loved to roll in the mud and pretend to shoot people with a toy gun. I remember reading these reports when I was a doctoral student in psychology at the University of Pennsylvania in the early 1980s. They were extraordinarily persuasive, not only to me but to everybody I knew who had read them.

The reports of "the boy who was raised as a girl" and the prestige of the Johns Hopkins School of Medicine were such that for about two decades, roughly from 1977 through 1997, most experts agreed that gender was indeed just a social construct, an invention of society. Applying that concept to boys born with cloacal exstrophy meant raising the boy as a girl. If a rudimentary penis was present, it was removed, and a blind sac simulating a vagina would be surgically created. Most of these boys were castrated as well, so that they would not have male hormones circulating in their system.

In 1997 Dr. Milton Diamond published a remarkable piece of medical detective work. Dr. Diamond had contacted Dr. Money years earlier, to ask what had happened to "the boy who was raised as a girl." Dr. Diamond wondered why there hadn't been any reports about this individual for several years. How was puberty going? Dr. Money replied that he had lost touch with the family after they had moved. Undeterred, Dr. Diamond tracked down the child, now a teenager, and learned that Dr. Money had lied. "The boy who was raised as a girl" had not adopted the female role happily. Brenda Reimer, as the child was called, was called "gorilla girl" and "cavewoman" by her classmates because of her masculine ways. She hated dolls and dresses. She liked to fight and she was fascinated by cars. She was completely miserable as a girl and twice attempted suicide. After the second suicide attempt, her parents finally told her the truth: that she had been born a boy but they had raised her as a girl on the advice of Dr. Money. Brenda immediately demanded to be allowed to transition to the male role, despite having no penis and no testicles, and despite having received female hormone supplements for several years.[4] Brenda chose the name "David," because he felt that his life had been a David versus Goliath battle.

David Reimer could have chosen to remain anonymous, but he chose to go public, explaining that he never wanted anyone else to be tortured the way that he had been tortured. In 2004 David Reimer committed suicide. (I dedicated the first edition of *Why Gender Matters* to David Reimer, out of respect for his courage in going public with his story.)

The fallout from Dr. Money's fabrication was substantial. The fact that he had lied to concoct evidence for his theory caused some people to doubt his theory. Maybe gender wasn't just a social invention after all. Maybe an XY male is *born* a boy. After all, raising Brenda Reimer as a girl had not helped her to live as a girl: despite the dresses and the Barbie dolls and the female hormones, and never having been told the truth about being born a boy, Brenda acted masculine, had masculine interests, and rejected everything about the female role.

But others did not agree that the revelation about Dr. Money's deceit had any implications for his theories. They continued to support Dr. Money's idea that gender is just an invention of society. They dismissed the case of Brenda/David Reimer as just an isolated case. They said, *What conclusions can you draw from just one case?* And they noted that the Reimers had not switched their son to the female role until seventeen months of age, when the child was a toddler. Maybe that was too late. Maybe the experiment would have worked better if only the parents had transitioned their child to the female role earlier.

Then, in 2004, Johns Hopkins urologist William Reiner published his report of sixteen boys with cloacal exstrophy. Despite being a colleague of Dr. Money's at Johns Hopkins, Dr. Reiner had come to believe that Dr. Money was mistaken about gender being just a social construct. The parents of all sixteen boys had been advised to raise their sons as girls, in accordance with Dr. Money's advice and the medical consensus in the 1980s and 1990s. The parents of two of the boys refused the advice and raised their sons as boys. (A third parent, who balked at the recommendation to raise his son as a girl, was threatened with child protective services—and possible loss of custody—if he did not comply with the recommendations of the experts.) The parents of the other fourteen boys complied with the expert recommendation, raising their sons as girls and legally changing their names. Each of the fourteen boys was castrated, and plastic surgeons created a simulated vagina for each boy.

Nevertheless, at follow-up in adolescence, eight of those fourteen boys were living as males. Every one of the fourteen boys had male-typical interests, despite having been raised as a girl. Of the six who were still living as female, "one had wished to become a boy but accepted her status as a girl. Later, her parents told her about her past, and she became angry and withdrawn, refusing to discuss the matter. Parents of the others are determined that the girls will never find out about their birth status. Three have become withdrawn, and a fourth has no friends."[5]

On page 246, I asked: what should parents be advised to do if their son is born with cloacal exstrophy? Based on the research of Dr. Reiner, the answer seems clear: they should raise their son as a boy, even if the surgeons can't construct a penis. If every cell in your body is XY male, then you're a male, even if you don't have a penis.

Most of us have the sense of being either female or male. We don't think about it much. We take it for granted. But it's hard to read stories like those of Brenda/David Reimer and the sixteen boys born with cloacal exstrophy without coming to the conclusion that gender identity is real. It's something you are born with, something programmed into your chromosomes. And real distress can result when the gender identity assigned to the child doesn't fit that child's hardwired gender identity. Today most doctors agree that when an intersex child is born, any sort of surgery on the genitals should be postponed until the child is old enough to express their true gender identity.

Transgender: Mike → Christine

Mike Penner had the job many men dream of: sportswriter for a major newspaper. He arrived at the *Los Angeles Times* in 1983. He covered Major League Baseball, NFL football, and professional tennis. While reporting on the U.S. Open tennis championship in 1984, he met another sportswriter, Lisa Dillman. They fell in love. In 1986 they married.

Family and friends agreed that Mike had always been crazy about sports. He was an avid soccer player. But there was another side to Mike that wasn't as well known: he liked to dress in women's clothes. As a boy, he would go into his mother's bedroom when she wasn't home and put on her things. As a man, he continued to cross-dress. It's not clear how and when his wife, Lisa, learned that her husband liked to wear women's clothes. Claire Winter, a friend of Penner's, said, "I'm pretty sure Lisa knew what [her husband] was doing." Lisa Dillman has never given a detailed interview about her relationship with her husband, so we don't know when she learned about her husband's cross-dressing.[6]

We do know that when Mike announced that he wanted to transition to being a woman, Lisa wasn't happy. Mike had been close to Lisa's family, but there were "blowout arguments" after Mike announced that he wanted to live as a woman. "How could he do this to her?" Lisa's parents demanded.

Although Mike got no backing from his wife regarding his desire to transition, he did get tremendous support from his employer, the *Los Angeles Times*. Mike offered to give up his job as a sportswriter, but his boss, Randy Harvey, encouraged him to stay on. Harvey also asked Mike to write a column explaining his decision. On April 26, 2007, the *Los Angeles Times* published Mike's essay titled "Old Mike, New Christine." "My brain was wired female," Penner explained.[7] He felt that he was a woman trapped in the body of a man. So he was going to leave Mike Penner behind. Christine Daniels took his place. The *Los Angeles Times* even hosted Daniels's blog about the transition process, titled Woman in Progress.

Christine Daniels, formerly known as Mike Penner, became a media sensation overnight. A friend from the sports world, Rick Reilly, wrote a glowing column for *Sports Illustrated* titled "Extreme Makeover." Reilly described the new Christine as "amazing" and "not bad-looking. Better than she ever was as a guy, put it that way."[8] Transgender activists promoted Daniels as their new high-profile mascot, with special kudos for the enlightened leadership shown by the *Los Angeles Times*. *Vanity Fair* arranged for the photographer Robert Maxwell to do a photo shoot for a major feature in the magazine, scheduled to be published alongside an interview by *Vanity Fair* reporter Evan Wright.

What happened next is a matter of dispute, although all sides agreed that the *Vanity Fair* project was a catastrophe. Photographer Maxwell asked afterward, "How do you tell someone who looks like a man, 'You're a beautiful woman'?" Maxwell's colleague Evan Wright said that Daniels seemed "suicidal" and that he wasn't sure how to cover Daniels without undermining her "fantasy conception ... [of] who she is." Wright and Maxwell said that they decided to pull the plug on the story. But Daniels and her friends claimed that *Vanity Fair* still wanted to proceed with the story after the photo shoot, and that Daniels had to demand that the story be canceled. Daniels said that Maxwell was determined to portray her as "a man in a dress."[9]

Around the same time, Daniels began to feel estranged from some in the transgender community, saying that she felt "used" by transgender activists to advance an agenda that was not her own. She canceled a speech she was scheduled to give for a Denver transgender conference. She didn't appear when she was nominated for an award by GLAAD, an LGBT advocacy group.

And her wife, Lisa Dillman, was not supportive of her husband's decision to transition to female. On May 23, 2007, just four weeks after publication of the "Old Mike, New Christine" essay, Dillman filed for divorce. She reportedly said, "I don't even want to see you around the office unless I absolutely have to. . . . I don't ever want to see you that way."[10] Everyone who knew Daniels agrees that Daniels was "crushed" by Dillman's lack of support.[11]

In April 2008 Daniels took medical leave from the *Los Angeles Times*, complaining of severe abdominal pain. In June 2008 she was hospitalized. Doctors concluded that her abdominal pain was due to stress and depression. They prescribed an antipsychotic medication, Zyprexa, along with an antidepressant, Elavil. Daniels canceled plans for sex-reassignment surgery (which is nowadays sometimes called "gender confirmation surgery"). "I can't do it anymore," Daniels told her friend Amy LaCoe. "Which part can't you do?" LaCoe asked. After a long silence, Daniels answered, "I had the perfect life with Lisa, and I threw it all away."[12]

In the summer of 2008, Daniels stopped taking female hormones and also stopped electrolysis treatments to remove hair. Christine Daniels slowly morphed back into Mike Penner. Penner gave away his women's clothes and jewelry and began presenting himself as a man again. His friends agreed that one motivation for the transition was Penner's hope that he could win his wife back again. "He hoped returning to [being] Mike could possibly lead to reconciliation with Lisa," his pastor said. "He loved Lisa, there was no doubt about that."[13]

Penner was hospitalized twice in 2009. One hospitalization occurred after his brother became concerned about comments Penner had made about trying to commit suicide. On November 27, 2009—exactly one year to the day after his divorce was finalized—Mike Penner put on a blue long-sleeved shirt, black jeans, and black and white Adidas sneakers, climbed into his Toyota Camry in the closed garage beneath his apartment, snaked a hose from the exhaust pipe into the car, and breathed carbon monoxide until he died.[14] According to the coroner's report, the suicide note expressed Penner's love for his ex-wife.

Transgender: Wyatt → Nicole

Wyatt and Jonas Maines were born identical twin boys. They were raised by their adoptive parents, Kelly and Wayne Maines, first in upstate New York and then in Maine.

Jonas loved everything Star Wars and Power Rangers. Wyatt loved everything Barbie. Jonas would play the "boy" character and Wyatt would play the "girl" character. Some of Wyatt's favorites included Dorothy from *The Wizard of Oz* and Ariel from *The Little Mermaid*. At age three Wyatt would run around the house with a red shirt on his head, trying to imitate Ariel's flowing red hair. At age four he told his parents that he wanted to be a girl. He began referring to himself as a "boy-girl" and asked his parents questions such as "When do I get to be a girl?" and "When will my penis fall off?"

When the family went shopping, Wyatt went straight to the girls' clothes and asked to buy dresses. In fourth grade, when the teacher asked every student to draw a self-portrait, Wyatt drew a girl with long curly hair, purple eye shadow, and jewelry. In fifth grade, with the approval of his parents, Wyatt officially changed his name to Nicole and began life as a girl. Shortly thereafter, in the summer before fifth grade, Nicole began complaining of stomachaches. "She just lies around moaning," her mother told the pediatrician. The doctor prescribed Prozac.

Nicole wanted to use the girls' bathroom, but the grandfather of a student at the school protested, so the school required her to use the teachers' bathroom, a private single-stall restroom. Nicole and her parents didn't like this arrangement, which Nicole felt singled her out as different. The parents were also unhappy about the lack of perceived support from the school district. After sixth grade the family moved south to Portland, and they filed a lawsuit against their old school district in Orono.

Nicole went "undercover" for the next two years at the public school in Portland. Nobody there knew that Nicole Maines had actually been born a boy and still had a penis and testicles. The stress of keeping the secret was a burden for Nicole, her brother, and her parents. In ninth grade Nicole enrolled at a private school and she and her parents decided to break cover. In fact, Nicole and her parents began lobbying the Maine state legislature in support of transgender rights. *The Boston Globe* ran a front-page feature profile, and Nicole Maines suddenly found that she had become a celebrity. She was invited to the White House along with other LGBT activists, where she and the other guests were greeted by President Obama.

The family was dealt a setback in September 2012, when the judge ruled against them in their lawsuit against the Maine public school. While the judge said that he was sympathetic to Nicole's plight, he concluded that the school's requirement that Nicole use the faculty single-stall restroom did not constitute "deliberate harassment," as required for their claim under state law. The Maines appealed to the state Supreme Court.

In January 2014 the state Supreme Court ruled in favor of

the Maines and awarded the family $75,000 in damages. After paying attorney's fees, the Maines took home $44,000 from the award. The family decided to use the money to pay for Nicole's gender-reassignment surgery: removal of the penis and testicles and creation of a five-inch-long closed-end tunnel in the perineum to simulate a vagina. Nicole underwent the surgery in July 2015. That same month, coincidentally, the Obama administration moved to lift the ban against transgender individuals serving in the U.S. armed forces.

As of this writing, in May 2017, Nicole Maines is reportedly healthy and happy, an undergraduate studying theater at the University of Maine.

Transgender: Anna → ?

Anna's parents recall her as a sweet, quiet, affectionate child. She could spend a long time concentrating on one task without fidgeting. She excelled in school and was something of a teacher's pet. She didn't require any prompting to do her homework, practice the piano, or go to soccer practice. As a teenager, she dressed in the same fashion as most of the other girls at her school, a casual no-makeup look. When the occasion permitted, she would wear a dress and put on makeup skillfully. In ninth grade she came out as lesbian, and at one point she cut her hair short. She eventually grew out her hair again and seemed feminine—not a girly girl but definitely not a tomboy. Her mom described her as "one hundred percent girl."

Then, during her junior year of high school, something changed. She stopped talking to everybody in the family: not only her parents but also her siblings and even the household pets. This went on for several weeks. With the help of a mediator, she started talking with her family again, but often with a resentful hostility that her parents could not understand.

She attended a highly selective university far away from home. The first year went okay. But when Anna came home the summer after that first year, she was different. Her mother found a journal Anna was keeping. The writing was impossibly small, about a five-point-font size and in a strange script. The contents were garbled and almost unintelligible. Her demeanor was different. Her parents called it "the dark mask."

The first semester of her sophomore year, she seemed to go off the rails. She was staying up almost all night without requiring sleep. She was cycling through majors rapidly, almost randomly, from history to astrophysics to women's studies. When her parents next saw her later that fall, she looked disheveled. She had always been careful with her appearance before, but now she didn't seem to care. She admitted that she had not combed her hair in months. She also had a noticeable mustache on her upper lip that she had never had before, as well as severe acne. She had always been in good shape and loved to go to the gym and attend yoga classes. Now she just lay around the house looking at her phone and her laptop. She didn't even want to walk the dog.

One day she simply disappeared. After much frantic texting and calling, her parents discovered that she had left the house with minimal belongings and Ubered to the airport to hop a flight back to the distant city where her university was located. She refused to speak to her parents or see them.

When the parents contacted the dean on call, they were informed, "Your daughter is in a *safe space*." Days later, Anna sent an e-mail notifying her parents that she had been diagnosed as bipolar and was with people who understood the disorder—she was referring to peers. The parents flew out to the university. Anna refused to meet with them. A psychologist from Student Counseling did agree to meet with the parents. When asked point-blank about their daughter and the mustache and the acne, the psychologist stated that gender-bending was popular on campus and it was possible to get sex-changing hormones via the student health clinic. The horrified mother asked if it could be possible for someone diagnosed with bipolar disorder to get sex-changing hormones. Yes, the psychologist replied. It was the policy of the college to support transgender students.

The parents received a short e-mail from their daughter over a month later: *Hi. I am now trans. I hope you guys are doing well.*

Transgender can mean many things. But if we're going to have a serious conversation about transgender, we must recognize that some psychiatric disorders—such as bipolar disorder and schizophrenia—can involve a delusion that one is the other sex. In one case, a thirty-nine-year-old schizophrenic man who was using LSD was absolutely convinced that he was a woman trapped in the body of a man. He wanted to undergo sex-reassignment surgery: to be castrated, to have his penis removed and an artificial vagina created. But when he stopped taking LSD and his schizophrenia was treated with a low dose of an antipsychotic medication, the transgender delusion went away.[15]

Right now we just don't know what proportion of transgender people are transgender as the result of a psychiatric disorder, but the proportion is certainly greater than zero. Cases like that thirty-nine-year-old man suggest that a minimum standard of care for any individual who believes that they are transgender should include at least a cursory evaluation to make sure that the individual is not bipolar or schizophrenic.

There are good clinicians out there who follow just such a sensible approach. They carefully evaluate each transgender individual to identify any underlying psychiatric diagnosis that might be relevant. We will meet one such clinician, Dr. Kenneth Zucker, toward the end of this chapter. We will also learn that Dr. Zucker was forced out of his position in part due to lobbying by transgender activists who labeled Dr. Zucker "transphobic" because he recognized, and publicly documented, cases in which the patient's transgender identity was a symptom of an underlying psychiatric disorder.[16]

The transgender activists seem to be motivated not primarily by data or research but by a belief: the belief that *transgender is a normal variation*. If that's true—if being transgender is a normal variation, just like being left-handed—then any effort to align a patient's gender identity with their biological sex would clearly be misguided, just as trying to make a left-handed person write with their right hand is misguided.

But transgender is not a normal variation. As we discussed in chapter 10, people with normal variations such as left-handedness do not require any professional intervention. But a transgender individual will require treatment with sex hormones and perhaps even sex-reassignment surgery in order to live in the other-sex role. Left-handed people don't need prescription medications or surgical intervention in order to live as left-handed people. But a transgender individual will need lifelong treatment with cross-sex hormones in order to pass as a member of the other sex.

Prior to 1942, prescription female hormones were not available. And without prescription hormones, an adult male wearing a dress looks like . . . a man in a dress. The modern conception of transgender—the notion that a child born male can, as an adult, be made to look like a woman and "pass" as a woman—rests on the ready availability of interventions such as electrolysis, plastic surgery, and prescription hormones. It is as much a creation of the modern world as the telephone and the digital computer.

The Best Interest of the Child

I'm a clinician. I see patients in the office. When I am meeting a patient for the first time, I try to answer questions such as: Does this patient have a medical or psychiatric problem, or is this just a variation of normal that doesn't require any intervention? If this patient does have a medical or psychiatric problem, what exactly is the problem? What are the options available for treatment? Which option is most likely to help the patient fulfill her or his potential?

Sometimes I conclude that a patient doesn't have a medical or psychiatric problem at all. For example: A mother and father asked me to evaluate their son, who was five years old. The school had sent a note home saying that the boy was fidgety and inattentive. On further evaluation, I learned that kindergarten at this school consisted of ninety-minute sessions devoted to learning phonics, during which time all children must sit still, be quiet, and pay attention. The school had abolished recess in order to allow more time for classroom instruction. When I evaluated this boy face to face, I concluded that he did not have ADHD or any other abnormality. The real pathology in this case lay not in the boy at all but in the school and in its unrealistic expectation that a five-year-old boy should sit still, be quiet, and pay attention for ninety uninterrupted minutes of instruction about diphthongs and digraphs.

What if parents bring in a five-year-old boy and report that this boy likes to dress up like a girl? And he said that he really *is* a girl. He also said that girls have more fun than boys. He said that all boys want to do is to fight or to pretend that they are fighting.

This boy is unusual. So a reasonable next question is *What do we know about such boys?* We know that most young boys who say that they are girls grow up to be men who do not think they are women and who do not want to be women. We now have many studies in which researchers have followed such boys for fifteen or twenty years, well into adulthood. In every study, the great majority of such boys grow up to be men who have no interest in becoming women.[17] In one of the largest such studies, of 139 boys who insisted in childhood that they were really girls trapped in the bodies of boys, only 12 percent still felt that way as adolescents or adults. In other words, 88 percent of the boys grew out of it.[18] Many of those boys grew up to be gay men. Some grew up to be straight men. But they are men. They don't need hormone supplements or surgery. They are capable of fathering children.

In other words, for the majority of young boys who say they are really girls, the desire to be a girl is just a phase. For such boys, allowing the boy to present himself as a girl will be a major stumbling block on his road to becoming a man (whether a gay man or a straight man). A reasonable first intervention in the case I just described—the five-year-old boy who wanted to dress as a girl—would be to connect the boy to a more diverse community of boys. This boy said that "all boys want to do is to fight or to pretend they are fighting." This particular boy likes to dance and do craft projects. (I myself loved to do macramé as a boy, as I mentioned in chapter 9; and I studied tap dancing for several years.) Broaden his understanding of what it means to be a boy. Boys can be great dancers. Boys can be great artists. Boys don't have to fight or pretend they are fighting.

I find that it's helpful to stay focused on *the best interest of the child*. What is in this child's best interest? When in doubt, **err on the side of normal variation.** If, after a careful evaluation, I am still uncertain whether this child is truly transgender, then I will err on the side of normal variation. If we proceed on the assumption that this boy, like most boys who say that they are girls, is experiencing a phase, then no medical or surgical intervention is required. No hormone shots. No surgery. No letters to the other parents at the school explaining that Wyatt is now Nicole. If, further down the road, it appears that this boy truly is transgender, then we can always reconsider and reassess.

By contrast, if we conclude that this child is transgender, and we allow the child to begin dressing like a girl and to assume a female persona, the child will require hormone shots. Medical treatment of a transgender child begins with injections of a synthetic gonadotropin-releasing hormone (GnRH) agonist such as Lupron, to delay the onset of puberty. Then, around the age of puberty, this child will begin receiving female hormones. Sex reassignment surgery will also need to be considered. Each of these steps constitutes a major medical intervention with significant consequences and risks. If this child later decides that he is really a boy after all, we have not served this child well by indulging the whim of a five-year-old or an eight-year-old.

The most common outcome for the five-year-old boy or eight-year-old boy who says that he is really a girl, twenty years down the road, is a boy who grows up to be a gay man. But a minority of such boys will persist in their transgender identity and grow up to be transwomen. How to tell who is who, at age five or age eight? It isn't easy. Most five-year-olds, and even most eight-year-olds, have little sense of their own sexual orientation prior to the onset of puberty. Many kids in that age group, when presented with the facts of life, just pronounce it all to be "yucky." Heterosexual intimacy and homosexual intimacy seem equally strange, and repellent, to many prepubescent kids. So it's very difficult for that eight-year-old boy who loves to dress up as a princess, who believes himself to be a girl, to know whether he might grow up to be a gay man and feel right as a gay man. Being a girl may seem more real and more comprehensible. He knows what girls are. He has met girls. He has friends who are girls. He may not really understand, at age five or age eight, what a gay man is. He may not even know a gay man. This approach—erring on the side of the normal variation rather than rushing to classify the child as transgender—seems to me to be commonsense best practice if there is any doubt at all regarding the child, particularly if the child is very young—say, less than nine years old. I will have more to say at the end of this chapter about what to say to a boy who says he's a girl, or a girl who says she's a boy.

Two Kinds of MtF

Earlier I shared the stories of Mike Penner/Christine Daniels and Wyatt/Nicole Maines. Both of these individuals were born as XY males. Both of them were convinced that they would be happier living as females. Both underwent medical treatment, including female hormones, to help them make that transition. Mike Penner was not happy living as Christine: he reverted to living as a man and ultimately committed suicide. Nicole Maines appears to be happy living as Nicole and has zero interest in reverting to a male role.

Aside from those obvious differences, there are other differences that are important in understanding the male-to-female (usually abbreviated "MtF") transsexual. Recall that Mike

Penner was an athlete who grew up to be a sportswriter. Wyatt Maines, by contrast, never liked boy-typical activities such as football. Also, Mike Penner always liked women; he never had any interest in sexual intimacy with men. Conversely, Nicole Maines likes men; she reports no interest in sexual intimacy with women.

Researchers who study MtF transsexuals have found that this distinction is robust. MtF transsexuals come in two varieties with little overlap. MtF transsexuals such as Wyatt/Nicole Maines are referred to as *homosexual* transsexuals, because their sexual orientation is homosexual relative to the sex they were born as: Wyatt Maines was born an XY male and has a sexual orientation toward intimacy with men, hence the term "homosexual." MtF transsexuals such as Mike Penner/Christine Daniels are referred to as *heterosexual* transsexuals, because their sexual orientation is heterosexual relative to the sex they were born with: Mike Penner was born an XY male and had a sexual orientation toward intimacy with women, hence the term "heterosexual."

Researchers find that heterosexual MtF transsexuals like Mike Penner typically have stereotypically masculine interests as boys and as men. They often like sports and may excel in athletics: they may even be champion athletes and win gold medals. Or they may enter the military, where they may serve as Navy SEALs or Green Berets. Conversely, homosexual MtF transsexuals like Nicole Maines often have hyperfeminine interests: they are more girly than most girls. They love princesses and glitter and high heels. They are often flamboyant and melodramatic.[19]

Today it is politically correct to pretend that *gender identity* and *sexual orientation* are two completely separate entities. The mantra that's usually heard is that "sexual orientation" refers to whom you go to bed *with*, and "gender identity" refers to who you go to bed *as*. While that may be politically correct, that notion is contradicted by the evidence. In reality, sexual orientation is inextricably tied up with sexual identity. With regard to MtF transsexuals, sexual orientation influences everything about the way these individuals deal with their gender identity. The homosexual MtF transsexual wants to appeal to men. So that individual is likely to pursue electrolysis, breast implants, female hormones, and surgery in an effort to present to the world, as convincingly as possible, as female. It's not unusual for a homosexual MtF transsexual to take classes to learn how to move like a woman and talk like a woman. (Yes, women do talk differently from men, on average, and it's not primarily about the pitch—higher-pitched for women and lower-pitched for men; women articulate words differently from men, on average.)[20]

The homosexual MtF transsexual usually presents very early in life, in childhood, as the boy who likes girly things, just as Wyatt/Nicole Maines did. The heterosexual MtF transsexual usually does not seek help in transitioning to the female role until adulthood, sometimes not until middle age (the Olympic champion Bruce Jenner was over sixty years old when he decided to become Caitlyn). Researchers refer to these types of MtF transsexuals as *early onset* and *late onset*.

"A Woman Trapped in the Body of a Man"

MtF transsexuals such as Nicole Maines say that they are girls trapped in the bodies of boys or women trapped in the bodies of men. What does the research show?

Let's start with interest in sex. In the previous chapter we met Professor J. Michael Bailey and learned about some of his research on gay men and straight men. He found, for example, that men—both gay and straight—were much more interested in casual sex, sex outside the context of a romantic relationship, than were women, whether straight or lesbian. Then Professor Bailey and his team asked MtF transsexuals—homosexual (early-onset) and heterosexual (late-onset)—about their interest in casual sex. The result: the transsexuals "respond pretty much like gay men and straight men."[21] They like the idea of casual sex.

What about sexual arousal? As we saw in the previous chapter, women are, on average, equally aroused by sexual pictures of men and sexual pictures of women. But homosexual MtF transsexuals are aroused only by sexual pictures of men and not at all by sexual pictures of women. Likewise, heterosexual MtF transsexuals are aroused only by sexual pictures of women and not at all by sexual pictures of men. These data contradict the current prevailing dogma that these individuals are "women trapped in the bodies of men." In terms of sexual arousal and sexual interest, they look like other men, not like women.

A similar pattern of results has been reported with regard to crime. After MtF transsexuals transition to the female role, they remain just as likely to commit crime, including violent crime, as other men are. Even though they are living as women, they are six times more likely to be convicted of a crime than are women who were born women. But when a woman transitions to being a man, she *does* become more likely to commit a crime.[22] Individuals who were born female but transition to being male—FtM transsexuals—receive testosterone to maintain a male persona; MtF transsexuals receive estrogen to maintain a female persona. We can reasonably conclude from these findings that extra testosterone can make you a criminal, but supplemental estrogen doesn't remove criminal tendencies.

Two chapters back, we learned that gender-atypical boys— feminine boys—have a difference in the androgen receptor gene compared with stereotypically masculine boys. Researchers have found a similar difference in the same gene in homosexual MtF transgender individuals.[23] This finding suggests that the homosexual MtF transsexual boy may just be an extreme version of the gender-atypical boy. That's the conclusion of Professor J. Michael Bailey, who writes, "Only a small minority of gay men become transgender, but homosexual transsexuals are a type of gay man."[24]

In the previous chapter I shared research showing that the more older brothers a boy has, the more likely that boy is to become homosexual; that's called the *fraternal birth order* effect, or FBO. Researchers have found a similar finding in early-onset MtF transsexuals, but not in female-to-male (FtM) transsexuals. The more older brothers a boy has, the more likely he is to become an early-onset transsexual.[25] Taken together, these findings strongly suggest that early-onset MtF transsexuals share more in common with other men, and specifically with gay men, than they do with women.

What About FtM?

There is much less published research on girls who want to be boys than there is on boys who want to be girls. But as is the case with boys who say they are girls, many girls who say they are boys grow up to be women who don't think they are men and who don't want to be men. Scholars study *persistence* and *desistence* among transgender individuals. "Persistence" means that the child who insists that they are transgender still insists, as an adult, that they are transgender. If a girl who believes she is a boy trapped in the body of a girl grows up to become a woman who believes she is a man trapped in the body of a woman, that is an example of *persistence*. If that girl changes her mind and no longer wants to live as a male but now prefers to live as a female and feels comfortable as a female, that is said to be an example of *desistence*. Researchers in the Netherlands studied 127 children who said in childhood that they were transgender: either a boy trapped in the body of a girl or a girl trapped in the body of a boy. The researchers then followed each kid into adolescence. The average age of each child was about nine years when first evaluated and just over sixteen years old at follow-up. Among the boys, 29 percent said that they were still transgender and wished to transition to the female role. Among the girls, 50 percent said that they were still transgender and wished to transition to the male role.[26] At least in this study, persistence appeared to be more common among FtM individuals—individuals born female who say they are male—than it was among MtF individuals—individuals born male who say they are female.

A team of Canadian researchers also followed girls with gender identity disorder, but with longer follow-up, right into adulthood. In the Canadian cohort only 12 percent of girls who had some kind of gender identity disorder in childhood were persisters: at follow-up, 88 percent of females in the Canadian study no longer wanted to be males and no longer felt themselves to be male.[27] (In 2013 the American Psychiatric Association discontinued the use of the diagnosis "gender identity disorder," replacing it with "gender dysphoria." I use "gender identity disorder" here because the Canadian researchers used that phrase—their paper was published in 2008.) It's unclear why the result of the Netherlands study—50 percent persistence—was so different from the result of the Canadian study: 12 percent persistence. One possibility is that the Canadians followed many of the girls well into adulthood—one of their subjects was thirty-six years old at follow-up—whereas the oldest girl in the Amsterdam study was nineteen years old at the time of follow-up. Perhaps some of the persisters in the Amsterdam study would have become desisters with longer follow-up. Another possibility is that the Canadian study included girls who weren't really transgender to begin with. Yet another possibility is that something about Canadian culture encourages desistence; or conversely that something about the culture of the Netherlands encourages persistence; or some combination of these two.

Researchers have found a sharp division among MtF transgender individuals, as we have already discussed: early-onset homosexual MtF individuals and later-onset heterosexual MtF individuals. There is some hint in the research of a similar division among FtM transgender individuals. While most FtM individuals present early and are homosexual relative to their sex at birth—meaning that they want to be intimate with women and not with men—there is a small proportion of FtM individuals who present later in life and who are heterosexual relative to their sex at birth, meaning that they want to be intimate with men and not with women.[28]

Transgender and Mental Illness

Individuals who identify as transgender—whether MtF or FtM—are at much higher risk of psychiatric disorders such as anxiety and depression than are nontransgender individuals. In her biography of Nicole Maines, *Becoming Nicole*, author Amy

Ellis Nutt acknowledges this reality. She then asserts: "The dysfunction arises not from their own confusion, but from being made to feel like freaks or gender misfits."[29] That's an interesting hypothesis, but it is probably not correct as stated. More likely the dysfunction arises *both* from their own confusion *and* from being made to feel like freaks.

Nutt goes on to claim that "there is no way to reconcile this conflict through psychological counseling or behavioral conditioning. There is only one way out of this alienation."[30] And that is transition to the other sex and sex-reassignment surgery. Nutt is perpetuating a popular notion about transgender individuals: namely, that sex-reassignment surgery reliably relieves the mental distress associated with being transgender. But researchers who have actually studied transgender individuals postsurgery have arrived at a different conclusion. As one investigator found, "even once the transsexual has achieved sex reassignment, the figure of being trapped in the wrong body, of being wrongly encased, continues to be evoked."[31]

Transgender adults who begin receiving hormonal therapy do benefit, on average, from that therapy: one year after starting hormonal therapy to transition to the desired gender, the rates of anxiety, depression, and impairment among transgender individuals are significantly reduced.[32] Nevertheless, even after sex-reassignment surgery and hormone treatment, the rate of mental illness such as anxiety, depression, and bipolar disorder among transgender individuals remains much higher than among the general population. "Sex reassignment is associated with more serious psychological sequelae and more prevalent regret than had previously been supposed," conclude other reviewers.[33] In the largest and longest follow-up available, researchers studied everybody who underwent sex-reassignment surgery in

Sweden between 1973 and 2003: 191 MtF individuals and 131 FtM individuals. These investigators found that 19 percent of MtF clients and 17 percent of FtM clients had been hospitalized for psychiatric problems prior to undergoing sex reassignment, compared with less than 4 percent of matched controls. After sex-reassignment surgery, transsexual clients were still nearly three times more likely than controls to be hospitalized for psychiatric problems other than gender dysphoria, even after adjustment for prior psychiatric problems. There was some benefit from sex-reassignment surgery, to be sure. Transsexuals who had undergone sex-reassignment surgery reported feeling less gender dysphoria—less of a sense of being trapped in the wrong body—and were somewhat less likely to be hospitalized for psychiatric problems than they were before the surgery.

But only somewhat. Even after sex-reassignment surgery, transsexual clients were still nearly five times more likely to have made a suicide attempt and nineteen times more likely to have died from suicide than were matched controls, again after adjusting for prior psychiatric problems. The researchers did not find any significant difference between MtF individuals and FtM individuals on any of these outcomes. Being transgender, even in Sweden and even after having sex-reassignment surgery, puts you at much greater risk of having major psychiatric problems, including death by suicide. This finding is consistent with multiple other studies.[34]

Being transgender also puts you at greater risk of death from natural causes. Individuals who undergo sex-reassignment surgery have shorter life expectancies years down the road, long after the scars from the surgery have healed. The graph on page 273 shows the survival curve for MtF transsexuals who underwent surgery and FtM transsexuals who underwent surgery, compared with age-matched male controls and age-matched female controls. Each death in the group drops the curve a notch. The lower the curve, the higher the risk of death. Control (nontransgender) females had the best life expectancy, with more than 90 percent of control females still alive at follow-up thirty years later. Control (nontransgender) males were next, with just under 90 percent still alive at thirty-year follow-up. Women who underwent FtM sex reassignment were next: for much of the follow-up period, these FtM individuals—who were living as men—continued to enjoy the female-typical advantage in life expectancy over MtF transsexuals, who were living as women. But at thirty-year follow-up, both FtM transsexuals and MtF transsexuals were much more likely to have died than were males and females who were not transsexual.[35]

There is today a widespread assumption that if a boy says he is really a girl, or if a girl says she is really a boy, that child will be happier, healthier, and more fulfilled if the grown-ups facilitate a transition to the other sex. **There is no long-term study that provides support for this assumption. Not one.** And there is compelling evidence that this assumption is often inaccurate. I recently exchanged e-mails with Anna's mom: she informed me that Anna is still transgender but has recently been hospitalized as an inpatient in a psychiatric unit. Of course, Anna also has bipolar disorder. Was she helped or hurt by the doctors who prescribed male hormones for her, at her request, shortly after the diagnosis of bipolar disorder was made?

Being transgender is associated with a high risk of bad outcomes: anxiety, depression, and premature death. Hormonal therapy and sex-reassignment surgery decrease the risk, but only somewhat. What are you supposed to do, then, if your son insists that he is really a girl or if your daughter insists that she is really a boy?

**Sex-Reassignment Surgery Is Associated with
Increased Risk of Death Many Years Later**

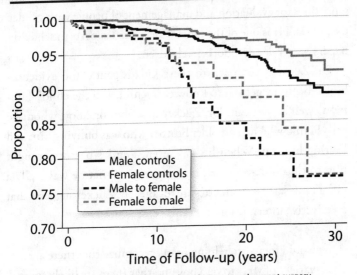

The rate of death is higher for individuals undergoing sex-reassignment surgery compared with age-matched controls; and the difference in death rates gets bigger, not smaller, as the years pass.
Source: Cecilia Dhejne and colleagues, "Long-Term Follow-up of Transsexual Persons Undergoing Sex Reassignment Surgery: Cohort Study from Sweden," PLOS One, 2011, Figure 1.

The Passion of
Dr. Kenneth Zucker

Dr. Kenneth Zucker is one of the world's leading experts on children with gender dysphoria: boys who say they are girls and girls who say they are boys. For more than three decades, he directed the Gender Identity Clinic in Toronto, which specialized in helping such children. He also is currently editor of the *Archives of Sexual Behavior*, one of the world's leading journals of research on sex and sexual identity, a position he has held since 2001. He was chair of the committee appointed by the American

Psychiatric Association to create new diagnostic criteria for gender dysphoria, and he helped to write the latest standard-of-care guidelines for evaluation and management of people with gender dysphoria. He is one of the most widely cited experts in scholarly papers on gender dysphoria in children.

Dr. Zucker's approach to these kids is gentle and evidence-based: begin by getting to know each child, and the child's family, as well as you can. Dr. Zucker describes one boy, whom he calls Frank, who had an older brother who was bullying him and beating him up. When he was seven, Frank's parents brought him to the clinic because Frank was saying that he was really a girl. Frank said that "all boys are mean." Dr. Zucker suggests that an effective intervention in Frank's case

> would focus on helping Frank recognize that there are a variety of ways to be a boy and that there are likely some boys in his social environment who are not pervasively mean or aggressive. Exposure of Frank to other boys whose temperament was more a match to his own could, in theory, help him to develop a more nuanced understanding of gender: that there are different ways to be a boy, that one does not have to be a girl as a fantasy solution to cope with his difficulties with his aggressive brother.[36]

Dr. Zucker advised gently redirecting kids away from other-gender activities. If your son wants to play with Barbies, offer plush animal toys instead. Focus on developing social skills: sign your child up for a group activity, like science club. Don't ever push your child into stereotypical activities aligned with their biological sex: don't force your son to play football or your daughter to play with Barbies. Bad idea. And if you occasionally allow your son to dress up in a princess outfit, keep it private. "Don't let the school make him a poster child," one mother recalls Dr. Zucker telling her. "Don't let them parade him around for pink assemblies. This is his personal journey and we don't know where he is going to end up."[37] Nobody knows whether this particular boy is going to grow up to be a straight man or a gay man; or whether he will persist in his transgender identity and become a transwoman. But if, like the majority of such boys, he will eventually become an adult man who doesn't want to be a woman, then you have done him no favors by putting him in a dress publicly at age six.

The most common outcome for boys who say that they are girls is that they grow up to be gay men. Accordingly, another major focus of Dr. Zucker's work was to help parents to support their son (or their daughter) no matter where the road led. He encountered many parents who were homophobic. If a boy overhears his father saying, "I'd rather my son be dead than be gay!" then it just might be easier for the boy to say (and to believe) that he is really a girl trapped in the body of a boy, rather than saying (and acknowledging to himself) that he is a gay boy. But, as I said earlier, it's very unusual to find a six-year-old boy who really understands what it means to be gay. If he is more familiar with girls than with gay men—as most young children are—then it will be easier for him to imagine becoming a girl than becoming a gay man.

Dr. Zucker knows all about the research presented in this chapter, of course. He has seen it firsthand. He is well aware of the increased risk of anxiety, depression, social impairment, and drug use among transgender adults, because he has followed some of his patients for thirty years or more. He also knows from firsthand experience that gender identity in childhood often is not fixed: on the contrary, in the majority of cases, Dr. Zucker finds that *gender identity can be changed* in the gender-dysphoric child. The XX female who insists she's a boy can come to be comfortable in the body of a girl: perhaps a lesbian girl, but still a girl. The XY male who insists that he's a girl can come to be comfortable in his own body, in the body of a boy: perhaps a gay boy, but still a boy. The gender dysphoria resolves.

With regard to children with gender dysphoria, Dr. Zucker finds that the younger the child, the less fixed gender identity tends to be. That's why he is strongly opposed to "transitioning" children at age six or age nine. He has thirty years of research and clinical experience and hundreds of case studies showing that many of these kids will grow out of it. On the other hand, Dr. Zucker is prepared to support the adolescent who adamantly insists on transitioning to the other gender. In fact, Dr. Zucker had just been awarded a $1 million grant to use MRI scans to study the brains of teenagers who were undergoing treatment with cross-sex hormones . . . when he was fired.

The morning of December 15, 2015, Dr. Zucker was summoned into an administrator's office at CAMH—the Centre for Addiction and Mental Health, Canada's largest psychiatric facility and Dr. Zucker's employer. He was told that he was being terminated, effective immediately, without notice. He was not permitted to return to his office to get his coat and his car keys: those items were given to him, and he was escorted off the premises.

CAMH explained in a press release that Dr. Zucker had been terminated because his approach was no longer "in step with the latest thinking."[38] "The latest thinking" refers to what is now called "gender affirmation," an approach to gender dysphoria that might be described as "the customer is always right." If a six-year-old boy tells you that he is actually a girl, "gender affirmation" means that you change his name to a girl's name and send him to school in a dress without any careful investigation to determine what factors might underlie this child's gender dysphoria. "Gender affirmation" represents a triumph of ideology over reality. In the next and final chapter, we will consider what sort of ideology is involved and what you need to know regardless of whether your child is straight, gay, lesbian, bisexual, or trans.

Bottom Line

As we saw in the previous chapter, lesbian women and gay men are normal variations, just as being left-handed is a normal variation. But being transgender is not a normal variation; it is a medical condition that will require prescription medication, surgery, and other interventions in order for the individual to achieve their desired goal of living as the other sex. And even after making the transition, the risk of mental illness and premature death remains many times higher than for nontransgender individuals.

As we saw above, the great majority of boys who say they are girls will grow up to be men who don't want to be women. Many girls who say they are boys will grow up to be women who don't want to be men. It follows that if you have a son who says he is a girl or a daughter who says she is a boy, you should gently redirect your son or your daughter to find other ways, short of surgery and prescription hormones, to accommodate your child's special needs. When your eight-year-old son tells you, "I'm really a girl," say to him, "I will always love you, no matter who you are. But for now, we're not changing your name, and you're not going to school in a dress. You're welcome to take a ballet class if you like, but you will study ballet as a boy, not as a girl, at least for now." If your son thinks that being a boy means that you have to like American football and violent video games, then find a wider community of boys who share his interests, whether those interests be dancing or painting or scrapbooking. If your daughter thinks that being a girl means you have to like Disney princesses and makeup, because that's the only kind of girl she knows, then find a wider community of girls who share her interests, whether those be martial arts or computer programming.

If you have a son who says he's a girl or a daughter who says she's a boy, and you want to seek professional help, be on your guard. Realize that if even internationally renowned experts like Dr. Zucker can be terminated without notice for violating the latest notions about gender, without regard to evidence, then your local practitioner may be vulnerable and she may act accordingly. Take the time to read Dr. Zucker's paper in which he explained his approach in detail: its title is "A Developmental, Biopsychosocial Model for the Treatment of Children with Gender Identity Disorder."[39] You can purchase it from the publisher for forty dollars, and I think it's well worth the price.

There's more than one way to be a woman. There's more than one way to be a man. Help your son to become the man he was meant to be. Help your daughter to become the woman she was meant to be. This advice, which would have seemed trivial and obvious twenty years ago, is now controversial, because our culture has become immersed in a peculiar confusion that I call "the male/female mistake."

CHAPTER 12

The Male/ Female Mistake

Ladies and Gentlemen, Skanks and Pimps

Several years ago, two high school boys in Steubenville, Ohio, were convicted of raping a sixteen-year-old girl while she was drunk and unconscious. The crime was documented by their friend Evan Westlake. Westlake's videos were circulated to friends and posted on Instagram and YouTube. When the two boys pleaded not guilty, the videos were among the evidence used to convict them. Mr. Westlake was granted immunity in return for cooperating as a witness for the state.

There is unfortunately nothing new about teenage boys sexually assaulting a drunk teenage girl. What was bizarre about this case was that almost nobody involved early on—neither the two boys, nor their friends who reposted the photos and the videos, nor the coaches who defended the boys—almost nobody seemed to have any sense that the boys had done anything wrong. Ohio attorney general Mike DeWine described encountering "unbelievable casualness about rape and about sex ... the belief that somehow there isn't anything wrong with any of this."[1]

Where did this come from?

Around the time of the Steubenville trial, coincidentally, *The New York Times* published a column by Lynn Messina, a regular contributor, in which she complained about a teacher at her four-year-old son's preschool who taught her son something about what it means to be a gentleman. Ms. Messina was angry that a teacher at her son's preschool would dare to use the word "gentleman." In Ms. Messina's opinion, teaching girls and boys to be Ladies and Gentlemen is a "first lesson in sexism." She admitted that when she shared her concern with other parents, not all agreed. "What's the harm in teaching little boys to respect little girls?" they asked. I would ask the same question. If you fail to teach little boys to respect little girls, some years later you are likely to have teenage boys who do not respect teenage girls.

But Messina had no doubts about the rightness of her position. The very suggestion of "Ladies" and "Gentleman" for her implies a double standard of behavior that "offends me as a mom," but "it's nothing compared with how much it infuriates me as a feminist."[2] Indeed. I have found that Messina's position has become the accepted wisdom at many leading universities in the United States, where you will not find any suggestion of teaching students to be Ladies and Gentlemen. These universities often advise students to obtain explicit verbal consent before engaging in any intimate or sexual act. Those policies are grounded in legalistic notions of rights and torts, not in any moral vision.[3]

In my visits to schools, I have sometimes conducted group conversations with teenagers on this topic. On one occasion I asked students, "What does it mean to be a gentleman?" One teenage boy answered, "A gentleman is someone who goes to gentlemen's clubs to watch women take their clothes off." He was trying to get a laugh from his peers, but underneath the veneer one finds merely ignorance. They truly don't know any answer that has substance. When I press them for a serious answer, they offer descriptions that are all about superficials. "A gentleman wears a three-piece suit."

I don't blame those boys. How should they know any substantive answer if they have received no instruction? No boy is born a gentleman. Boys have to be taught. We used to teach them. We no longer do. The result is, predictably, boys who have no idea of what it means to be a gentleman; boys whose sense of right and wrong is mostly about what's right for *me* and what's harmful to *me*. When the two boys in Ohio heard the judge pronounce the guilty verdict, one of the boys, Ma'lik Richmond, sobbed, "My life is over."[4] Perhaps, but what about the victim? Does Richmond still have no regret about what he did to her? Or does he merely regret being caught? The message some boys will take away from the verdict in the Ohio rape case may be merely *Don't take photos or video of anything you do with a girl, and don't send texts about it.* They are not learning to be gentlemen. They are learning to hide the evidence.

My warning to Messina and other critics of teaching girls and boys what it means to be Ladies and Gentlemen: be careful what you wish for. The popular culture of young Americans today is quickly becoming a culture nearly devoid of Ladies and Gentleman. But what has replaced Ladies and Gentleman is not the neutered Virtuous Citizen that Messina assumes will be the result of gender-blind instruction, but rather a culture of Skanks and Pimps: girls who think they have to get drunk in order to be cool, and boys who think that the best thing to do with an unconscious girl is to molest her.

I am not recommending a return to the 1950s. That era was

racist and sexist. We need to create a new understanding of what it means to be a lady or a gentleman. A lady has respect for herself and for her own body. That means she doesn't post nude or seminude photos of herself on Instagram for strangers to see. A gentleman never takes advantage of a woman when the woman is drunk, no matter what. These rules are gender-specific because men and women experience different temptations. Some men may be tempted to fondle a woman who is drunk and unconscious, lying in a pool of her own vomit. (Many porn sites offer just these sort of images—Google "sexy girl drunk vomit," if you dare, and you will get more than one million hits.) Most women do not feel strong temptations to fondle the genitals of a man who is drunk and unconscious, lying in a pool of his own vomit. We do no one any favors by pretending that these male/female differences do not exist. Ignoring reality always comes at a cost.

In order to affirm that a gentleman has obligations different from those of a lady, you must also affirm that gender matters, and that gender is real: that 99.98 percent of humans are either male or female. That reality is now under attack.

The War on Male and Female

Judith Butler is a professor at the University of California at Berkeley. She believes that we should challenge the "traditional" division of the human race into male and female. In the name of personal freedom, Professor Butler encourages individuals to construct their own gender identity, without regard to their biological sex. According to Butler, notions such as "boy" and "girl," "man" and "woman," "father" and "mother" are all mere inventions of a sexist society created in order to support the patriarchy and "heteronormativity"—the preference for straight people over gay and lesbian people (Butler herself is lesbian). Butler has been awarded the Guggenheim Fellowship, the Rockefeller Fellowship, and the Andrew W. Mellon Award (a $1.5 million prize), among many other honors.[5]

Butler and her followers—and they are now legion—show no awareness of sex differences in vision, sex differences in hearing, sex differences in risk taking, or sex differences in sex itself. An international conference recently concluded that all claims of hardwired differences between men and women are based on "prejudices and stereotyped roles for men and women."[6] They did not attempt to refute any of the research documenting hardwired male/female differences in hearing, vision, risk taking, etc. The elites at the conference showed no interest in any of the research, or even any awareness of it. Their theorizing is almost entirely driven by ideology. But their theorizing is now the dominant worldview at many leading universities in the developed world.

Butler was not the first to argue that the male/female distinction is harmful. A pioneer in the field was Sandra Bem, who was a professor of psychology at Cornell for more than thirty years. Dr. Bem was convinced that masculine boys and feminine girls were likely to have all kinds of problems, because they were stuck in traditional notions of male and female. Dr. Bem believed that boys would benefit from being more feminine, and girls would benefit from being more masculine. Dr. Bem's beliefs were very influential in the 1980s and 1990s and continue to be widely accepted today.

But a few researchers had the courage to test Dr. Bem's beliefs. They surveyed a large group of kids to determine how gender-typical or -atypical each kid was. They also measured how satisfied each girl and each boy was with their gender, separately from whether the child was gender-typical or -atypical. They then followed the kids for a year to see whether a kid who was gender-typical would become more anxious or develop lower self-worth, as Dr. Bem would predict.

The results were just the opposite of what Dr. Bem's theories would lead you to expect. Gender-typical kids, both girls and boys, were *less* likely to become anxious and had higher self-worth, compared with gender-atypical kids. Separately, kids who were content with their gender also were found to develop higher self-worth and were also more likely to become more popular with their peers, compared with kids who were not content with their gender. The authors concluded that their results "pose a serious challenge to a conceptualization of gendered self-concept that has dominated the field for the past quarter century—Bem's."[7] These researchers found that *being content* with your gender predicted good outcomes, separate from being *gender typical*. Likewise, these researchers found that kids who reported pressure to conform to gender stereotypes were more likely to become anxious.

From this research we can reasonably conclude that a sensible, evidence-based approach to parenting a girl or a boy is to help your daughter or your son to be comfortable being a girl or a boy, respectively. But don't pressure your daughter or your son to conform to gender stereotypes. If your son wants to take ballet classes or learn macramé (as I did), cheer him on. If your daughter wants to study martial arts and computer programming, sign her up. Teach your son that there are all kinds of men in the world, including men who excel at ballet and macramé. Teach your daughter that there are all kinds of women in the world, including women who are masters of karate and of computer programming.

Unfortunately, that's not what's happening. Throughout the developed world, there is now a growing tendency to ask whether the boy who loves ballet or the girl who likes violent combat might possibly be *transgender*. Rather than counseling these kids and helping them to become more content with their gender, a growing number of schools and universities are promoting what they call the "trans revolution," the embrace of all things transgender.[8] The writer and cultural critic Lionel Shriver observes that many elementary schools now sponsor "Transgender Days" the way that schools used to sponsor bake sales.[9]

I recently received an e-mail from an administrator at a highly selective university (we were negotiating an upcoming speaking engagement). At the end of her e-mail, under her name and alongside her university affiliation, was written: "my preferred pronouns are she/her/hers." This practice is becoming widespread. Liz Reis is a professor of gender studies at the City University of New York. She writes that at some universities, "it's [now] common for students to introduce themselves, whether in class or in student group meetings, by name, followed by a string of pronouns. 'I'm Lizzie; she/her/hers,' for example."[10]

This may seem enlightened (to some). But it is not. It is harmful. It makes gender a problem. It makes being female or male the boring, conformist option and being transgender the enlightened, creative option. It actively encourages kids to wonder about their gender identity, to be less content with their gender—even though we have good evidence that kids who are not content with their gender are more likely to become anxious or depressed. It leads to confusion about what it means to be a man or a woman.

The traditional constructions of femininity and masculinity are now under attack. In one classroom in California, a male teacher was meeting with a group of boys, sharing with the boys his ideas about what it means to be a good man. The teacher said:

> We talked about strength, and we talked about self-control and being able to control your emotions and making sacrifices for others. You know we talked about if you have a family and you only have enough money for two cheeseburgers, you're not going to eat. . . . You know you're going to feed your wife and your kids and you wait.[11]

Unfortunately for this teacher, three scholars hired by the Ford Foundation were observing his classroom. The scholars condemned this teacher for daring to reinforce traditional notions of gender. The scholars were disappointed that the boys "were told that they should learn to be strong men and take care of their wives. In most cases, traditional gender role stereotypes were reinforced, and gender was portrayed in an essentialist manner."[12]

This teacher was trying to provide the boys with a healthy image of what a man should be. He told them that the husband, the father, should wait to eat until he's taken care of his wife and kids. He was trying his best to give those boys some guidance, some idea of what it means to be a man.

Not all traditional gender roles deserve to be condemned as gender stereotypes. There are life-affirming gender roles, and there are gender stereotypes that are harmful and destructive. The "dumb blonde" is a negative and destructive gender stereotype, as is the "dumb jock." But no one should condemn the ideal of the husband and father who sacrifices himself for the sake of his wife and children. Instead, that ideal should be affirmed as a role model, as one among several.

"Deconstructing" all images of the ideal husband and father is not likely to result in a father who insists on his wife sharing equally in all sacrifices. The result is more likely to be a selfish young man who doesn't feel any strong obligation to the children he has fathered. In the United States more than 40 percent of babies are now born to unmarried women.[13] The growing trend away from married couples with children cuts across almost all demographic boundaries. Married couples with one or more children now constitute less than 20 percent of American households.[14]

What I find troubling about the scholars' condemnation of that teacher in California is their willingness to reject the traditional role of father as self-sacrificing provider while putting *nothing* in its place. These educated elites have no suggestions for what boys *should* be taught about becoming a man. Their suggestions are entirely negative: boys should *not* be taught to be traditional husbands and fathers.

But nature abhors a vacuum. If the grown-ups do not provide positive instruction for boys, then boys will turn to the Internet and to social media for guidance. And what they find there is a culture of disrespect, a culture in which it's cool for boys to play violent video games and surf the Web for pornography.[15]

Gender is a reality. Gender matters. You can ignore that reality if you like, but ignoring it doesn't make it go away. When girls and boys are given no guidance, the result often is girls who present themselves as sexual objects and boys who engage in reckless physical risk taking. As we saw in the chapter on risk, that particular default—reckless physical risk taking for boys—appears to be hardwired across various species of primates, including our own. Preaching to children about the harms of risk taking has little proven benefit in terms of diminishing risk taking among susceptible boys. The key to successful outcomes is not to ignore gender, but to guide and inform your child's development into constructive rather than self-destructive channels.

Ignoring gender, and pretending that gender doesn't matter, has not yielded a utopian culture of virtuous citizens. What it has produced instead is a confused culture in which girls and boys are trying to figure out on their own, without adult guidance, what it means to be a real man or a real woman. One common result of that confusion is boys playing violent video games while girls send sexy photos via Snapchat.

Gender is more fragile than we knew. Though perhaps we should have known better. Most cultures have taken great care in teaching gender norms. We no longer do. On the contrary, our learned professors now actively deconstruct and tear down every gender guidepost, in the name of individual liberty, with no awareness of the costs. We need to be careful about the norms we teach, of course. We don't want to perpetuate stereotypes like the dumb jock or the dumb blonde. We need to create new ideals of manhood and womanhood that make sense in the twenty-first century. But "personhood" won't fly. Boys don't want to be "persons." Neither do girls. Boys want to be men. Girls want to be women. We have to teach them what that means.

Is Gender a Social Construct?

Simone de Beauvoir, the celebrated feminist author, famously wrote that a woman is not born, she is made.[16] In other words: gender is just a social construction, an invention of society, completely malleable. That assertion became a staple of the feminist movement and of gender studies. But in just the past few years, the mainstream consensus has added a footnote: gender is just a social construction, completely malleable—*unless* you happen to be *transgender*, in which case your gender identity is inviolate, hardwired, and impossible to change. This claim, like de Beauvoir's original assertion, is based less in science than in ideology.

The contradiction between these two positions has contributed to a growing tension between traditional feminists and the transgender community. Transgender activists have been vocal in their claim that an XY male who transitions to the female role is just as much a woman as a woman who was born an XX female. "Transwomen are women, period" is one of the slogans employed by the activists. Male-to-female activist Mari Brighe asserts that anyone who describes a transwoman—a male-to-female transsexual—as "biologically male" is a bigot.[17] For Brighe and other activists, having male (XY) chromosomes and a penis and testicles is irrelevant. A transwoman is a normal variation, just another way of being a woman. For the transgender activists, gender is all about how you feel. If you feel yourself to be a woman, then you are a woman.

Transgender activists use the acronym "TERF"—trans-exclusionary radical feminist—to describe feminists who don't agree with their claim that a transwoman is just another way of being a normal woman.[18] Transgender activists have lobbied successfully for women's colleges to admit transwomen.[19] They have stopped production of the play *The Vagina Monologues* at some women's colleges, arguing that a play about women who have vaginas excludes transwomen, who don't have vaginas. Mount Holyoke College, a women's college in Massachusetts, dutifully agreed no longer to present the play. The Mount Holyoke theater group explained that a play with a title like *The Vagina Monologues* "is inherently reductionist and exclusive."[20] Erin Murphy, chair of the theater group, wrote that the play offered an "extremely narrow perspective on what it means to be a woman." The feminist journalist Elinor Burkett responded:

Let me get this right: the word "vagina" is exclusionary and offers an extremely narrow perspective on womanhood, so the 3.5 billion of us who have vaginas, along with the trans people who want them, should describe ours with the politically correct terminology trans activists are pushing on us: "front hole" or "internal genitalia"?[21]

Traditional feminists argue that individuals who have lived most of their lives as men simply haven't had many of the defining experiences that most women have had. For example, transgender women can't menstruate or become pregnant. In her essay for *The New York Times* titled "What Makes a Woman?" Burkett wrote, "People who haven't lived their whole lives as women . . . shouldn't get to define us. That's something men have been doing for much too long. Their truth is not my truth."[22]

Here's what's peculiar about the debate between the traditional feminists and the transgender activists: both sides are mistaken about some basic facts. The feminists are mistaken in their claim that gender is primarily a social construct, an invention of society. In reality, gender is not primarily a social construct. It is a biological fact of our species, just as it is for gorillas and chimpanzees and every other primate. That is not to say that all girls are alike any more than it is to say that all female chimps are alike. Some female chimps kill and eat monkeys; most female chimps do not. Many male chimps kill and eat monkeys, though a few do not.[23] A primate researcher who ignored these differences would be a poor researcher. But a researcher studying humans who dares to highlight similar differences among humans, and to suggest that those differences might be hardwired—as they clearly are in chimpanzees—is now likely to be denounced as a reactionary tool of the patriarchy.

It is now common to hear educated people refer to biological sex, female or male, as being "assigned" at birth. For example, schools and universities refer to transgender individuals as people who identify themselves as belonging to a gender different from the gender "assigned" at birth. But gender—male or female—is not "assigned" at birth. It is more accurate to say that gender is "recognized" at birth.[24] When the obstetrician delivers a newborn, sees a penis, and announces, "It's a boy!" that is not an arbitrary assignment but the recognition of a fact. (In rare cases when an intersex child is born with ambiguous genitalia, the sex of the child may be difficult to recognize. As I explained in the chapter on intersex, the contemporary standard of care is to wait until the correct gender can be recognized. Such cases are, as I explained, extremely rare, less than two out of 10,000 live births.)

The transgender activists are mistaken in their claim that being transgender is a normal variation, no different from being left-handed. A boy, an XY male, who becomes convinced that he is a girl trapped in the body of a boy has a serious problem. The notion that you can fix his problem by pretending that he is actually an XX girl rather than an XY boy is contradicted by the evidence we considered in the previous chapter. For many of those boys, submitting to their belief may not be in their best interest at all and may increase the risk of bad outcomes, as it did for Mike Penner. (Recall from the previous chapter that Mike Penner was the sportswriter who transitioned to being a woman, then had regrets and ultimately committed suicide.)

Gender is not alien to human nature, nor is it accidental, nor is it an arbitrary invention of society. It is close to the core of human identity. Gender matters. As the author G. K. Chesterton wrote, "You can free things from alien or accidental laws, but not from the laws of their own nature. . . . Do not free a camel of the burden of his hump; you may be freeing him from being a camel. Do not go about as a demagogue, encouraging triangles to break out of the prison of their three sides. If a triangle breaks out of its three sides, its life comes to a lamentable end."[25] If you encourage a boy to break out of the prison of being a boy and to "transition" to being a girl, you may not succeed in creating a happy, well-adjusted girl. As we saw in the previous chapter, long-term outcomes for individuals who undergo sex reassignment are not uniformly positive. You are more likely to be successful, based on the evidence we have available, if you help that boy to become more comfortable being a boy, which may require that you broaden his understanding of what it means to "be a boy." Being a boy doesn't have to mean liking football or playing rough-and-tumble games. It can include ballet and knitting and scrapbooking. The contemporary assumption—that every such boy will be better off in the long term if we put him in a dress, castrate him, and give him female hormones—does not have a strong basis in evidence.

Some Tips

Be patient with other grown-ups. I have found that many people, not just kids, are now seriously confused about gender. If you encounter a physical education instructor or camp counselor who thinks every boy should enjoy whacking other kids with lightsabers, but your son doesn't like to hit or to be hit, then you should talk to the instructor and explain that there are different kinds of boys, and that's okay. Lend the instructor your copy of this book, with instructions to read chapter 9.

Don't preach. If your neighbors have a four-year-old boy who insists that he's a girl, and they decide to start dressing their son in girls' clothes and insist that you now call him Emily instead of Jason, don't give unsolicited advice. Unless they have asked for your opinion, don't pester them about the studies we considered in the previous chapter, showing that most boys who say they are girls grow up to be men who don't want to be women. Your neighbors aren't likely to listen to you, and there's a good chance that you will create tension where there used to be friendship.

Focus on your own child. For your own child, you can be a fearless advocate. But it's not your job to educate other parents about the new science of gender differences. If you insist on offering advice when you haven't been asked to, you aren't likely to accomplish much.

With regard to gender and the understanding of gender: our culture is going in the wrong direction, and the changes are being driven not by science but by ideology. Again quoting Lionel Shriver, "We're in the process of taking a giant cultural step backwards. The women's liberation movement of my adolescence advocated a release from gender roles, and now we are entrenching them—pigeonholing ourselves with picayune precision on a continuum of gender identity, as if arriving at the right relationship to cliché is tantamount to self-knowledge." Shriver writes that as a girl she "scrabbled in the dirt with my brothers playing with model cars and making toy trains crash spectacularly from a height. I shunned Barbies and detested baby dolls. I reviled dresses, spurning lace and flounces for jeans and flannel shirts. At fifteen, I changed my name from Margaret to Lionel. Were I to have grown up fifty, sixty years later, it's entirely possible that my parents would have taken me to see a therapist and put me on hormone therapy."[26] Even in the scholarly literature, "gender-nonconforming" is becoming almost a synonym for "transgender." The girl who likes to whack other kids with light-sabers and "scrabble in the dirt" is now likely to be asked whether she might not prefer to be a boy instead of a girl.[27]

There's been an explosion in the proportion of people who identify as transgender. The fourth edition of the DSM—the American Psychiatric Association's *Diagnostic and Statistical Manual of Mental Disorders*—published in 1994, stated that "there are no recent epidemiological studies to provide data" on the number of transgender individuals in the United States but that studies in Europe showed that "1 per 30,000 adult males and 1 per 100,000 adult females seek sex-reassignment surgery."[28] We do have a study from the Netherlands, published in 1993, in which researchers estimated a prevalence of 1 out of every 11,900 males seeking to transition to being a female and 1 out of every 30,400 females seeking to transition to being a male, a prevalence that the authors themselves described as "relatively high" in comparison with other countries.[29]

A prevalence of 1 in 10,000 works out to 0.01 percent. Things have changed since the 1990s. In 2011 the estimated prevalence of transgender individuals in the United States was 0.3 percent; by 2016, just five years later, that proportion had more than doubled, to more than 0.7 percent.[30] I just received a medical journal in the mail; an article in the journal suggested that the true incidence of transgender might be as high as 5 percent.[31] If the correct figure is indeed now 5 percent, that would represent a five-hundred-fold increase in less than thirty years. (Five percent is 500 times 0.01 percent.)

Some have suggested that this rapid and astonishing rise reflects the declining stigma associated with being transgender. Those advocates claim that lots of transgender people have always been with us, but that now they feel free to come out of the closet.

As someone who has been a medical doctor for more than thirty years, I am not convinced. For eighteen years I ran a primary care medical practice in suburban Maryland, which I grew from zero to more than seven thousand patients, almost every one of whom I met personally, most of them on multiple occasions. We had many gay and lesbian patients, a few of whom confided their sexual orientation only to me, not even to their (straight) spouse. If transgender individuals comprised even 0.7 percent of the population, then roughly forty-nine of our patients (0.7 percent of seven thousand) should have been transgender. There wasn't even one.

If the rise in the proportion of the population identifying as transgender isn't due to people who were always transgender coming out of the closet, then how to explain it? One part of the answer may simply be the confusion surrounding the word "transgender." Lindsay Collin and her colleagues recently reviewed twenty-seven studies of the prevalence of transgender individuals. They found that if you define "transgender" to mean strictly "individuals who wish to become members of the opposite sex—females who want to become males, and males who want to become females"—then the best estimate of prevalence is 9 per 100,000, which works out to just under 0.01 percent. But if you define "transgender" more loosely to mean that you *feel yourself* to be a member of the opposite sex but you're not necessarily planning to *transition* to being a member of the opposite sex, then the prevalence soars to 871 per 100,000, which works out to 0.87 percent.[32] At least part of the rise in the prevalence of individuals who say that they are transgender may be a change over the past decade in what people understand the term "transgender" to mean. Ten years ago, "transgender" might have meant that you planned to transition to presenting yourself as a member of the opposite sex. Today, for many people, "transgender" may just mean that you *feel* yourself to be a member of the opposite sex . . . whatever that means.

The Male/Female Mistake

Do you feel yourself to be a member of the opposite sex?

I am uncomfortable with the phrase "the opposite sex." Throughout this book I have shared with you a great deal of evidence that the average boy is different from the average girl in many ways. But on most of these parameters, the average boy is not the *opposite* of the average girl, just different. And there's lots of variation *among* boys and lots of variation among girls, as we saw especially in chapter 9.

But opposite? Apples and oranges are different from each other, but they are not the *opposite* of each other. They are both fruits. They are both nourishing and good for you, though in somewhat different ways: oranges are a better source of vitamin C and folic acid; apples are a better source of catechin and pectin. They are not the same. If you try to make an apple pie using oranges instead of apples, you will be disappointed with the result.

The notion of "the opposite sex" assumes that you are *either* masculine *or* feminine. It assumes a one-dimensional continuum:

Feminine ⟵⟶ MASCULINE

But researchers have known for more than forty years that that notion just isn't accurate.[33] Gender isn't one-dimensional. It's two-dimensional.

Feminine	Androgynous
Undifferentiated	**MASCULINE**

A particular human can be very feminine, or not; very masculine, or not; both feminine and masculine—that's *androgynous*—or neither feminine nor masculine—that's *undifferentiated*. In reality, most of us are scattered somewhere on this two-dimensional plane.[34] We're all a mix. A particular girl might be more masculine than she is feminine, while a particular boy might be more feminine than he is masculine. Differences do not imply an order of rank. A feminine girl isn't better or worse than a masculine girl (a tomboy). They're just different.

We should celebrate those differences. They expand the range of human experience, making all of us more three-dimensional, more real. In my own marriage, my wife fixes the lawn tractor and does most of the outdoor chores, while I shop for groceries. I like to shop for groceries, and she doesn't. She enjoys fixing the tractor, while I wouldn't know where to begin. But she has a much better eye for colors than I do, and I am better at targeting a moving object than she is. People are a mix.

If you're a parent, you want to help your child to find their own spot on this two-dimensional map. Professor Sandra Bem believed that we should encourage every child to be androgynous, an equal mix of male and female. As we have seen, Dr. Bem's assumption that androgyny is best for every child doesn't stand up well to empirical test. Some kids are happy being androgynous, but most kids are happier somewhere else on the two-dimensional plane. Some boys are happier being more feminine than masculine, although they still have masculine elements. Some girls are happier being more masculine than feminine, although they still have feminine elements.

The explosion in the proportion of people who believe that they are transgender may well represent a failure to understand that gender is two-dimensional, not one-dimensional. If you are a man who has some (or many) feminine qualities, or you are a woman who has some (or many) masculine qualities, that doesn't mean that you are transgender. It means that you are a human being.

Although many aspects of gender are hardwired, *gender identity* itself is more fragile than we knew. A man may see like a man, hear like a man, and experience sexual desire as a man (gay or straight); but if he finds himself in a culture that promotes an either/or construction of gender—*either* you're a guy who loves football and World Wide Wrestling, *or* you're a girl who loves makeup and prom dresses—then he may conclude that he is transgender. He is mistaken. He is confused by the culture in which he is immersed, a culture that has an impoverished, binary, either/or understanding of gender. We can call that the male/female mistake: the notion that you have to be *either* a tough guy who loves fighting and street racing or a girly girl who cries over romantic comedies and wears too much mascara. The best intervention you can offer this man is not to castrate him and put him in a dress, but to expand his understanding of gender.

The Stay-at-Home Dad

When I talk about the importance of acknowledging gender differences and celebrating gender differences, some critics assert that I'm trying to turn back the clock, to take us back to the 1950s. But I'm not. The challenges today are different. We need to help young men to be better stay-at-home dads, if that's what works best for their family. There's a growing gender gap in academic achievement, as I mentioned in chapter 5 and as I document at length in my book *Boys Adrift*. There's a growing number of couples where the woman earns more than the man. Child care in many regions of the United States is exorbitantly expensive, often more than the lower-earning parent can earn. If that couple is going to raise children, it might make more sense for the young man to stay at home and be a full-time parent, rather than working at a job that might not even cover the cost of child care. In that case, that young man needs to understand that a stay-at-home parent must take primary responsibility for changing diapers, vacuuming the floor, doing the laundry, preparing the meals, etc.

We are not doing a good job at preparing young men to be stay-at-home dads, in part because many young men want to be *men* and they don't see role models—in their video games or their pornography or their social media—of young men who are good stay-at-home dads. What young men need today is going to be different from what young men needed in 1955. There's very little understanding that *gender matters* today every bit as much as it did in 1955, but that the culture must respond differently today than it did in that earlier era. Instead, the leading universities try to "deconstruct" gender, with the result that many young men are spending their free time playing video games and looking at porn. They are adrift, with no guideposts directing them to productive manhood.

I have seen firsthand the results of neglecting gender in this way. Over more than thirty years as a physician, I have seen many marriages end. If your knowledge of the world comes primarily from TV and movies and Instagram and Beyoncé, you might think that adultery is the most common reason why marriages end. But in my observation, many couples are just too busy for that sort of thing. Here's a more common scenario.

A married couple has two young children, one still in diapers. Mom is a bank executive, working sixty-plus hours a week. Dad is, at the moment, out of work, so he is functioning as a stay-at-home dad even though that wasn't the plan when the couple married. But Dad doesn't want to watch the kids, so the two children are at a day care. Mom picks the kids up from day care on her way home from work. She comes home to find the house a mess and supper not made. The baby is crying with a dirty diaper. Dad is on the couch, watching TV. Mom is exasperated but she doesn't explode, not yet. She says, "Caitlyn's diaper needs to be changed. You change her diaper while I make supper."

Dad doesn't know how to change a diaper, but something in his wife's tone of voice warns him not to protest. He gets off the couch and puts the baby on the changing table. He starts changing the diaper but gets poop on the baby's clothes.

Now Mom does explode. "Don't you even know how to change a diaper? Can't you do *anything*? You're just making more work for me. Get outta here!" It doesn't take long for that mom to begin wondering whether she might be better off, with less stress and less shouting, if she evicted her unmotivated husband and hired a nanny instead.

In defense of that dad: how are you supposed to know how to change a diaper if you have never been instructed? Nobody is born knowing how to change a diaper. You have to be taught. Girls learn from their moms and from babysitting or from asking friends or watching a YouTube video. Boys are less likely to have worked as a babysitter and perhaps less likely to watch a YouTube video about changing diapers, maybe because they don't think that's something that real guys do, maybe because they don't recognize that changing a diaper is serious business that needs to be taken seriously.

How can we change that? How can we improve the odds that boys will grow up knowing how to change a diaper? What would an enlightened approach look like? An approach that embraced gender differences instead of trying to pretend that they don't exist?

To understand the answer—and with it a good strategy for avoiding the male/female mistake—it's helpful to consider what some psychologists call *group contrast effects*.[35] Group contrast effects mean that when members of two different groups are put together, the members of each group tend to exaggerate the differences between the two groups. Boys and girls categorize themselves as "boys" and "girls" whether or not it's politically correct to do so. When girls are around, boys are less willing to exhibit any behavior that might be considered feminine. When boys are around, girls are reluctant to exhibit behaviors that might be considered boyish.[36]

Let me give you an example from one school that I have visited on three occasions: Stonewall Jackson Middle School in Charleston, West Virginia. One sixth-grade teacher there told me how she brought a rabbit into her sixth-grade classroom for one day, just for the children to see the rabbit close up, as part of the biology unit on mammals. As soon as the teacher brought the rabbit into the room, one of the girls said, "Oh it's so *cute*! Can I pet it?" Then one of the boys said, "I'd like to blow its head off with a bazooka." From the moment that boy made that comment, no other boy in the classroom showed any interest in petting the bunny. The gender lines had been drawn. Girls pet bunnies. Boys blow off bunnies' heads with bazookas (or at least, boys claim that they want to). No boy stepped forward to pet the bunny, despite the teacher's coaxing.

Then the same teacher was allowed to introduce single-gender classrooms. Once again she brought in a bunny to a room of sixth-grade boys; but this time there were no girls present. This time about half the boys wanted to pet the bunny, which this teacher told me wasn't much different from the girls' classroom, where about half the girls wanted to pet the bunny.

I don't think that there are large hardwired differences between boys and girls in how much they like to pet bunnies. But we live in a sexist society. Despite the best efforts of some professors to deconstruct gender, many boys still want to be seen as men, and many girls still want to be seen as women. Because we provide so little guidance, boys today now often construct masculinity *negatively*. In the absence of any positive guidance, being a real man comes to mean *not* doing whatever girls want to do. If girls want to pet bunnies, then I don't want to. If girls are careful not to take crazy physical risks, then I will skate my skateboard off the high ledge onto the concrete pavement below, with everybody watching. If girls care about turning in the homework on time, then I will make a point of playing video games instead of doing the homework.

How to apply this understanding to the problem of getting boys to learn to change diapers and to master other tasks that stay-at-home dads need to know?

If you offer an optional after-school class on babysitting, including a segment on learning to change diapers, you won't get many boys to sign up. Most boys regard babysitting and changing diapers as things girls do. Group contrast effects kick in: most boys won't sign up even if they would like to. Few boys want to be the only boy in a babysitting class with twelve girls.

I learned a better approach when I visited University School, a boys' private school in northeastern Ohio. They told me about their *all-boys* babysitting elective, which was very popular with the boys, including the jocks. They teach the boys that changing a diaper is a high-stakes game with three objectives:

1. Don't allow the baby to fall onto the floor.

2. Don't get any poop on the baby's penis or vagina, because of the risk of urinary tract infection.

3. Don't get any poop on the baby's clothes.

The class is taught by real parents, first using life-size dolls, then using real babies (see the photo on page 304).

The boys love it. The truth is, it can be great fun to play with a baby, to feed a baby, to teach a baby. Boys can enjoy it just as much as girls enjoy it. But the best way to engage boys in that activity is different from the best way to engage girls in that activity. If you don't understand that—if you pretend that gender doesn't matter—you end up with boys who think changing diapers is for girls. And the result is fathers who don't know how to change a diaper.

The same principle applies with regard to helping girls to break through gender stereotypes. As I mentioned in chapter 5, the most effective strategies to motivate girls in computer coding are different from the most effective strategies for boys. In an all-girls computer coding class, you can deploy those strategies free

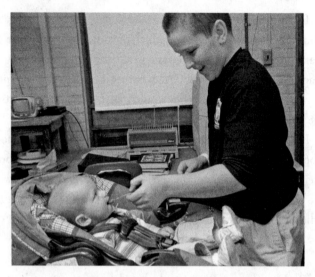

If you want to get boys to sign up for a babysitting class, try an all-boys class.
Photo courtesy of University School, Hunting Valley, Ohio.

from group contrast effects. In the United States, boys taking AP Computer Science now outnumber girls by more than three to one, as we discussed in chapter 5. If there are three girls in a class with eleven boys, those three girls may feel like they don't belong, and no amount of preaching about gender equity is going to change that. But if the class is just girls, you may get more girls to sign up, and the girls will be more comfortable and will likely gain more confidence. There are a number of programs already in existence that embody these simple truths, programs like Girls Who Code. The late Dr. Sally Ride devoted much of her professional life to creating Sally Ride Science Camps, all-girls science camps, because Dr. Ride—the first American woman to fly in space—understood this concept. But programs like these are too few and too far between.

I am not here making a general case for single-sex education in all content areas. I am making the point that in view of what we know about group contrast effects and the confusion about gender in contemporary American society, if you want to engage girls and boys specifically in areas that the contemporary culture deems gender-atypical—babysitting for boys or computer science for girls—then you would do well to consider offering those programs in gender-specific formats, such as an all-boys babysitting class or an all-girls computer coding class, teaching those topics using gender-aware strategies. If you want to break down gender stereotypes, you have to begin by understanding gender differences and working *with* those differences rather than ignoring them or pretending they don't exist.

Preventing Sexual Assault and Sexual Harassment

I began this chapter with the story of two high school boys who were convicted of raping a girl who was drunk and unconscious. How best to prevent sexual assault and sexual harassment? At most middle schools, high schools, and universities, students hear a series of secular sermons about treating everybody with respect, coupled with warnings about the terrible consequences for those who don't obey the rules, often with details about the difficulty of getting into a good school or finding a good job once you have been convicted of a sex crime. In my observations at more than four hundred schools, the most common outcome of such harping is a growing proportion of teenage boys who stay in their bedrooms, masturbating over pornography. Many boys have told me that the instructor in their high school sex-ed class openly encouraged them to choose masturbation over actual sexual encounters, explaining that when you masturbate, you don't have to worry about affirmative consent.

There's a better way. In my observation, the schools that are most effective in preventing sexual assault and sexual harassment, without scaring boys away from sexual intimacy altogether, are those schools that teach girls and boys to be ladies and gentlemen. A gentleman does not harass a lady, and a lady will not tolerate harassment. How, then, to teach boys to be gentlemen? Or more precisely: how to inspire boys to want to behave like gentlemen, in a culture that celebrates disrespect, seminude selfies, and pornography?

I delivered the commencement address at Avon Old Farms, a boys' school in Connecticut. I noticed that there were many teenage girls in the audience—far outnumbering the boys. "You guys all seem to have about four sisters apiece," I said to some of the boys.

"Those aren't our sisters, Dr. Sax," one of the boys told me. "Those are friends."

"You mean girlfriends?"

"Some of them are girlfriends; most of them are just friends," he said.

This piqued my interest. I spoke with some of the girls. A few were from Miss Porter's School, a girls' school about five miles away, but most were from Westminster, a nearby coed school.

"A coed school?" I said. "So what are you girls doing here? Why would you want to hang out here at a boys' school when you have boys at your own school?"

One girl rolled her eyes. "The boys at our school are all such total losers," she said. "Being around them is like being around my younger brother. They're loud and obnoxious and annoying.

And they think they're so tough. It's—*nauseating*." The other girls laughed and nodded their agreement.

"And the boys here are really that different?" I asked.

They all nodded again. "Totally," another girl said. "The boys here are, like, *gentlemen*. I know that sounds really weird and old-fashioned, but that's just the way it is. Like, they stand up when you come in the room. They open doors for you."

"And they don't interrupt you," another girl said, interrupting. "I hate trying to talk to guys at our school 'cause they are *always* interrupting."

"You should come here some weekend, Dr. Sax," another girl said. "You would totally not even know that this is a boys' school. There are probably more girls here than boys on the weekend. We just totally mob the place. Not even to hang with the guys necessarily. Last week a bunch of us girls went down to the indoor hockey rink here at the school just to slide around on the ice. Just us girls."

"But why bother to come to this school at all? You could have just gone to a public ice-skating rink," I said.

She shook her head "no." "It wouldn't be the same. It's fun to hang out here, because—"

"Because it's like we're family," another girl said.

"Because it feels safe," another girl said.

This school is not unique. I have heard similar comments from other girls who like to congregate at boys' schools, for example at Georgetown Prep in Bethesda, Maryland. I hasten to add that I have heard very different comments at other boys' schools: I have heard girls say that they would never, ever in a million years hang out at certain boys' schools. Just establishing a boys' school doesn't make that school a place where girls like to gather. On the contrary, when you put teenage boys together in groups, without the right kind of adult leadership, they can easily become a gang of bullies and thugs who consider sexual assault an amusing pastime.

Leadership from responsible adults makes the difference between schools where girls feel safe and welcome, and schools where girls feel unsafe (because they *are* unsafe). Schools like the one in Connecticut where I spoke don't leave this to chance. They make a point of teaching boys to be gentlemen. At this particular school the boys are taught the school's eight "core values," which are:

- Scholarship

- Integrity

- Civility

- Tolerance

- Altruism

- Sportsmanship

- Responsibility

- Self-discipline

"It's not enough for a boy to become a man. We want him to become a *gentleman*," the headmaster, Kenneth LaRocque, explained to me. At this school LaRocque and his colleagues explicitly teach the rules that they believe define a gentleman: A gentleman doesn't make pretend farting noises to amuse his buddies. A gentleman doesn't harass girls or women. A gentleman doesn't interrupt a girl when she is speaking. A gentleman defends a weak or unpopular person against a bully. A gentleman stands up when a girl or woman enters the room. At this school all these points are explicitly taught to the boys. "You can't assume that boys today know these things. Many of them don't. But they can be taught," Mr. LaRocque said. "A boy does not naturally grow up to be a gentleman. You need a community of men showing boys how to behave. And that's what we provide here."[37]

I'm not suggesting that Mr. LaRocque is the guru. I'm not suggesting that he has all the answers. But he has *an* answer: he and his colleagues have developed one particular way of teaching boys to become gentlemen. There are other core values you might choose and other ways of teaching those values. Heather Haupt, mother of three boys, sent me a draft of her book *Knights in Training: Ten Principles for Raising Honorable, Courageous, and Compassionate Boys*. Her principles include, among others: protect the weak; respect women; and speak the truth. I don't necessarily agree with all ten of her principles, and not all of her principles are gender specific. All children, both girls and boys, should be taught to speak the truth. But Haupt includes a lengthy section explaining why "respecting women" means that a gentleman does not look at pornography.[38] That's something boys need to be taught. It's less important to teach that to girls, because girls are less likely than boys to want to spend hours a day looking at pornography. (Reread chapter 6 if you're unsure of that finding.) For the girls' side of this story, I recommend *Girls Gone Mild: Young Women Reclaim Self-Respect and Find It's Not Bad to Be Good*, by Wendy Shalit; and *Strong Fathers, Strong Daughters*, by my friend Dr. Meg Meeker.

Almost every culture of which we have detailed knowledge takes great care in guiding girls and boys through the transition to womanhood and manhood, respectively. One example: The !Kung bushmen of southwest Africa, who call themselves "the

working to make sure that differences don't become disadvantages.

We know that human females, like females in other primate species, are less likely than males to take risks (see chapter 3). So: Work with girls to empower them to take risks. Learn from programs like the one at St. Michael's Collegiate School in Tasmania (which I shared in chapter 3), which culminates in girls happily and confidently rappelling down a sheer cliff over the Pacific Ocean at Freycinet.

We know that human males, like males in other primate species, are more likely than females to engage in risky and aggressive activities (see chapters 3 and 4). So: work with boys to channel their aggression into constructive behavior.

Let me tell you a story that illustrates what I mean.

Thunder Bay is a small town on the north shore of Lake Superior. A teenage boy there—let's call him David—fell in with a bad group of kids, a gang. To earn membership in the gang, a boy had to commit a crime. So David broke into an old woman's house while she was out shopping and stole some of her jewelry. David then sold the jewelry at a local pawn shop. When the woman reported the crime to police, it didn't take the detective long to track the stolen goods back to David. David was promptly arrested and convicted. He was sent to juvenile detention.

The warden of the facility had a friend who owned a lumberyard. The friend mentioned to the warden that he had a pile of lumber that was warped and could not be sold for construction purposes, although it would make good firewood. The warden also knew of a nonprofit group that helped the elderly. The head of the nonprofit had mentioned to him that some of the elderly in Thunder Bay still heated their homes with wood, but firewood was expensive, so the homes of some of these elderly people were colder than they ought to be. The warden asked his friend at the lumberyard whether he would be willing to cut up and donate the warped lumber for free, and he said that he would.

Now all that was needed was some way to deliver the wood to the homes of the elderly who needed it. The warden asked for volunteers to help. Three teenage boys volunteered, including David. It was a bitterly cold and windy day in mid-December. (If you have spent some time on the north shore of Lake Superior, you know what I'm talking about.) In a small town like Thunder Bay, the warden does lots of chores himself, so the warden himself was driving the pickup truck to deliver the wood, and the three boys were with him. They had made just two deliveries when the warden said, "Hey, guys, it's way too cold today. This is ridiculous. The wind's gusting. It's freezing. If we stay out here, we're all gonna die. Let's head back and get inside. We can try to finish some other day when it's not so crazy cold."

But David said, "No way! We still have deliveries to make! Those old folks are expecting us *today*. We can't let them down!" The warden was impressed by David's passion. And so they continued on.

The next house on the list turned out to be the very same home that David had broken into. So there was David, stacking wood in freezing cold and gusty wind, for the same woman whose home he had broken into a few months before.[41]

Boys want to be men. If we can channel that heroic/aggressive/risk-taking drive in a good way, the result may be a boy gallantly stacking wood for an old woman on a winter's day. If we fail to channel that drive, if we pretend that gender doesn't matter, the result is a boy breaking into an old woman's house to prove to himself and to his peers that he's a real man.

Beyond Pink and Blue

Back in 2003 a group of distinguished scholars convened at Dartmouth Medical School to discuss, among other topics, how our society's neglect of gender differences has caused great harm. Adults need to get serious about the question of gender, the scholars concluded. "The need to attach social significance and meaning to gender appears to be a human universal," they wrote, and one that "deeply influences well-being."[42]

These researchers acknowledged that many people view gender not as an innate biological characteristic but as a socially constructed role. After reviewing the evidence, these experts concluded that such a perspective is "seriously incomplete." Gender "runs deeper, near to the core of human identity and social meaning—in part because it is biologically primed and connected to differences in brain structure and function, and in part because it is so deeply implicated in the transition to adulthood."[43]

The transition to adulthood. More than in any other realm, that's where our society now lets kids down. We offer our daughters and sons little guidance about what it means to become a woman or a man. In traditional societies, the transition to a gendered adulthood is a matter of great importance, observed with ceremonies and rituals that are markedly different for girls and boys—so the scholars convened at Dartmouth observed. Female rites of passage "tend to celebrate entry into womanhood.... For young women, many world rituals suggest that with menarche comes heightened introspective powers, greater spiritual access, and an enriched inner life.... Male rites of passage are often more punishing, typically involving suffering and endurance. Such rituals seek to help the boy connect with spiritual and mythic meaning and totemic sponsorship from which he will draw strength to control his own aggression and to direct it toward the pro-social goals of his community."[44]

One hundred years from now, scholars may look back at the cultural disintegration manifest in the first half of the twenty-first century and conclude that a fundamental cause for the unraveling of our social fabric was the neglect of gender in the raising of our children. I wonder what those future historians will say about how long it took us to recognize our mistake, to realize that what girls need is different from what boys need, to understand that *gender matters.*

I hope that the blinders are coming off at last. In 2017, the *Journal of Neuroscience Research* devoted an entire issue to sex differences in every aspect of brain function, from vision to learning to mental illness. The issue was 791 pages long, with seventy-three different scholarly articles.[45] Larry Cahill, a professor of neuroscience at the University of California at Irvine who served as editor for the special edition, wrote:

> Due to a deeply ingrained, implicit (but false) assumption that "equal" means "the same," most neuroscientists *knew*, and even feared that establishing that males and females are not the same in some aspect of brain function meant establishing that they were not equal. This assumption is false and deeply harmful, in particular to the health of women, but remains deeply impactful nonetheless.
>
> The past 15 to 20 years in particular witnessed an explosion of research (despite the prevailing biases against the topic) documenting sex influences at *all* levels of brain

function. So overpowering is the wave of research that the standard ways of dismissing sex influences (e.g., "They are all small and unreliable," "They are all due to circulating hormones," "They are all due to human culture," and "They don't exist on the molecular level") have all been swept away, at least for those cognizant of the research.

[The seventy-three papers in this volume] forcefully document the fact that sex influences on brain function are ubiquitous, regularly reshaping findings—hence conclusions—at all levels of our field, and powerfully demonstrating how much "sex matters."

The notion that sex matters fundamentally, powerfully, and pervasively for *all* of neuroscience (not just for reproduction) is an idea whose time indeed has come.[46]

So perhaps the neuroscientists, or at least some of them, are finding the courage to allow reality rather than ideology to guide their research.

You and I are not neuroscientists. We have an even bigger job. Our job now is to create a society that has the courage and the wisdom to cherish and celebrate the innate differences between the sexes, while at the same time enabling equal opportunities for every child.

Gender is central to the human experience. But as in every other domain, girls and boys need guidance from grown-ups if they are to grow up to be the women and men they were meant to be. Help your daughter to become a confident and authentic woman: a lady. Help your son to become a courteous and respectful man: a gentleman. That won't be easy. It never has been. And contemporary culture—with the determined blindness to gender shown by the elites, coupled with the stereotyped caricatures of tough dudes and sexy girls pervasive on social media—makes the parent's job today that much harder.

I don't claim to have all the answers. But I think I'm asking the right questions.

We live in an era with new challenges. The answers of the 1950s won't work. We don't want to push girls and boys back into 1950s-style pink and blue cubbyholes, and we couldn't do so even if we wanted to. As a society and as parents, we face a challenge without precedent. We have to help girls and boys make the transition to a gendered adulthood, to adult life as women and men, in a culture in which women can do anything—including being rocket scientists—and men can do anything—including staying home to raise the baby. We have to find ways to value and cherish gender differences without restricting freedom of opportunity. We have to acknowledge that gender matters, without allowing gender to limit our children's horizons.

It won't be easy. But I think it can be done.

EXTRA STUFF:
SEX DIFFERENCES
IN HEARING

Researchers have learned that girls and boys, women and men, differ significantly (on average) in how they hear. One researcher made this comment about those sex differences:

> Intuition handles well the idea that complex behaviors and structures—higher order functions—can differ between the sexes, but it stumbles over the existence of sex differences in what are regarded to be simple, low-level functions and structures. Why this counterintuition? Perhaps because the existence of sex differences in simple, low-level abilities carries the implication that they—both the sex differences and the abilities—have, all along, been more important than has been appreciated.[1]

Stevens' *n*

How loudly is that teacher speaking? It seems like a simple question that should be easy enough to answer. The amplitude, or volume, of a sound is usually measured in decibels (dB). Go to an electronics store and purchase a sound meter. Sit in a classroom with your sound meter switched on (as I have done on a few occasions when visiting classrooms) and record how loud the teacher's voice is, as heard at the back of the classroom. I find that one soft-spoken teacher registers around fifty-four dB on my sound meter. Another teacher with a louder voice registers about sixty-four dB on the meter. So I have documented an objective difference of roughly ten dB in the loudness of these two teachers' voices. But how big a difference is ten dB?

The physical amplitude of a sixty-four dB sound is ten times greater than that of a fifty-four dB sound. A ten dB difference always represents a tenfold difference in amplitude. A twenty dB difference represents a hundredfold difference in amplitude. A thirty dB difference represents a thousandfold difference in amplitude.

But a student is a human being, not an automated sound meter. The student's subjective experience of the sound is not a linear function of the objective amplitude. No human being experiences an eighty-five dB sound as being a thousand times louder than a fifty-five dB sound. The eighty-five dB sound is louder, certainly, but not a thousand times louder. How much louder is it?

To explain how an *increment* in the amplitude of a sound affects the subjective loudness of the sound, I have found that it's useful to make an analogy to vision. Imagine a windowless room. It's totally dark. Now you switch on a light, a single lightbulb. Wow, what a difference. You can see!

Now suppose you switch on a second lightbulb identical to the first. The room becomes brighter. You switch on a third. A little brighter still. And a fourth. A fifth. By the time you switch on the fifth lightbulb, the incremental change in brightness might seem small. Objectively, however, the difference in illumination between the fourth lightbulb and the fifth lightbulb, compared with the difference between no lightbulb and the first lightbulb, is the same: in each case it's one lightbulb brighter, or about eight hundred lumens brighter if you are using conventional incandescent sixty-watt lightbulbs. To put this in technical language: the subjective experience of brightness is not a linear function of the objective stimulus.

Psychophysics is the part of psychology that is about understanding the relationship between an objective stimulus—in this case, the light from a lightbulb or the sound of the teacher's voice—and the subjective experience—in this case, the perceived brightness of the lightbulb or the perceived loudness of the teacher's voice.

J. J. Stevens, a professor at Harvard, recognized fifty years ago that for most visual and auditory stimuli, the subjective experience can be related to the objective stimulus by a relationship generally referred to today as "Stevens' Power Law" or just "Stevens' Law."[2] In the case of sound, Stevens' Law relates the subjective loudness of a tone L to the physical amplitude of the tone ϕ:

$$L = k\phi^n$$

where k is a scaling constant and Stevens' n is some number less than one. The value of n varies from one individual to the next and therefore must be measured for each person individually. Stevens' n is a measure of how sensitive a person is to sound. The higher the value of n, the more sensitive the person is to sound.

In one study researchers measured the variability in subjects' identification of the loudness of tones at different intensities and were thereby able to derive estimates of n for their subjects. Averaging across all frequencies and intensities, they found that the average value of Stevens' n for women was nearly 38 percent higher than the value of Stevens' n for men. This difference between women and men was highly significant.[3] In another study researchers used a different approach to measuring Stevens' *n*. In this second study, the average value of Stevens' *n* for women was between 44 percent and 49 percent higher than the value of Stevens' *n* for men, depending on the amplitude of the sound being tested. Again, these were highly significant differences.[4]

Researchers noted that the higher value of *n* for women compared with men "implies that females are more sensitive to a given physical range of tones than are males."[5] An earlier study from Stanford provides direct support for that assertion. Stanford researcher Diane McGuinness measured the sensitivity of women and men to loud tones. Across a wide range of frequencies, from 250 Hz to 8 kHz, she found that women's average maximum comfort level was consistently about eight dB lower than that of

Most Boys and Men Need the Sound Turned Up

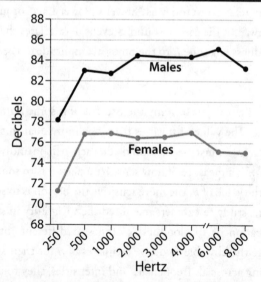

Equal loudness curves for young men and young women, across the frequency spectrum.
Source: Diane McGuinness, "Equating Individual Differences for Auditory Input,"
Psychophysiology, *volume 11, pp. 115–120, 1974.*

men (see the figure on page 320).[6] A British researcher, Colin Elliott, reported similar girl/boy differences in children as young as five years old.[7]

Another group measured subjects' most comfortable listening level and subjects' acceptable background noise level. Their subjects included twenty-five females and twenty-five males, all between nineteen and twenty-five years of age and all with normal hearing. The most comfortable listening level for females was 36.2 dB; for males it was 42.1 dB, or about six dB louder, a significant difference. In other words, males preferred speakers to speak about six dB louder, on average, than the loudness preferred by females. Likewise, the acceptable background noise level for females was 24.8 dB, while for males it was 31.7 dB, or about seven dB louder; again, a significant difference.[8] To put this finding another way: males tolerated significantly louder background noise than females did.

Psychophysical investigations in which subjects' sensitivity to sound is measured directly, as in each of the studies mentioned above, consistently find that the average female is more sensitive to sound than the average male. However, different results are obtained when researchers just *ask* subjects whether or not they are sensitive to sound. For example, a psychologist named Neil Weinstein devised a questionnaire back in 1978 to assess noise sensitivity. Weinstein would categorize you as being insensitive to noise if you agreed with statements such as "I wouldn't mind living on a noisy street if the apartment I had was nice," "No one should mind much if someone turns up his stereo full blast once in a while," or "In a library, I don't mind if people carry on a conversation if they do it quietly." Conversely, Weinstein would categorize you as being "noise-sensitive" if you agreed with statements such as "I get mad at people who make noise that keeps me from falling asleep or getting work done" or "I get annoyed when my neighbors are noisy." Weinstein showed no awareness of how the social construction of gender might influence subjects' answers to his questionnaire.[9] In the 1970s, when Weinstein administered this questionnaire, young women were probably less likely than males to agree with any statements that began "I get mad at people who . . ." Getting mad at people was not a desirable trait for young women in the 1970s. Likewise, other things being equal, young women in the 1970s would have been more likely than young men to agree with statements that began with "I don't mind if . . ." or "No one should mind if . . ." Giving in, not minding, and letting the other person have their way are well-documented attributes of traditional femininity in patriarchal cultures, a category that arguably includes American culture in the 1970s. No wonder that women in Weinstein's study were not more likely to identify themselves as sensitive to noise. There have been other claims that gender doesn't matter with regard to noise sensitivity, and those claims are unpersuasive for similar reasons.[10]

Applications

In chapter 2 I hinted that sex differences in hearing could make a big difference in the classroom. The sex differences noted here suggest that **the average boy may need the teacher to speak more loudly**—roughly six to eight decibels more loudly—**if the average boy is to hear the teacher as well as the average girl hears the teacher.**

If a particular classroom is arranged with children sitting in the same seats day after day, and the teacher is at the front of the classroom, then moving an inattentive boy from the back of the classroom to the front may be beneficial. I have personally been involved in the evaluation and ongoing supervision of boys in my own practice whose academic performance improved substantially after they were moved from the back row to the front. However, in my experience this intervention is reliably effective only with the youngest boys, in kindergarten or first grade. It is less likely to be helpful for older boys and may even be counterproductive for boys in middle school and high school. How come?

If girls and boys are allowed to sit wherever they like in the classroom, typically there will be one or two studious boys in the front row, with most of the girls in the front or middle rows; the gender-typical boys are more likely to sit toward the back of the room, with the rowdiest boys typically occupying the back row of seats. If a teacher in a classroom of eighth graders moves an inattentive boy from the back row to the front, then that boy's first priority often may be to prove to his buddies in the back row that he is not a teacher's pet. As a result, he may become more defiant and inattentive in the front row than he was in the back row. So that simple strategy doesn't work well with older boys. Moving your son to a different classroom, with a teacher who runs around the room and speaks more loudly, might be a better strategy.

Each of the studies cited earlier, demonstrating sex differences in Stevens' *n*, also documented substantial variation *among* males and *among* females. Some males are very sensitive to sounds, including background noise; and some females are less sensitive than some males are. Not all boys benefit when the teacher speaks more loudly. Some boys are acutely sensitive to sound. These boys may have an auditory processing disorder, also referred to as central auditory processing deficit or central auditory processing disorder.[11] Such a boy may be disadvantaged by being placed in a classroom with a teacher who speaks more loudly. That boy would likely do better with a soft-spoken teacher.

Another application of the sex differences in hearing noted here is that **boys typically tolerate a higher level of background noise in the classroom than girls do**: about six to eight decibels higher. The hum of a buzzing fan or the sound of fingers tapping on a desk may be quite annoying to a girl or to the (female) teacher but is less likely to annoy a boy.

If your son's teacher tells you that your son is always tapping his pencil on the desk, and it's very distracting, you might share this book with the teacher. Suggest that the teacher read the section titled Extra Stuff: Sex Differences in Hearing (the section you are reading now). The teacher may not be aware that there are, in fact, sex differences in the amount of noise the average boy will tolerate compared with the average girl. When the teacher tells your son to stop tapping his pencil, and he does stop, but five minutes later he's tapping his pencil again, he isn't necessarily being defiant or disrespectful. He's just not hearing the tapping the way that the (female) teacher and the girls are hearing it. Offer a suggestion: pipe cleaners. Pipe cleaners give your son something to tap, without making any noise on the desk.

Don't ignore sex differences. Work with them. The benefits may be substantial. The six-year-old boy who told you he hated school last week now says that he loves school. I've seen it happen.

EXTRA STUFF: SEX DIFFERENCES IN VISION

Would You Rather Play with a Truck or a Doll?

If you took a course in developmental psychology at almost any university in the past fifty years, odds are good that you learned about a number of classic experiments done in the 1960s through the 1990s. All these experiments were some variation on the following: the experimenter offers a young child, perhaps three or four years old, a choice between playing with a doll or some other "girly" toy and playing with a truck or some other "boy" toy. Girls typically show a slight preference for the doll over the truck. Boys typically show a great preference for trucks rather than dolls.[1]

The graph on page 326 shows a typical result from one of these studies. The black bar indicates the amount of time the child spent playing with a "masculine" toy such as a truck. The gray bar indicates the amount of time the child spent playing with a "feminine" toy such as a doll. Girls spend slightly more time playing with the doll than with the truck. Boys, on the other hand, typically spend a great deal more time playing with the truck rather than with the doll. Very few boys spend even a minute playing with the doll. The boys greatly prefer the truck; the girls slightly prefer the doll.[2]

When I learned about those studies thirty-seven years ago as a graduate student earning my Ph.D. in psychology at the University of Pennsylvania, we were taught that "the social construction of gender" is the appropriate framework in which to understand these results. My professor at Penn, Justin Aronfreed, explained it to me this way: "We give girls a fairly consistent message that girls are supposed to play with dolls and not with trucks. So when offered a choice, girls will be more likely to play with dolls rather than trucks. But if a girl picks up a truck, it's not a catastrophe."

Young Girls Slightly Prefer to Play with Dolls Rather Than Trucks; Young Boys Greatly Prefer to Play with Trucks Rather Than Dolls

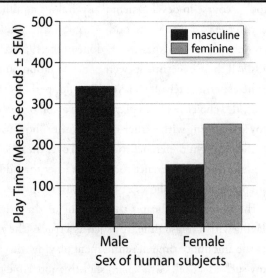

Young girls spend somewhat more time playing with "feminine" toys such as dolls, on average, whereas young boys spend much more time playing with "masculine" toys such as trucks.
Source: Janice Hassett, Erin Siebert, and Kim Wallen, "Sex Differences in Rhesus Monkey Toy Preferences Parallel Those of Children," Hormones and Behavior, *volume 54, pp. 359–364, 2008.*

With boys, Professor Aronfreed explained, the stakes are higher. "We send boys a much stronger message about what a boy is and is not supposed to do. Boys are *not* supposed to play with dolls. Boys get that message loud and clear. So boys are much more likely to play with trucks rather than dolls."

When Professor Aronfreed gave me that explanation, I didn't question it. It seemed like common sense.

In 2008 Kim Wallen and his colleagues at the Yerkes National Primate Research Center in Atlanta decided to do this familiar study again, with a little twist: instead of offering human children a choice between dolls and trucks, they gave that choice to monkeys. They gave monkeys the opportunity to play with a

Similar Sex Differences Are Seen with Monkeys

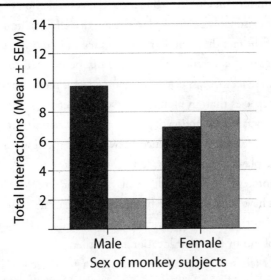

Male monkeys spend more time playing with "masculine" toys such as trucks rather than with "feminine" toys such as dolls.

Source: Janice Hassett, Erin Siebert, and Kim Wallen, "Sex Differences in Rhesus Monkey Toy Preferences Parallel Those of Children," Hormones and Behavior, *volume 54, pp. 359–364, 2008.*

"boy toy" such as a truck or with a "girl toy" such as a doll. Their results are shown on the previous page.

As you can see, the basic pattern of results was similar to the pattern seen with human children.[3] The female monkeys slightly prefer to play with dolls rather than trucks. The males substantially prefer to play with trucks rather than dolls.

It is difficult to invoke the social construction of gender to accommodate this finding. You would have to assert that a monkey in authority, maybe a parent, is saying to a young male monkey, *Don't let me catch you playing with a doll!* But in fact nothing of the sort happens. Monkeys don't appear to care whether other monkeys, female or male, are playing with trucks or with dolls. And yet the main effect—the preference of the male to play with a truck rather than with a doll—is clearly present in monkeys, as it is in human children. But the social construction of gender cannot reasonably be invoked to explain this effect in humans, in view of the fact that a similar effect is present in monkeys.[4]

The social construction of gender *can* be invoked to explain the difference *across* species. The main effect is more pronounced in our species than in monkeys, as you can see from the graphs. So the social construction of gender in our species can reasonably help to explain the difference between our species—in which culture plays a significant role in the construction of gender—and monkeys, in which culture plays little or no role. Monkeys do not have "culture" in the human sense, meaning customs and behaviors that are not genetically programmed and that may differ profoundly from one location to another.

Dr. Melvin Konner sums it up nicely in just three words: "culture *stretches* biology."[5] The main effect—the preference of the male to play with a dull gray truck rather than with a colorful doll—has to be hardwired, because it is conserved across different species. But that effect is more pronounced in our species because culture stretches biology, because human culture and the social construction of gender exaggerate and exacerbate the hardwired difference.

All right. So we've explained, perhaps, the difference in this finding between humans and monkeys. But we still haven't explained the main effect, found in both humans and monkeys: why is it the case that juvenile males, whether humans or monkeys, greatly prefer to play with a dull gray truck rather than with a colorful plush doll?

Monkeys, Girls, Boys, and Toys[6]

Developmental psychologist Gerianne Alexander thinks she might know. Professor Alexander actually was the first to offer monkeys a choice of playing with "boy toys" or with "girl toys." Just like Dr. Wallen's group, Professor Alexander found sex differences among monkeys similar to the sex differences we see among human children.[7] In 2003, one year after she published her monkey study, Professor Alexander published her theory explaining *why* female and male monkeys—as well as female and male humans—might prefer to play with different toys.[8]

Scientists have known for more than thirty years that our visual system is actually two separate systems operating in parallel, beginning at the level of the ganglion cells in the retina and extending back to the visual cortex and visual association cortex.[9] One system is devoted to answering the question *What is it?* What's its color? What's its texture? The other system is devoted to answering the question *Where is it going?* And how fast is it moving? These two systems in the brain are often referred to as the "what" system and the "where" system.[10]

Professor Alexander was the first to suggest that hardwired

sex differences in the visual system may explain findings such as the observed sex differences in the toy preferences of children (as well as monkeys). She conjectured that maybe girls have more resources in the "what" system, while boys have more resources in the "where" system. Girls are more likely to play with a doll rather than with a dull gray truck because the doll has a more interesting color and texture. Boys are more likely to play with the dull gray truck because it has *wheels*. It moves.

Professor Alexander's hypothesis helps to make sense of many findings that otherwise are hard to explain. For example, baby girls (three to eight months of age), but not baby boys of the same age, prefer to look at dolls rather than at toy trucks.[11] When researchers show women and men different colors and ask them to name the colors, "women respond faster and more accurately than men."[12] When researchers test men and women to see how accurately they can target a moving object, men are significantly more accurate than women.[13] Some might argue that male/female differences in targeting moving objects merely reflect differences in preferred pastimes: boys are more likely than girls to play games where they throw things at moving objects; boys have more practice targeting moving objects than girls do, so boys are better at it. But there is an intersex condition called congenital adrenal hyperplasia (CAH), in which a female baby is exposed to male hormones while in her mother's womb. Those male hormones masculinize the girl's brain in utero. CAH girls are much better than normal girls at targeting moving objects; in fact, the CAH girls are just as accurate as the boys.[14] Finally, researchers in Germany have reported dramatic sex differences in the anatomy of the human visual cortex in adults, with significantly more resources devoted to the "where" system in men than in women, even after adjusting for any overall size differences in the brain.[15]

All these findings fit Professor Alexander's hypothesis. Researchers who recently reviewed this research concluded that there is now "a large body of evidence indicating that sex differences in visual perception and its neural basis are real and [lend] support to the folk belief that males and females really do see the world differently, even if only to a degree."[16]

But why should you care about any of this?

I find that Professor Alexander's hypothesis helps me to understand the gender differences I have seen firsthand, in schools from Edinburgh to Toronto to Dallas to Auckland, in gender-specific best practices for teaching subjects as diverse as physics, creative writing, visual arts, and even modern foreign languages. The best way to teach physics to boys is pretty much the way we do teach physics to boys: keep the focus on *action*—cars accelerating, football players colliding, etc. Action engages the "**where** is it going" system, the system that appears to predominate in males. The best way to teach physics to girls appears to be focusing on answers to question like "**What** is it? **What** is light made out of? **What** is matter made out of? **What** laws govern the universe? **Why** those laws and not others?" (Please see chapter 5 of this book for some practical applications of this approach.)

How we see influences how we perceive the world. It influences what we like to read and how we like to write, particularly when we are young. In my book *Boys Adrift* I explored how a lack of awareness of this point disengages boys in subjects such as creative writing and visual arts. Some boys want to write stories with an emphasis on action; but they lose their enthusiasm when the teacher says, *Tell me more about your characters, Justin: What do they look like? What kind of clothes are they wearing?* The teacher wants Justin to emphasize the features that engage the "what" visual system, but Justin wants to tell a story that engages the "where is it going" visual system.

Most teachers don't know anything about sex differences in

the visual system. How could they? Very few schools of education provide any instruction on this topic, or on anything related to sex differences in best practices for teaching various subjects.[17] The general lack of awareness of gender differences disadvantages both girls and boys, but it disadvantages them in different ways. When teachers don't understand these gender differences, the result too often is a school where the boys think creative writing is for girls and the girls think physics is for guys. When teachers understand these gender differences, they can break down gender stereotypes. I've seen it firsthand.

Chapter 1: Differences

1. Anne Fausto-Sterling, *Sexing the Body: Gender Politics and the Construction of Sexuality* (New York: Basic Books, 2000), pp. 31, 3.
2. Claudia Dreifus, "Anne Fausto-Sterling: Exploring What Makes Us Male or Female," *New York Times*, January 2, 2001, p. F3. See also Courtney Weaver, "Birds Do It," *Washington Post*, March 26, 2000, p. X6; and Marc Breedlove, "Sexing the Body," *New England Journal of Medicine*, volume 343, p. 668, August 31, 2000.
3. This recommendation is made by Susan Hoy Crawford in her book *Beyond Dolls and Guns: 101 Ways to Help Children Avoid Gender Bias* (Portsmouth, NH: Heinemann, 1995). See also *William's Doll* by Charlotte Zolotow (New York: Harper & Row, 1972).
4. Deborah Tannen, *You Just Don't Understand: Women and Men in Conversation*, rev. ed. (New York: HarperCollins, 2001), p. 245.

Chapter 2: Smelling, Seeing, and Hearing

1. See Jeanmarie Diamond, Pamela Dalton, Nadine Doolittle, and Paul Breslin, "Gender-Specific Olfactory Sensitization: Hormonal and Cognitive Influences," *Chemical Senses*, volume 30 (supplement 1), pp. i224–i225, 2005. See also Pamela Dalton, Nadine Doolittle, and Paul Breslin, "Gender-Specific Induction of Enhanced Sensitivity to Odors," *Nature Neuroscience*, volume 5, pp. 199–200, 2002; and also Nassima Boulkroune and colleagues, "Repetitive Olfactory Exposure to the Biologically Significant Steroid Androstadienone Causes a Hedonic Shift and Gender Dimorphic Changes in Olfactory-Evoked Potentials," *Neuropsychopharmacology*, volume 32, pp. 1822–1829, 2007.
2. For an introduction to the emerging evidence on the importance of glial cells, see the review by Nicola Allen and Ben Barres, "Glia: More Than Just Brain Glue," *Nature*, volume 457, pp. 675–677, February 5, 2009. See also Baljit Khakh and Michael Sofroniew, "Diversity of Astrocyte Functions and Phenotypes in Neural Circuits," *Nature Neuroscience*, volume 18, pp. 942–952, 2015.
3. Ana Oliveira-Pinto and colleagues, "Sexual Dimorphism in the Human Olfactory Bulb: Females Have More Neurons and Glial Cells Than Males," *PLOS One*, November 5, 2014, http://journals.plos.org/plosone/article?id=10.1371/journal.pone.0111733.
4. This story is adapted from "The Royal Pigeon" in Anthony de Mello, *The Song of the Bird* (New York: Doubleday, 1982). I am grateful to Philomena Roy for sharing this book with me.
5. The College Board offers three AP exams in Studio Art: Studio Art Drawing, Studio Art 2-D Design, and Studio Art 3-D Design. In 2015—the most recent year for which data are available—1,504 boys and 4,059 girls took the AP exam in Studio Art Drawing; 2,247 boys and 7,238 girls took the AP Exam in Studio

Art 2-D Design; 402 boys and 1,307 girls took the AP exam in Studio Art 3-D Design. Adding the figures across all three exams, 4,153 boys and 12,604 girls took an AP exam in Studio Art. Boys therefore composed 24.8 percent of the total, slightly below one in four students. These figures are drawn from the College Board's Program Summary Report for 2015, available at https://secure-media.collegeboard.org/digitalServices/pdf/research/2015/Program-Summary-Report-2015.pdf.

6. See, for example, Simone Alter-Muri and Stephanie Vazzano, "Gender Typicality in Children's Art Development: A Cross-Cultural Study," *Arts in Psychotherapy*, volume 41, pp. 155–162, 2014.

Chapter 3: Risk

1. The full translation of this passage from Nietzsche's *Die Fröhliche Wissenschaft*, section 283, is "The secret to harvesting the greatest fruitfulness and the most fun from life, is: *to live dangerously*. Build your cities on the slopes of Vesuvius! Send your ships into unknown seas! Live at war with your peers and with yourselves!" The translation is my own. The emphasis is in the original.

2. See Richard Sorrentino, Erin Hewitt, and Patricia Raso-Knott, "Risk-Taking in Games of Chance and Skill: Informational and Affective Influences on Choice Behavior," *Journal of Personality and Social Psychology*, volume 62, pp. 522–533, 1992.

3. This phenomenon is seen with young girls and boys just as it is seen with adults. Psychologists David Miller and James Byrnes demonstrated this effect with third, fifth, and seventh graders in their paper, "The Role of Contextual and Personal Factors in Children's Risk Taking," *Developmental Psychology*, volume 33, pp. 814–823, 1997.

4. The largest meta-analysis of sex differences in risk taking remains the article by James Byrnes, David Miller, and William Schafer, "Gender Differences in Risk Taking: A Meta-analysis," *Psychological Bulletin*, volume 125, pp. 367–383.

5. J. H. Kerr and J. Vlaminkx, "Gender Differences in the Experience of Risk," *Personality and Individual Differences*, volume 22, pp. 293–295, 1997.

6. See, for example, Paul Poppen, "Gender and Patterns of Sexual Risk Taking in College Students," *Sex Roles*, volume 32, pp. 545–555, 1995. See also Debra Murphy and colleagues, "Adolescent Gender Differences in HIV-Related Sexual Risk Acts, Social-Cognitive Factors and Behavioral Skills," *Journal of Adolescence*, volume 21, pp. 197–208, 1998.

7. Barbara Morrongiello and Tess Dawber, "Toddlers' and Mothers' Behaviors in an Injury-Risk Situation: Implications for Sex Differences in Childhood Injuries," *Journal of Applied Developmental Psychology*, volume 19, pp. 625–639, 1998.

8. William Pickett and colleagues, "Multiple Risk Behavior and Injury: An International Analysis of Young People," *Archives of Pediatrics and Adolescent Medicine*, volume 156, pp. 786–793, 2002.

9. Anna Waller and colleagues, "Childhood Injury Deaths: National Analysis and Geographic Variations," *American Journal of Public Health*, volume 79, pp. 310–315, 1989. See also Susan Sorenson, "Gender Disparities in Injury Mortality: Consistent, Persistent, and Larger Than You'd Think," *American Journal of Public Health*, volume 101, pp. S353–S358, 2011.

10. Barbara Morrongiello, "Children's Perspectives on Injury and Close-Call Experiences: Sex Differences in Injury-Outcome Processes," *Journal of Pediatric Psychology*, volume 22, pp. 499–512, 1997.

11. Lizette Peterson and colleagues, "Gender and Developmental Patterns of Affect, Belief, and Behavior in Simulated Injury Events," *Journal of Applied Developmental Psychology*, volume 18, pp. 531–546, 1997.

12. Jonathan Howland and colleagues, "Why Are Most Drowning Victims Men? Sex Differences in Aquatic Skills and Behaviors," *American Journal of Public Health*, volume 86, pp. 93–96, 1996. These numbers are drawn from figure 1 of that paper, whose full text is available at www.ncbi.nlm.nih.gov/pmc/articles /PMC1380371/pdf/amjph00512-0095.pdf.

13. Howland and colleagues (previous citation). The quote comes from page 96.

14. "Thunderstorm-Related Deaths Occur Mainly in Men and Involve Sports or Vehicles, Reports University of Pittsburgh Researcher" (news release), UPMC/ University of Pittsburgh Schools of the Health Sciences Media Relations, April 28, 2003, www.upmc.com/media/NewsReleases/2003/Pages/thunder -storm-death-study.aspx.

15. Barbara Morrongiello and colleagues, "Gender Biases in Children's Appraisals of Injury Risk and Other Children's Risk-Taking Behaviors," *Journal of Experimental Child Psychology*, volume 77, pp. 317–336, 2000.

16. Linda Marie Fedigan and Sandra Zohar, "Sex Differences in Mortality of Japanese Macaques: Twenty-one Years of Data from the Arashiyama West Population," *American Journal of Physical Anthropology*, volume 102, pp. 161– 175, 1997.

17. For a different perspective on the possible explanations for the underrepresentation of women among top CEOs, see Margaret Heffernan, "Why Do Only 26 Fortune 500 Companies Have Female CEOs?" *Fortune*, December 8, 2014, http://fortune.com/2014/12/08/competition-gap-women -leaders/.

18. Robert J. Samuelson, "What's the Real Gender Pay Gap?" *Washington Post*, April 24, 2016.

19. Ariane Hegewisch and Asha DuMonthier, "The Gender Wage Gap by Occupation 2015 and by Race and Ethnicity," Institute for Women's Policy Research, April 2016, www.iwpr.org/publications/pubs/the-gender-wage-gap-by -occupation-2015-and-by-race-and-ethnicity.

20. Linda Babcock and Sara Laschever, *Women Don't Ask: Negotiation and the Gender Divide* (Princeton, NJ: Princeton University Press, 2003).

21. Margrét Pála Ólafsdóttir, "Kids Are Both Girls and Boys in Iceland," *Women's Studies International Forum*, volume 19, pp. 357–369, 1996.

Chapter 4: Aggression

1. General Patton spoke these words in a speech to American soldiers in England on June 5, 1944, the day before the invasion of Normandy. The full passage reads: "You are here today for three reasons. First, because you are here to defend your homes and your loved ones. Second, you are here for your own self-respect, because you would not want to be anywhere else. Third, you are here because you are real men and all real men like to fight." The speech is widely available online, for example at www.pattonhq.com/speech.html.

2. Rachel Simmons, *Odd Girl Out: The Hidden Culture of Aggression in Girls* (New York: Harcourt, 2002), p. 75.

3. The German original is "Die Großen Epochen unsres Lebens liegen dort, wo wir den Mut gewinnen, unser Böses als unser Bestes umzutaufen," section 116 from Jenseits von Gut und Böse (*Beyond Good & Evil*).

4. See two articles by Janet Lever: "Sex Differences in the Games Children Play," *Social Problems*, volume 23, pp. 478–487, 1976, and "Sex Differences in the Complexity of Children's Games," *American Sociological Review*, volume 43, pp. 471–83, 1978.

5. Quoted in Deborah Blum's book *Sex on the Brain: The Biological Differences Between Men and Women* (New York: Penguin, 1998), pp. 73–74.

6. Tracy Collins-Stanley and colleagues, "Choice of Romantic, Violent, and Scary Fairy-Tale Books by Preschool Girls and Boys," *Child Study Journal*, volume 26, pp. 279–302, 1996.

7. Kai von Klitzing and colleagues, "Gender-Specific Characteristics of 5-Year-Olds' Play Narratives and Associations with Behavior Ratings," *Journal of the American Academy of Child and Adolescent Psychiatry*, volume 39, pp. 1017–1023, 2000.

8. David Perry, Louise Perry, and Robert Weiss, "Sex Differences in the Consequences That Children Anticipate for Aggression," *Developmental Psychology*, volume 25, pp. 312–319, 1989.

9. See, for example, Sheri Berenbaum and Elizabeth Snyder, "Early Hormonal Influences on Childhood Sex-Typed Activity and Playmate Preferences," *Developmental Psychology*, volume 31, pp. 31–42, 1995. See also Sheri Berenbaum and Melissa Hines, "Early Androgens Are Related to Childhood Sex-Typed Toy Preferences," *Psychological Science*, volume 3, pp. 203–206, 1992.

10. Anna Servin and colleagues, "Prenatal Androgens and Gender-Typed Behavior: A Study of Girls with Mild and Severe Forms of Congenital Adrenal Hyperplasia," *Developmental Psychology*, volume 39, pp. 440–450, 2003. See also Melissa Hines, "Sex-Related Variation in Human Behavior and the Brain," *Trends in Cognitive Science*, volume 10, pp. 448–456, 2010, full text available at https://www.ncbi.nlm.nih.gov/pmc/articles/PMC2951011/.

11. Maria Van Noordwik and associates, "Spatial Position and Behavioral Sex Differences in Juvenile Long-Tailed Macaques," in Michael Pereira and Lynn Fairbanks (editors), *Juvenile Primates* (New York: Oxford University Press, 2002), pp. 77–84.

12. Carolyn Crockett and Theresa Pope, "Consequences of Sex Differences in Dispersal for Juvenile Red Howler Monkeys," in Pereira and Fairbanks, *Juvenile Primates* (see previous note), pp. 104–118; see especially "Infant Care by Juvenile Females," pp. 112–113. See also David Watts and Anne E. Pusey, "Behavior of Juvenile and Adolescent Great Apes," in *Juvenile Primates*, pp. 148–172, especially "Alloparenting," p. 162.

13. Niels Bolwig, "A Study of the Behaviour of the Chacma Baboon," *Behaviour*, volume 14, pp. 136–162, 1959.

14. Jennifer Lovejoy and Kim Wallen, "Sexually Dimorphic Behavior in Group-Housed Rhesus Monkeys at 1 Year of Age," *Psychobiology*, volume 16, pp. 348–356, 1988.

15. Sonya Kahlenberg and Richard Wrangham, "Sex Differences in Chimpanzees' Use of Sticks as Play Objects Resemble Those of Children," *Current Biology*, volume 20, pp. R1067–R1068, 2010. See also Elizabeth Lonsdorf and colleagues, "Boys Will Be Boys: Sex Differences in Wild Infant Chimpanzee Social Interactions," *Animal Behavior*, volume 88, pp. 79–83, 2014, full text online at www.ncbi.nlm.nih.gov/pmc/articles/PMC3904494/.

16. Dario Maestripieri and Suzanne Pelka, "Sex Differences in Interest in Infants Across the Lifespan: A Biological Adaptation for Parenting?" *Human Nature*, volume 13, pp. 327–344, 2002. In the text, I summarize these authors' findings this way: "women over forty-five are less interested in infants compared with

younger women, teenage girls, or younger girls." This summary is based on figure 1(a) from this study. See also Rodrigo Cardenas and colleagues, "Sex Differences in Visual Attention Toward Infant Faces," *Evolution and Human Behavior*, volume 34, pp. 280–287, 2013.

17. When psychologists Hugh Lytton and David Romney reviewed 172 studies involving 28,000 children, they found no evidence that parents' child rearing has any measurable effect on the gender-typical behavior of their children. See their paper, "Parents' Differential Socialization of Boys and Girls: A Meta-analysis," *Psychological Bulletin*, volume 109, pp. 267–296, 1991.

18. Michael Meaney, Elizabeth Lozos, and Jane Stewart, "Infant Carrying by Nulliparous Female Vervet Monkeys," *Journal of Comparative Psychology*, volume 104, pp. 377–381, 1990.

19. See for example the article by Jane Goodall and her associates in the *American Journal of Physical Anthropology*, "Patterns of Predation by Chimpanzees on Red Colobus Monkeys in Gombe National Park, 1982–1991," volume 94, pp. 213–228, 1994. They found that adolescent male and adult male chimps often kill colobus monkeys. Goodall and her colleagues never saw an *adolescent* female chimp kill a monkey, and even adult female chimps rarely killed monkeys. The anthropologists identified fifteen different male chimps each of whom killed three or more monkeys, and nine male chimps each of whom killed more than ten monkeys each. One male killed seventy-six monkeys. By contrast, only two female chimps killed more than two monkeys: one female killed four monkeys, and one (a female who never mated or became pregnant) killed ten monkeys. See their Table 3, p. 220. See also Michael Hopkin's article, "Girl Chimps Learn Faster than Boys," *Nature*, April 15, 2004, online at www.nature.com /news/2004/040412/full/news040412-6.html. In this article primatologist Andrew Whiten is quoted as saying, "While termites are a valuable food for females, males often catch larger animals such as monkeys. Their rough-and-tumble play may be a way to hone their hunting skills."

20. J. Dee Higley, "Aggression," in Dario Maestripieri (editor), *Primate Psychology* (Cambridge, Mass.: Harvard University Press, 2003), pp. 17–40. Dr. Higley explained this finding to me in detail when we were neighbors in Montgomery County, Maryland.

21. See, for example, "Dodgeball Banned After Bullying Complaint," *Headline News*, March 28, 2013, online at www.hlntv.com/article/2013/03/28/school -dodgeball-ban-new-hampshire-district. For an earlier report, see Tamala Edwards, "Scourge of the Playground: It's Dodgeball, Believe It or Not. More Schools Are Banning the Childhood Game, Saying It's Too Violent," *Time*, May 21, 2001, p. 68.

22. Marc Fisher, "Skittish Schools Need to Take a Recess," *Washington Post*, November 23, 2003, p. C1.

23. John Gehring, "Snowball's Chance," *Education Week*, January 21, 2004, p. 9. For example, the Morning Glory Public School of the York Region District School Board in Ontario, Canada, reminds students that "snow must stay out of hands and on the ground at all times." This rule was stated in a newsletter from the Morning Glory school in December 2013 posted at www.yrdsb.ca/schools /morningglory.ps/NewsEvents/Documents/Dec%202013%20vol%201%20 mgps.pdf.

24. The Rutherford Institute, "Victory: School Officials to Lift Suspension from 10-Year-Old Who Shot Imaginary Arrow at Pennsylvania Elementary School," January 6, 2014, www.rutherford.org/publications_resources/Press%20Release

/victory_school_officials_to_lift_suspension_from_10_year_old_who_shot _imagi. See also Liz Klimas, "10-Year-Old Suspended for an Imaginary Weapon," *The Blaze*, December 9, 2013, www.theblaze.com/stories/2013/12/09/10-year -old-suspended-for-shooting-imaginary-bow-and-arrow/.

25. This line is a quotation from the *Epistles* of Horace (I, 10). The original Latin is *Naturam expellas furca, tamen usque recurret.*

26. Adam Bellow, *In Praise of Nepotism: A Natural History* (New York: Doubleday, 2003), pp. 341–342.

27. Albert Beveridge, *Abraham Lincoln, 1809–1859* (Boston: Houghton-Mifflin, 1928), pp. 120–221.

28. Bellow, *In Praise of Nepotism*, p. 342.

29. Rachel Simmons, *Odd Girl Out: The Hidden Culture of Aggression in Girls* (New York: Harcourt, 2002), p. 75.

30. John Bishop and colleagues, "Nerds and Freaks: A Theory of Student Culture and Norms," in *Brookings Papers on Education Policy, 2003*, Diane Ravitch, editor (Washington, DC: Brookings Institution Press, 2003), pp. 141–213. The quote is from page 158.

31. See the review by Jon Sutton and colleagues, "Bullying and 'Theory of Mind': A Critique of the Social Skills Deficit View of Anti-Social Behaviour," *Social Development*, volume 8, pp. 117–127, 1999. These authors observe that "the stereotype of a bully as a powerful but 'oafish' person with little understanding of others" may be a good description of the typical *boy* who bullies but rarely describes the *girl* who bullies. Girls who bully "need good social cognition and theory of mind skills in order to manipulate and organize others, inflicting suffering in subtle and damaging ways while avoiding detection themselves." For a different perspective on sex differences in bullying, see the article by Anthony Volk and colleagues, "Is adolescent bullying an evolutionary adaptation?" *Aggressive Behavior*, volume 38, pp. 222–238, 2012.

32. See my article "The Unspeakable Pleasure," *The World & I*, February 2000.

33. Rachel Simmons, *Odd Girl Out: The Hidden Culture of Aggression in Girls*, revised edition, (Boston: Mariner, 2011), p. 162.

Chapter 5: School

1. See Tricia Valeski and Deborah Stipek, "Young Children's Feelings About School," *Child Development*, volume 72, pp. 1198–1213, 2001. See also Eva Pomerantz, Ellen Altermatt, and Jill Saxon, "Making the Grade but Feeling Distressed: Gender Differences in Academic Performance and Internal Distress," *Journal of Educational Psychology*, volume 94(2), pp. 396–404, 2002; and also Laura McFarland and colleagues, "Student-Teacher Relationships and Student Self-Concept: Relations with Teacher and Student Gender," *Australian Journal of Education*, volume 60, pp. 5–25, 2016.

2. Elizabeth Lonsdorf, Lynn Eberly, and Anne Pusey, "Sex Differences in Learning in Chimpanzees," *Nature*, volume 428, pp. 715–716, 2004. See also Elizabeth Lonsdorf and colleagues, "Boys Will Be Boys: Sex Differences in Wild Infant Chimpanzee Social Interactions," *Animal Behaviour*, volume 88, pp. 79–83, 2014; and also Lonsdorf and colleagues, "Sex Differences in Wild Chimpanzee Behavior Emerge During Infancy," *PLOS One*, June 9, 2014, DOI: 10.1371/ journal.pone.0099099.

3. Pomerantz and colleagues (citation above), p. 402.

4. Diane Halpern and Mary LeMay, "The Smarter Sex: A Critical Review of Sex

Differences in Intelligence," *Educational Psychology Review*, volume 12, pp. 229–246, 2000.

5. Angela Duckworth and Martin Seligman, "Self-Discipline Gives Girls the Edge: Gender in Self-Discipline, Grades, and Achievement Test Scores," *Journal of Educational Psychology*, volume 98, pp. 198–208, 2006.

6. This observation—that girls' friendships are face to face while boys' friendships are shoulder to shoulder—has been made by many scholars, most accessibly by Deborah Tannen, *You Just Don't Understand: Women and Men in Conversation*, rev. ed. (New York: HarperCollins, 2001); and by Helen Fisher, *Why We Love: The Nature and Chemistry of Romantic Love* (New York: Henry Holt, 2004).

7. See Kathryn Dindia and Mike Allen's review of 205 studies on this topic: "Sex Differences in Self-Disclosure: A Meta-analysis," *Psychological Bulletin*, volume 112, pp. 106–124, 1992. See also Tong Yu, "Gender Differences on Self-Disclosure in Face-to-Face Versus E-mail Communication," *International Conference on Education, Language, Art and Intercultural Communication*, 2014, online at www.atlantis-press.com/php/download_paper.php?id=12632.

8. See, for example, the chapter by Deborah Belle and Joyce Benenson, "Children's Social Networks and Well-Being," chapter 45 in the book *Handbook of Child Well-being*, edited by A. Ben-Arieh and colleagues, (New York: Springer, 2014).

9. Shelley Taylor and associates, "Biobehavioral Responses to Stress in Females: Tend-and-Befriend, Not Fight-or-Flight," *Psychological Review*, volume 107, pp. 411–429, 2000. The quotation comes from page 418.

10. John Bishop and colleagues, "Nerds and Freaks: A Theory of Student Culture and Norms," in *Brookings Papers on Education Policy, 2003*, Diane Ravitch, editor (Washington, DC: Brookings Institution Press, 2003), pp. 141–213. The quotation is from pages 182–183.

11. First Samuel 18:3–4 and 23:17 (NIV).

12. This rule works with most white girls and most black girls. It is less reliably effective with Latina girls, especially Latina girls who trace their ancestry to the indigenous peoples of the Americas as opposed to Spain. This strategy is also less reliably effective with East Asian, Southeast Asian, and South Asian girls, especially those raised in traditional families with close ties to Asian culture.

13. Daphna Joel and colleagues, "Sex Beyond the Genitalia: The Human Brain Mosaic," *Proceedings of the National Academy of Sciences*, volume 112, pp. 15468–15473, 2015.

14. Kate Wheeling, "The Brains of Men and Women Aren't Really That Different, Study Finds," *Science*, November 30, 2015.

15. Adam Chekroud and colleagues, "Patterns in the Human Brain Mosaic Discriminate Males from Females," *Proceedings of the National Academy of Sciences*, volume 113, p. E1968, 2016.

16. Marek Glezerman, "Yes, There Is a Female and a Male Brain: Morphology Versus Functionality," *Proceedings of the National Academy of Sciences*, volume 113, p. E1971, 2016.

17. Todd Elder, "The Importance of Relative Standards in ADHD Diagnoses: Evidence Based on Exact Birth Dates," *Journal of Health Economics*, volume 29, pp. 641–656, 2010, full text online at www.msu.edu/~telder/2010-JHE.pdf.

18. Rhoshel Lenroot and colleagues, "Sexual Dimorphism of Brain Developmental Trajectories During Childhood and Adolescence," *Neuroimage*, volume 36, pp. 1065–1073, 2007. The figure shown is Figure 2(a) from the article.

19. Chris Boyatzis, Elizabeth Chazan, and Carol Ting, "Preschool Children's

Decoding of Facial Emotions," *Journal of Genetic Psychology*, volume 154, pp. 375–382, 1993.

20. For a review of how the kindergarten curriculum accelerated between 1980 and 2000, and how this change has been especially harmful to boys, see my paper "Reclaiming Kindergarten: Making Kindergarten Less Harmful to Boys," *Psychology of Men and Masculinity*, volume 2, pp. 3–12, 2001.

21. See Deborah Stipek and associates, "Good Beginnings: What Difference Does the Program Make in Preparing Young Children for School?" *Journal of Applied Developmental Psychology*, volume 19, pp. 41–66, 1998. See also D. Burts and associates, "Observed Activities and Stress Behaviors of Children in Developmentally Appropriate and Inappropriate Kindergarten Classrooms," *Early Childhood Research Quarterly*, volume 7, pp. 297–318, 1992.

22. See Tricia Valeski and Deborah Stipek, "Young Children's Feelings About School," *Child Development*, volume 72, pp. 1198–1213, 2001. Quotations are from page 1199. See also Professor Stipek's chapter "Pathways to Constructive Behavior: Importance of Academic Achievement in the Early Elementary Grades," in the book she edited entitled *Constructive and Destructive Behavior: Implications for Family, School, and Society* (Washington, DC: American Psychological Association, 2001).

23. For a brief review, see John Holloway's article, "When Children Aren't Ready for Kindergarten," *Educational Leadership*, April 2003, pp. 89–90. See also my paper, "Reclaiming Kindergarten: Making Kindergarten Less Harmful To Boys," *Psychology of Men and Masculinity*, volume 2, pp. 3–12, 2001.

24. See my book *The Collapse of Parenting: How We Hurt Our Kids When We Treat Them Like Grown-Ups* (New York: Basic Books, 2015), pp. 59–61, for supporting calculations and sources.

25. As important as I believe "the medicalization of misbehavior" to be, it is by no means the only factor driving the rise in the proportion of American kids on medication for ADHD. Another factor is the collapse of American parenting. In chapter 3 of my book *The Collapse of Parenting*, I show how the abdication of parental authority creates a vacuum of authority: the physician, armed with a prescription pad, steps into that vacuum. Medication is used to regulate behavior. Another factor is the marketing of prescription medications such as Adderall and Vyvanse directly to consumers, a practice that is prohibited by law in every other developed country with the sole exception of New Zealand.

26. This section is adapted from my discussion of this topic in chapter 3 of my book *The Collapse of Parenting*.

27. When I rattle off the list of stimulant medications—Adderall, Vyvanse, Concerta, Focalin, Metadate, Daytrana, Ritalin, and Quillivant—it sounds as though I am mentioning eight different medications. In fact these eight medications are just two medications. Adderall and Vyvanse are two proprietary **amphetamines**. Ritalin, Concerta, Focalin, Metadate, Quillivant, and Daytrana are all different versions of **methylphenidate**. There is consensus that methylphenidate works by increasing the action of dopamine in the synapse: see, for example, Nora Volkow and colleagues, "Imaging the Effects of Methylphenidate on Brain Dopamine: New Model on Its Therapeutic Actions for Attention-Deficit/Hyperactivity Disorder," *Biological Psychiatry*, volume 57, pp. 1410–1415, 2005. And it has long been recognized that amphetamine mimics the action of dopamine in the brain, and that the dopamine system is key to ADHD: see for example James Swanson and colleagues, "Dopamine and Glutamate in Attention Deficit Disorder," pp. 293–315 in the book *Dopamine*

and Glutamate in Psychiatric Disorders, edited by Werner Schmidt and Maarten Reith (New York: Humana Press, 2005), pp. 293–315.

28. See Mónica Franco Emch, "Ventro-Striatal/Nucleus Accumbens Alterations in Adult ADHD: Effects of Pharmacological Treatment. A Neuroimaging Region of Interest Study" (bachelor's thesis, Universitat Pompeu Fabra, 2015). See especially Figure 2 from this study. The full text is online at http://repositori .upf.edu/bitstream/handle/10230/24651/Franco_2015.pdf?sequence=1. See also Elseline Hoekzema and colleagues, "Stimulant Drugs Trigger Transient Volumetric Changes in the Human Ventral Striatum," *Brain Structure and Function*, volume 219, pp. 23–34, 2013.

29. L. J. Seidman and colleagues, "Dorsolateral Prefrontal and Anterior Cingulate Cortex Volumetric Abnormalities in Adults with Attention Deficit/ Hyperactivity Disorder Identified by Magnetic Resonance Imaging," *Biological Psychiatry*, volume 60, pp. 1071–1080, 2006. See also Emch, 2015 (previous citation).

30. See Nicolas Carriere and colleagues, "Apathy in Parkinson's Disease Is Associated with Nucleus Accumbens Atrophy: A Magnetic Resonance Imaging Shape Analysis," *Movement Disorders*, volume 29, pp. 897–903, 2014. See also Robert Paul, Adam Brickman, Bradford Navia, and colleagues, "Apathy is associated with volume of the nucleus accumbens in patients infected with HIV," *Journal of Neuropsychiatry and Clinical Neuroscience*, volume 17, pp. 167–171, 2005.

31. Susan Price, "The Tech Gender Gap Is Getting Worse," *Forbes*, October 29, 2016.

32. In 2015, 48,994 students took the AP exam in computer science: 10,778 girls and 38,216 boys. Boys thus composed 78 percent of the total, girls 22 percent. These data come from the College Board Web site: https://secure-media.collegeboard .org/digitalServices/pdf/research/2015/Program-Summary-Report-2015.pdf.

33. Caitlin Kelleher, "Barriers to Programming Engagement," *Advances in Gender & Education*, volume 1, pp. 5–10, 2009, online at www.mcrcad.org/Web_Kelleher .pdf.

34. Trudi Hammel Garland, *Fascinating Fibonaccis: Mystery and Magic in Numbers* (Parsippany, NJ: Pearson, 1987).

35. Nicole Fortin and colleagues, "Leaving Boys Behind: Gender Disparities in High Academic Achievement," *The Journal of Human Resources*, volume 50, pp. 549–579, 2015.

36. Eva Pomerantz and colleagues, "Making the Grade but Feeling Distressed: Gender Differences in Academic Performance and Internal Distress," *Journal of Educational Psychology*, volume 94, pp. 396–404, 2002. See also Fortin and colleagues, "Leaving Boys Behind."

37. You can read the full text of Professor Summers' remarks at www.harvard.edu /president/speeches/summers_2005/nber.php.

38. See Linda Chavez, "The Shibboleths of Academe," January 19, 2005, https:// townhall.com/columnists/lindachavez/2005/01/19/the-shibboleths-of -academe-n1062361. See also Cathy Young's essay "Summers Spoke the Truth," *Boston Globe*, February 28, 2005.

39. Harvard physics professor Howard Georgi reportedly said: "It's crazy to think that it's an innate difference. It's socialization. We've trained young women to be average. We've trained young men to be adventurous." Quoted in Sara Rimer and Patrick Healy, "Furor Lingers as Harvard Chief Gives Details of Talk on Women," *New York Times*, February 18, 2005.

40. The faculty vote of March 15, 2005, marked the first time in Harvard's (then) 370-year history that the faculty had taken any such action against the president

of the college or university. The faculty has no authority to appoint or depose the president. More than one observer noted the coincidence, if it was a coincidence, that the faculty vote fell on the Ides of March.

41. I am referring to AP Physics C, which has two sections: Mechanics is one section, and Electricity and Magnetism is the other section. In most high schools, the Mechanics portion of AP Physics C is taught in the fall, with the Electricity and Magnetism portion of AP Physics C taught in the spring. The wave-particle duality of light is often taught, as I said, just a week or two before the exam is administered. But there is no reason why a school could not do Electricity and Magnetism in the fall, with Mechanics in the spring, and begin with the wave-particle duality of light. Korowa in Melbourne, along with a number of high schools in New South Wales, Australia, begin with Electricity and Magnetism and move on to Newtonian Mechanics in the second semester.

42. Quoted in Debra Viadero, "New Studies Suggest Why Women Avoid STEM Fields," *Education Week*, June 17, 2009, p. 15.

43. Kim Tolley, *The Science Education of American Girls: A Historical Perspective* (New York: RoutledgeFalmer, 2003). "Science for the Ladies, Classics for Gentlemen" is the title of chapter 2 of Tolley's book.

44. Anat Zohar and David Sela, "Her Physics, His Physics: Gender Issues in Israeli Advanced Placement Physics Classes," *International Journal of Science Education*, volume 25, pp. 245–268, 2003.

Chapter 6: Sex

1. Anne Jarrell, "The Face of Teenage Sex Grows Younger," *New York Times*, April 2, 2000.

2. This paragraph is excerpted from pages 218 and 219 of *Seventeen* magazine's August 2003 survey and report on oral sex, entitled *Oral Report*. The lead author was Noelle Howey.

   Newer references are available. For example, Peggy Orenstein's book *Girls and Sex: Navigating the Complicated New Landscape* (New York: Harper, 2016) was widely hailed, and deservedly so, for shining a light on how the hookup culture, with its emphasis on oral sex, has transformed the lived experience of American teenagers compared with Orenstein's own experience coming of age in the 1970s (she was born in 1961). However, the hookup culture and the commonness of oral sex are no longer new: both were already dominant in the early 2000s when I was writing the first edition of *Why Gender Matters*. I have deliberately kept many of the older references in this chapter specifically to highlight the fact that these issues, while important, have been with us at least since 2000 or thereabouts.

3. Howey and colleagues, "Oral Report," p. 220.

4. Gladys Martinez and colleagues, "Teenagers in the United States: Sexual Activity, Contraceptive Use, and Childbearing, 2006–2010 National Survey of Family Growth," Hyattsville, Maryland: National Center for Health Statistics, *Vital Health Statistics*, volume 23, number 31, 2011, https://www.cdc.gov/nchs/data/series/sr_23/sr23_031.pdf.

5. Alexandra Hall, "The Mating Habits of the Suburban High School Teenager," *Boston*, May 2003.

6. Dr. Kass made this remark in an interview on the PBS program *The Merrow Report*, November 29, 2000, "Lessons in Courtship and Marriage."

7. This quote comes from her article, "Forget Sex in the City, Women Want Romance in Their Lives," *Washington Post*, February 9, 2003, p. B2.

8.   Hall, "Mating Habits" (cited above).

9.   Lisa Diamond, "What Does Sexual Orientation Orient? A Biobehavioral Model Distinguishing Romantic Love and Sexual Desire," *Psychological Review*, volume 110, pp. 173–192, 2003.

10. Two early reports are Sherif Karama and associates, "Areas of Brain Activation in Males and Females during Viewing of Erotic Film Excerpts," *Human Brain Mapping*, volume 16, pp. 1–13, 2002; and Stephan Hamann and colleagues, "Men and Women Differ in Amygdala Response to Visual Sexual Stimuli," *Nature Neuroscience*, volume 7, pp. 411–416, 2004. More recent reports have confirmed and extended these findings: see for example Serge Stoleru and colleagues, "Functional Neuroimaging Studies of Sexual Arousal and Orgasm in Healthy Men and Women: A Review and Meta-analysis," *Neuroscience & Biobehavioral Reviews*, volume 36, pp. 1481–1509, 2012. See also David Sylva and colleagues, "Neural Correlates of Sexual Arousal in Heterosexual and Homosexual Women and Men," *Hormones and Behavior*, volume 64, pp. 673–684, 2013.

11. See Stoleru and colleagues, "Functional Neuroimaging Studies of Sexual Arousal and Orgasm," previous citation; and also Sylva and colleagues, "Neural Correlates of Sexual Arousal in Heterosexual and Homosexual Women and Men," previous citation.

12. Marisela Hernandez-Gonzalez and colleagues, "Sexual Arousal Decreases the Functional Synchronization Between Cortical Areas in Young Men," *Journal of Sex & Marital Therapy*, volume 39, pp. 264–279, 2013.

13. Letitia Anne Peplau, "Human Sexuality: How Do Men and Women Differ?" *Current Directions in Psychological Science*, volume 12, pp. 37–44, 2003.

14. Neil Malamuth, "Rape Proclivity Among Males," *Journal of Social Issues*, volume 37, pp. 138–157, 1981.

15. Neil Malamuth, "Testing Hypotheses Regarding Rape: Exposure to Sexual Violence, Sex Differences, and the 'Normality' of Rapists," *Journal of Research in Personality*, volume 14, pp. 121–137, 1980.

16. Ana Bridges and colleagues, "Aggression and Sexual Behavior in Best-Selling Pornography Videos: A Content Analysis Update," *Violence Against Women*, volume 16, pp. 1065–1085, 2010.

17. Taylor Kohut and colleagues, "Is Pornography *Really* About 'Making Hate to Women'? Pornography Users Hold More Gender Egalitarian Attitudes Than Nonusers in a Representative American Sample," *Journal of Sex Research*, volume 53, pp. 1–11, 2016.

18. Sarah Murnen and colleagues, "A Meta-analytic Review of the Research That Relates Masculine Ideology to Sexual Aggression," *Sex Roles*, volume 46, pp. 359–375, 2002.

19. Anthony Bogaert and colleagues, "Intellectual Ability and Reactions to Pornography," *Journal of Sex Research*, volume 36, pp. 283–291, 1999.

20. Erik Hedegaard, "The Dirty Mind and Lonely Heart of John Mayer," *Rolling Stone*, June 6, 2012, www.rollingstone.com/music/news/the-dirty-mind-and-lonely-heart-of-john-mayer-20120606.

21. Roy Baumeister, "Gender Differences in Erotic Plasticity: The Female Sex Drive as Socially Flexible and Responsive," *Psychological Bulletin*, volume 126, pp. 247–274, 2000.

22. Joan Jacobs Brumberg, *The Body Project: An Intimate History of American Girls* (New York: Random House, 1997), p. 190.

23. Anne Jarrell, "The Face of Teenage Sex Grows Younger," *New York Times*, April 2, 2000.

24. Peggy Orenstein, *Girls and Sex: Navigating the Complicated New Landscape* (New York: Harper, 2016), p. 54.

25. Stephen Eyre and Susan Millstein, "What Leads to Sex? Adolescent Preferred Partners and Reasons for Sex," *Journal of Research on Adolescence*, volume 9, pp. 277–307, 1999.

26. This quote comes from Whitehead's article "Forget Sex in the City, Women Want Romance in Their Lives," *Washington Post*, February 9, 2003, p. B2.

27. Natalie Kitroeff, "In Hookups, Inequality Still Reigns," *New York Times*, November 11, 2013, http://well.blogs.nytimes.com/2013/11/11/women -find-orgasms-elusive-in-hookups/?_r=0. See also Elizabeth Armstrong, Paula England, and Alison Fogarty, "Orgasm in College Hookups and Relationships," *Families As They Really Are* (New York: W. W. Norton, 2009), pp. 362–377.

28. Dr. Pinsky made these remarks as a guest on the NPR program *Fresh Air*, September 24, 2003. To listen, go to http://www.npr.org/programs/fresh-air /archive?date=9-24-2003, scroll down to "Dr. Drew Pinsky" and click the play button. See also Dr. Pinsky's book *Cracked: Putting Broken Lives Together Again* (New York: HarperCollins, 2003), especially chapter 10, pp. 111–117.

29. Catherine Grello, Deborah Welsh, and Melinda Harper, "No Strings Attached: The Nature of Casual Sex in College Students," *Journal of Sex Research*, volume 43, pp. 255–267, 2006.

30. Hanna Rosin, "Boys on the Side," *The Atlantic*, September 2012, www .theatlantic.com/magazine/archive/2012/09/boys-on-the-side/309062/.

31. Peter Wood, "The Meaning of Sex," *Weekly Standard*, May 4, 2015, www .weeklystandard.com/the-meaning-of-sex/article/928461.

32. B. Bradford Brown, "'You're Going Out with WHO?' Peer Group Influences on Adolescent Romantic Relationships," in Wyndol Furman, B. Bradford Brown, and Candice Feiring, editors, *The Development of Romantic Relationships in Adolescence* (New York: Cambridge University Press, 1999), pp. 291–329.

33. For a lucid, book-length exploration of the health benefits of marriage, which scholars call the "marriage advantage," please see Tara Parker-Pope's book *For Better: How the Surprising Science of Happy Couples Can Help Your Marriage Succeed* (New York: Plume, 2011). Parker-Pope emphasizes that the marriage advantage seems not to apply to miserable couples or to divorcing couples.

34. K. Joyner and J. Udry, "You Don't Bring Me Anything But Down: Adolescent Romance and Depression," *Journal of Health and Social Behavior*, volume 41, pp. 369–391, 2000. See also Joanne Davila, "Depressive Symptoms and Adolescent Romance: Theory, Research, and Implications," *Child Development Perspectives*, volume 2, pp. 26–31, 2008; and also Lisa Starr and Constance Hammen, "Genetic Moderation of the Association Between Adolescent Romantic Involvement and Depression: Contributions of Serotonin Transporter Gene Polymorphism, Chronic Stress, and Family Discord," *Development and Psychopathology*, volume 28, pp. 447–457, 2016.

35. Denise Hallfors and colleagues, "Which Comes First in Adolescence—Sex and Drugs or Depression?" *American Journal of Preventive Medicine*, volume 29, pp. 163–170, 2005.

36. Jane Mendle and colleagues, "Depression and Adolescent Sexual Activity in Romantic and Nonromantic Relational Contexts: A Genetically-Informative Sibling Comparison," *Journal of Abnormal Psychology*, volume 122, pp. 51–63, 2013.

37. See, for example, Aubrey Spriggs and Carolyn Halpern, "Sexual Debut Timing and Depressive Symptoms in Emerging Adulthood," *Journal of Youth and Adolescence*, volume 37, pp. 1085–1096, 2008.

38. See, for example, Catherine Grello and colleagues, "No Strings Attached," cited above.

39. Brian Soller, "Caught in a Bad Romance: Adolescent Romantic Relationships and Mental Health," *Journal of Health and Social Behavior*, volume 55, pp. 56–72, 2014.

40. Wyndol Furman and Elizabeth Wehner, "Adolescent Romantic Relationships: A Developmental Perspective," in *Romantic Relationships in Adolescence: Developmental Perspectives*, edited by Shmuel Shulman and Andrew Collins (San Francisco: Wiley/ Jossey-Bass, 1997), pp. 23, 27.

41. National Campaign to Prevent Teen Pregnancy, *14 and Younger: The Sexual Behavior of Young Adolescents* (Washington, DC: 2003), summary at http://thenationalcampaign.org/resource/14-and-younger-sexual-behavior -young-adolescents. See also Conduct Problems Prevention Research Group, "Trajectories of Risk for Early Sexual Activity and Early Substance Use in the Fast Track Prevention Program," *Prevention Science*, volume 15, pp. 33–46, 2014.

Chapter 7: Drugs and Alcohol

1.   CASA: Center on Addiction and Substance Abuse, *The Formative Years: Pathways to Substance Abuse Among Girls and Young Women Ages 8–22*. In chapter 5, see the heading "Concerns about Weight and Appearance Increase Risk," on pp. 42–45. The report is online at www.centeronaddiction.org /addiction-research/reports/formative-years-pathways-substance-abuse-among -girls-and-young-women-ages.

2.   Dreama Moon and associates, "Ethnic and Gender Differences and Similarities in Adolescent Drug Use and Refusals of Drug Offers," *Substance Use and Misuse*, volume 34, pp. 1059–1083, 1999.

3.   Elisabeth Simantov, Cathy Schoen, and Jonathan Klein, "Health-Compromising Behaviors: Why Do Adolescents Smoke or Drink?" *Archives of Pediatrics and Adolescent Medicine*, volume 154, pp. 1025–1033, 2000.

4.   Emmanuel Kuntsche and colleagues, "Drinking Motives Mediate Cultural Differences but Not Gender Differences in Adolescent Alcohol Use," *Journal of Adolescent Health*, volume 56, pp. 323–329, 2015. See also Emmanuel Kuntsche and colleagues, "Disentangling Gender and Age Effects on Risky Single Occasion Drinking During Adolescence," *European Journal of Public Health*, volume 16, pp. 670–675, 2006.

5.   See, for example, Kirsti Kumpulainen and Saija Roine, "Depressive Symptoms at the Age of 12 Years and Future Heavy Alcohol Use," *Addictive Behaviors*, volume 27, pp. 425–436, 2002. See also John Hoffmann and Susan Su, "Stressful Life Events and Adolescent Substance Use and Depression: Conditional and Gender Differentiated Effects," *Substance Use and Misuse*, volume 33, pp. 2219–2262, 1998.

6.   Michele Moore and Chad Werch, "Sport and Physical Activity Participation and Substance Use Among Adolescents," *Journal of Adolescent Health*, volume 36, pp. 486–493, 2005. In an earlier study Deborah Aaron and her colleagues at the University of Pittsburgh found that boys who played sports were slightly *more* likely to drink alcohol, whereas playing sports had a *protective* effect for the girls. Playing sports decreased the likelihood that a girl would smoke cigarettes, for example. See Deborah Aaron and associates, "Physical Activity and the Initiation of High-Risk Health Behaviors in Adolescents," *Medicine and Science in Sports & Exercise*, volume 27, pp. 1639–1645, 1995.

7.   Katherine M. Keyes, Guohua Li, and Deborah S. Hasin, "Birth Cohort Effects

and Gender Differences in Alcohol Epidemiology: A Review and Synthesis," *Alcoholism: Clinical and Experimental Research*, volume 35, pp. 2101–2112, 2011.

8.   My discussion of alcohol use in this section is adapted and updated from chapter 3 of my book *Girls on the Edge* (New York: Basic Books, 2011).

9.   See Almila Erol and Victor Karpyak, "Sex and Gender-Related Differences in Alcohol Use and Its Consequences: Contemporary Knowledge and Future Research Considerations," *Drug and Alcohol Dependence*, volume 156, pp. 1–13, 2015. See also Enrique Baraona and colleagues, "Gender Differences in Pharmacokinetics of Alcohol," *Alcoholism: Clinical and Experimental Research*, volume 25, pp. 502–507, 2001; and also the National Institute on Alcohol Abuse and Alcoholism, "Are Women More Vulnerable to Alcohol's Effects?" *Alcohol Alert*, number 46 (1999), online at http://pubs.niaaa.nih.gov/publications/aa46 .htm. For an investigation of similar sex differences in laboratory animals, see Silvia Alfonso-Loeches and colleagues, "Gender Differences in Alcohol-Induced Neurotoxicity and Brain Damage," *Toxicology*, volume 311, pp. 27–34, 2013.

10.   See, for example, Krista Medina and colleagues, "Prefrontal Cortex Volumes in Adolescents with Alcohol Use Disorders: Unique Gender Effects," *Alcoholism: Clinical and Experimental Research*, volume 32, pp. 386–394, 2008. These researchers found that teenage girls (ages fifteen to seventeen) with alcohol-use disorders had smaller prefrontal cortices than girls who didn't drink; but that wasn't true for male adolescents. Among adults, men and women who drink heavily both have smaller PFCs than nondrinkers. See also K. Mann and colleagues, "Neuroimaging of Gender Differences in Alcohol Dependence: Are Women More Vulnerable?" *Alcoholism: Clinical and Experimental Research*, volume 29, pp. 896–901, 2005. They concluded that "brain atrophy [caused by alcohol] seems to develop faster in women."

11.   Krista Lisdahl Medina and colleagues, "Prefrontal cortex volumes in adolescents with alcohol use disorders: unique gender effects," *Alcoholism: Clinical and Experimental Research*, volume 32, pp. 386–394, 2008.

12.   See Timo Kvamme and colleagues, "Sexually Dimorphic Brain Volume Interaction in College-Aged Binge Drinkers," *NeuroImage: Clinical*, volume 10, pp. 310–317, 2016. Similar dimorphic findings reported by Lindsay Squeglia and colleagues, "Binge Drinking Differentially Affects Adolescent Male and Female Brain Morphometry," *Psychopharmacology*, volume 220, pp. 529–539, 2012. For a review, see Lynda Sharrett-Field, "Sex Differences in Neuroadaptation to Alcohol and Withdrawal Neurotoxicity," *European Journal of Physiology*, volume 465, pp. 643–654, 2013.

13.   K. T. Foster and colleagues, "Gender Differences in the Structure of Risk for Alcohol Use Disorder in Adolescence and Young Adulthood," *Psychological Medicine*, volume 45, pp. 3047–3058, 2015.

Chapter 8: Social Media and Video Games

1.   I've had some interesting conversations with students on this topic. Sometimes, after the end of my public conversation with the students, a student will come up to me and tell me that she *does* keep a diary, but she didn't want to raise her hand and say so publicly, in front of the other students, because keeping a diary is now seen as something that only geeks do. So it is possible that the number of hands raised in a public setting may lead to an underestimate of the number of kids who are keeping a diary.

2.   Susan Herring and Sanja Kapidzic, "Teens, Gender, and Self-Presentation in

Social Media" in *International Encyclopedia of Social and Behavioral Sciences*, 2nd ed., ed. J. D. Wright (Oxford: Elsevier, 2015), pp. 146–152, full text online at http://info.ils.indiana.edu/~herring/teens.gender.pdf.

3.   Jessica Ringrose and colleagues, "Teen Girls, Sexual Double Standards, and Sexting: Gendered Value in Digital Image Exchange," *Feminist Theory*, volume 14, pp. 305–323, 2013.

4.   Nicola Doring and colleagues, "How Gender-Stereotypical Are Selfies? A Content Analysis and Comparison with Magazine Adverts," *Computers in Human Behavior*, volume 55, pp. 955–962, 2016. These scholars found that on several dimensions, girls' self-presentation on Instagram was *more* sexist and objectified than what was typical in magazine advertisements. See also the recent scholarly paper by Izaskun Sarabia and Ana Estevez, "Sexualized Behaviors on Facebook," *Computers in Human Behavior*, volume 61, pp. 219–226, 2016.

5.   Elizabeth Daniels and Eileen Zurbriggen, "The Price of Sexy: Viewers' Perceptions of a Sexualized Versus Nonsexualized Facebook Profile Photography," *Psychology of Popular Media Culture*, volume 5, pp. 2–14, 2016.

6.   Marsha Gabriel and colleagues, "Narcissistic Illusions in Self-Evaluations of Intelligence and Attractiveness," *Journal of Personality*, volume 62, pp. 143–155, 1994.

7.   Sarah Kate Bearman, Erin Martinez, and Eric Stice, "The Skinny on Body Dissatisfaction: A Longitudinal Study of Adolescent Girls and Boys," *Journal of Youth and Adolescence*, volume 35, pp. 217–229, 2006.

8.   Sylvia Beyer, "Gender Differences in Self-Perception and Negative Recall Biases," *Sex Roles*, volume 38, pp. 103–133, 1998.

9.   Emily Grijalva, "Gender Differences in Narcissism: A Meta-analytic Review," *Psychological Bulletin*, volume 141, pp. 261–310, 2015. Researchers have noted that the neural substrate for narcissism may differ, quite radically, for females compared with males: see the article by Wenjing Yang and colleagues, "Gender Differences in Brain Structure and Resting-State Functional Connectivity Related to Narcissistic Personality," *Scientific Reports*, volume 5, article number 10924, 2015, online at www.nature.com/articles/srep10924.

10. Jacqueline Nesi and Mitchell Prinstein, "Using Social Media for Social Comparison and Feedback-Seeking: Gender and Popularity Moderate Associations with Depressive Symptoms," *Journal of Abnormal Child Psychology*, volume 43, pp. 1427–1438, 2015.

11. Susan C. Herring and Sanja Kapidzic, "Teens, Gender, and Self-Presentation in Social Media," *International Encyclopedia of Social and Behavioral Sciences*, 2nd edition, pp. 146–152, 2015.

12. Amanda Kimbrough and colleagues, "Gender Differences in Mediated Communication: Women Connect More Than Do Men," *Computers in Human Behavior*, volume 29, pp. 896–900, 2013.

13. Robert Fairlie, "Do Boys and Girls Use Computers Differently, and Does It Contribute to Why Boys Do Worse in School Than Girls?" IZA Discussion Papers, No. 9302, 2015, online at www.econstor.eu/bitstream/10419/120955/1/dp9302.pdf.

14. In the *Phaedo* Socrates tells Simmias that "a true philosopher" will "depart [from life] with joy" and that philosophy itself is "the practice of death," i.e., facing the prospect of one's own death cheerfully. The full text of the *Phaedo* is online at http://classics.mit.edu/Plato/phaedo.html.

15. Here is the link to the latest AAP guidelines for children under five years of

age, "Media and Young Minds": http://pediatrics.aappublications.org/content /pediatrics/138/5/e20162591.full.pdf. Here is the link to the AAP guidelines for children ages five to seventeen, "Media Use in School-Aged Children and Adolescents": http://pediatrics.aappublications.org/content/pediatrics/138/5 /e20162592.full.pdf.

16. Robert Fairlie, "Do Boys and Girls Use Computers Differently, and Does It Contribute to Why Boys Do Worse in School than Girls?" IZA Discussion Papers, No. 9302, 2015, online at www.econstor.eu/bitstream/10419/120955/1 /dp9302.pdf. See also Karla Hamlen, "Re-examing Gender Differences in Video Game Play: Time Spent and Feelings of Success," *Journal of Educational Computing Research*, volume 43, pp. 293–308, 2010.

17. Mark Griffiths and Nigel Hunt, "Dependence on Computer Games by Adolescents," *Psychological Reports*, volume 82, pp. 475–480, 1998. See also Rani Desai and colleagues, "Video Game Playing in High School Students: Health Correlates, Gender Differences and Problematic Gaming," *Pediatrics*, volume 126, pp. e1414–e1424, 2010; also Mark Griffiths and colleagues, "Video Game Addiction: Past, Present, and Future," *Current Psychiatry Reviews*, volume 8, pp. 308–318, 2012; also Gi Jung Hyun and colleagues, "Risk Factors Associated with Online Game Addiction: A Hierarchical Model," *Computers in Human Behavior*, volume 48, pp. 706–713, 2015; and also Sacip Toker and Meltem Baturay, "Antecedents and Consequences of Game Addiction," *Computers in Human Behavior*, volume 55, pp. 668–679, 2016.

18. Yvonne Yau and colleagues, "Are Internet Use and Video-Game-Playing Addictive Behaviors? Biological, Clinical, and Public Health Implications for Youths and Adults," *Minerva psichiatrica*, volume 53, pp. 153–170, 2012. See also Jeanne Funk and colleagues, "Preference for Violent Electronic Games, Self-Concept and Gender Differences in Young Children," *American Journal of Orthopsychiatry*, volume 70, pp. 233–241, 2000.

19. Fumiko Hoeft, "Gender Differences in the Mesocorticolimbic System During Computer Game-Play," *Journal of Psychiatric Research*, volume 42, pp. 253–258, 2008.

20. I have adapted much of the information in this section from chapter 3 of my book *Boys Adrift: The Growing Epidemic of Unmotivated Boys and Underachieving Young Men* (New York: Basic Books, Second Edition, 2015).

21. The simplest way to watch the commercial is to go to YouTube and enter "Greatness Awaits, PS4" in the search box.

22. Marc Sestir and Bruce Bartholow, "Violent and Nonviolent Video Games Produce Opposing Effects on Aggressive and Prosocial Outcomes," *Journal of Experimental Social Psychology*, volume 46, pp. 934–942, 2010. See also Muniba Saleem, Craig Anderson, and Douglas Gentile, "Effects of Prosocial, Neutral, and Violent Video Games on College Students' Affect," *Aggressive Behavior*, volume 38, pp. 263–271, 2012.

23. Bruce Bartholow and colleagues, "Chronic Violent Video Game Exposure and Desensitization to Violence: Behavioral and Event-Related Brain Potential Data," *Journal of Experimental Social Psychology*, volume 42, pp. 532–539, 2006. See also Tom Hummer and colleagues, "Short-Term Violent Video Game Play by Adolescents Alters Prefrontal Activity During Cognitive Inhibition," *Media Psychology*, volume 13, pp. 136–154, 2010.

24. Christopher Barlett and Christopher Rodeheffer, "Effects of Realism on Extended Violent and Nonviolent Video Game Play on Aggressive Thoughts,

Feelings, and Physiological Arousal," *Aggressive Behavior*, volume 35, pp. 213–224, 2009.

25. Craig Anderson and colleagues, "Violent Video Game Effects on Aggression, Empathy, and Prosocial Behavior in Eastern and Western Countries: A Meta-analytic Review," *Psychological Bulletin*, volume 136, pp. 151–173, 2010. For a thoughtful comment on this paper—observing that some doubters will never be persuaded, no matter how strong the evidence—see L. Rowell Huesmann, "Nailing the Coffin Shut on Doubts That Violent Video Games Stimulate Aggression: Comment on Anderson et al. 2010," *Psychological Bulletin*, volume 136, pp. 179–181, 2010.

26. See Craig Anderson, "Violent Video Games: Myths, Facts, and Unanswered Questions," *Psychological Science Agenda*, volume 16, October 2003; full text available online at www.apa.org/science/about/psa/2003/10/anderson.aspx.

27. *Brown v. Entertainment Merchants Association*, 564 U.S. 786 (2011) (Alito, S., dissenting). The full text of the case, including Justice Alito's concurrence, is online at www.supremecourt.gov/opinions/10pdf/08-1448.pdf; the quotes in this paragraph come from pp. 12 and 14 of the concurrence.

28. You can read Professor Anderson's guidelines in full at this link: www.psychology.iastate.edu/faculty/caa/VG_recommendations.html.

29. Patrick Welsh, "It's No Contest: Boys Will Be Men, and They'll Still Choose Video Games," *Washington Post*, December 5, 2004, p. B1.

30. Tamar Lewin, "At Colleges, Women Are Leaving Men in the Dust," *New York Times*, July 9, 2006, pp. A1, A18, A19.

31. Lewin, "At Colleges, Women Are Leaving," pp. A18, A19.

32. Craig Anderson, Douglas Gentile, and Katherine Buckley, *Violent Video Game Effects on Children and Adolescents* (New York: Oxford University Press, 2007), p. 66.

33. Griffiths and Hunt, "Dependence on Computer Games by Adolescents."

Chapter 9: Gender Nonconforming

1. Wendy Waters, Michael Ziegler, and Janice Meck, "Postspaceflight Orthostatic Hypotension Occurs Mostly in Women and Is Predicted by Low Vascular Resistance," *Journal of Applied Physiology*, volume 92, pp. 586–594, 2002. More recent research suggests that individuals prone to orthostatic hypotension (both men and women) can be helped by customized training protocols: see for example Nandu Goswami and colleagues, "Effects of Individualized Centrifugation Training on Orthostatic Tolerance in Men and Women," *PLOS One*, May 28, 2015, http://journals.plos.org/plosone/article?id=10.1371/journal.pone.0125780.

2. Kagan called these boys "highly reactive," but that term can be confusing because in some circumstances these boys are shy, passive, and withdrawn while other boys are outgoing and assertive.

3. Jerome Kagan and colleagues, "Temperament and Allergic Symptoms," *Psychosomatic Medicine*, volume 53, pp. 332–340, 1991. See also Iris Bell and colleagues, "Is Allergic Rhinitis More Frequent in Young Adults with Extreme Shyness?" *Psychosomatic Medicine*, volume 52, pp. 517–525, 1990; and also Anne-Charlotte Lilljeqvist, Dag Smørvik, and Asbjørn Faleide, "Temperamental Differences Between Healthy, Asthmatic, and Allergic Children Before Onset of Illness," *Journal of Genetic Psychology*, volume 163, pp. 219–227, 2002.

4. Doreen Arcus and Jerome Kagan, "Temperament and Craniofacial Variation in the First Two Years," *Child Development*, volume 66, pp. 1529–1540, 1995.

5. Shawn Geniole and colleagues, "Fearless Dominance Mediates the Relationships Between the Facial Width-to-Height Ratio and Willingness to Cheat," *Personality and Individual Differences*, volume 57, pp. 59–64, 2014.

6. See for example Vit Trebicky and colleagues, "Further Evidence for Links Between Facial Width-to-Height Ratio and Fighting Success," *Aggressive Behavior*, volume 41, pp. 331–334, 2015.

7. Jerome Kagan, *Galen's Prophecy: Temperament in Human Nature* (New York: Basic Books, 1994), especially chapter 6, "Early Predictors of the Two Types."

8. Patricia Cayo Sexton, *The Feminized Male: Classrooms, White Collars, and the Decline of Manliness* (New York: Random House, 1969).

9. The song is "I Am a Rock," from the Simon & Garfunkel album *Sounds of Silence*, first released in January 1966.

10. Sexton, *Feminized Male*, p. 35.

11. Jerome Kagan, *Galen's Prophecy: Temperament in Human Nature* (New York: Basic Books, 1994), p. 205.

12. Kagan, *Galen's Prophecy*, pp. 204–207.

13. Sexton, *Feminized Male*, p. 129.

14. When I say "or from themselves," I am thinking of the extraordinary case of Theodore Roosevelt. As a child, Teddy Roosevelt was frail and timid, stayed indoors, and avoided sports. He was asthmatic. Late in adolescence he deliberately reinvented himself as a warrior. He became an outdoorsman and a cowboy, a Rough Rider. And he outgrew his asthma. The Cuban revolutionary Che Guevara may also fit this pattern.

15. Sexton, *Feminized Male*, p. 93.

16. Katherine Green and Malcolm Gynther, "Blue Versus Periwinkle: Color Identification and Gender," *Perceptual and Motor Skills*, volume 80, pp. 27–32, 1995. See also Dimitris Mylonas, Galina Paramei, and Lindsay MacDonald, "Gender Differences in Colour Naming," Section III, pp. 225–239 in *Colour Studies: A Broad Spectrum*, edited by Wendy Anderson and colleagues, Amsterdam: John Benjamins Publishing, 2014.

17. See my comments about Theodore Roosevelt and Che Guevara, note 14 above.

18. See, for example, Bonnie Auyeung and colleagues, "Prenatal and Postnatal Hormone Effects on the Human Brain and Cognition," *European Journal of Physiology*, volume 465, pp. 557–571, 2013.

19. Hyu Jung Kang and colleagues, "Spatio-temporal Transcriptome of the Human Brain," *Nature*, volume 478, pp. 483–489, 2011.

20. Anton Aluja and colleagues, "Interactions Among Impulsiveness, Testosterone, Sex Hormone Binding Globulin and Androgen Receptor Gene CAG Repeat Length," *Physiology & Behavior*, volume 147, pp. 91–96, 2015. See also Michael Zitzmann and Eberhard Nieschlag, "The CAG Repeat Polymorphism Within the Androgen Receptor Gene and Maleness," *International Journal of Andrology*, volume 26, pp. 76–83, 2003.

21. Stuart Seidman and colleagues, "Testosterone Level, Androgen Receptor Polymorphism, and Depressive Symptoms in Middle-Aged Men," *Biological Psychiatry*, volume 50, pp. 371–376, 2001.

22. Aluja, 2015 (cited above).

23. See for example Marina Butovskaya and colleagues, "Androgen Receptor Gene Polymorphism, Aggression, and Reproduction in Tanzanian Foragers and Pastoralists," *PLOS One*, August 20, 2015, http://dx.doi.org/10.1371/journal

.pone.0136208; and also Singh Rajender and colleagues, "Reduced CAG Repeats Length in Androgen Receptor Gene Is Associated with Violent Criminal Behavior," *International Journal of Legal Medicine*, volume 122, pp. 367–372, 2008.

24. Akitsugu Konno and colleagues, "Androgen Receptor Gene Polymorphisms Are Associated with Aggression in Japanese Akita Inu," *Biology Letters*, volume 7, pp. 658–660, 2011, full text online at http://rsbl.royalsocietypublishing.org /content/roybiolett/7/5/658.full.pdf.

Chapter 10: Lesbian, Gay, Bisexual

1. I have updated this story from the first edition of *Why Gender Matters*. The actual story, as this boy's parents told it to me around 2000, was that Mom found gay porn *magazines* under her son's bed. However, boys today rarely look at porn in printed magazines. They are much more likely to look at porn on their phones.

2. J. Michael Bailey and colleagues, "Sexual Orientation, Controversy, and Science," *Psychological Science in the Public Interest*, volume 17, pp. 45–101, 2016.

3. Lillian Faderman, *The Gay Revolution: The Story of the Struggle* (New York: Simon & Schuster, 2015), p. 546.

4. Siobhan Fenton, "LGBT Relationships Are Illegal in 74 Countries, Research Finds," *Independent*, May 17, 2016.

5. David McCullough, *Truman* (New York: Simon & Schuster, 1993), p. 43.

6. J. Michael Bailey and Richard Pillard, "A Genetic Study of Male Sexual Orientation," *Archives of General Psychiatry*, volume 48, pp. 1089–1096, 1991.

7. J. Michael Bailey and colleagues, "Genetic and Environmental Influences on Sexual Orientation and Its Correlates in an Australian Twin Sample," *Journal of Personality and Social Psychology*, volume 78, pp. 524–536, 2000.

8. Niklas Långström and colleagues, "Genetic and Environmental Effects on Same-Sex Sexual Behavior: A Population Study of Twins in Sweden," *Archives of Sexual Behavior*, volume 39, pp. 75–80, 2010.

9. Bailey and colleagues, "Sexual Orientation, Controversy, and Science," 2016.

10. Ray Blanchard and Anthony Bogaert, "Homosexuality in Men and Number of Older Brothers," *American Journal of Psychiatry*, volume 153, pp. 27–31, 1996.

11. Anthony Bogaert, "Biological Versus Nonbiological Older Brothers and Men's Sexual Orientation," *Proceedings of the National Academy of Sciences*, volume 103, pp. 10771–10774, 2006.

12. Roy Blanchard and colleagues, "The Relation of Birth Order to Sexual Orientation in Men and Women," *Journal of Biosocial Science*, volume 30, pp. 511–519, 1998.

13. Ray Blanchard, "Fraternal Birth Order and the Maternal Immune Hypothesis of Male Homosexuality," *Hormones and Behavior*, volume 40, pp. 105–114, 2001. See also Anthony Bogaert and Malvina Skorska, "Sexual Orientation, Fraternal Birth Order, and the Maternal Immune Hypothesis," *Frontiers in Neuroendocrinology*, volume 32, pp. 247–254, 2011.

14. J. Michael Bailey, "Gay Femininity," in *The Man Who Would Be Queen: The Science of Gender-Bending and Transsexualism* (Washington, DC: National Academies Press, 2003), pp. 61–84.

15. Nicholas Fonseca, "They're Here! They're Queer! And They Don't Like Your End Tables!" *Entertainment Weekly*, August 8, 2003, pp. 24–28. This was the cover story for the August 8 issue of *Entertainment Weekly*. The cover proclaimed the show to be the "summer's outrageous breakout hit." The last episode of the

broadcast show aired in October 2007, although there is word that Netflix may revive the series: see http://ew.com/tv/2017/01/24/netflix-queer-eye-for-the -straight-guy/.

16. Louis Bayard, "Not All of Us Can Accessorize," *Washington Post*, August 10, 2003, p. B2.

17. Anthony D'Augelli and colleagues, "Gender Atypicality and Sexual Orientation Development Among Lesbian, Gay, and Bisexual Youth," *Journal of Gay & Lesbian Mental Health*, volume 12, pp. 121–143, 2008. See also Daryl Bem, "Is There a Causal Link Between Childhood Gender Nonconformity and Adult Homosexuality?" *Journal of Gay & Lesbian Mental Health*, volume 12, pp. 61–79, 2008.

18. Kenneth Zucker, "Reflections on the Relation Between Sex-Typed Behavior in Childhood and Sexual Orientation in Adulthood," *Journal of Gay & Lesbian Mental Health*, volume 12, pp. 29–59, 2008. See also Richard Green, "Childhood Cross-Gender Behavior and Adult Homosexuality," *Journal of Gay & Lesbian Mental Health*, volume 12, pp. 17–28, 2008.

19. Alan Bell, Martin Weinberg, and Sue Hammersmith, *Sexual Preference: Its Development in Men and Women* (Bloomington: Indiana University Press, 1981).

20. Letitia Anne Peplau and Mark Huppin, "Masculinity, Femininity and the Development of Sexual Orientation in Women," *Journal of Gay & Lesbian Mental Health*, volume 12, pp. 145–165, 2008.

21. Gerulf Rieger and colleagues, "Sexual Orientation and Childhood Gender Nonconformity: Evidence from Home Videos," *Developmental Psychology*, volume 44, pp. 46–58, 2008.

22. J. Michael Bailey and colleagues, "Effects of Gender and Sexual Orientation on Evolutionarily Relevant Aspects of Human Mating Psychology," *Journal of Personality and Social Psychology*, volume 66, pp. 1081–1093, 1994.

23. William Masters and Virginia Johnson, *Homosexuality in Perspective* (Philadelphia: Lippincott, Williams & Wilkins, 1979).

24. Donald Symons, *The Evolution of Human Sexuality* (New York: Oxford University Press, 1979), p. 300.

25. Meredith Chivers, J. Michael Bailey, and colleagues, "A Sex Difference in the Specificity of Sexual Arousal," *Psychological Science*, volume 15, pp. 736–744, 2004. These comments are based on Figure 2, p. 740.

26. Again, see Chivers and colleagues 2004, Figure 2, p. 740 (previous citation).

27. And once again, see Chivers and colleagues 2004, figure 2, p. 740. See also Meredith Chivers and colleagues, "Gender and Sexual Orientation Differences in Sexual Response to Sexual Activities Versus Gender of Actors in Sexual Films," *Journal of Personality and Social Psychology*, volume 93, pp. 1108–1121, 2007.

28. J. Michael Bailey, "What Is Sexual Orientation and Do Women Have One?" in D. A. Hope (editor), *Contemporary Perspectives on Lesbian, Gay, and Bisexual Identities* (New York: Springer, 2009), pp. 43–63.

29. *Huffington Post*, "Ke$ha Bisexual: Pop Star Says She Doesn't 'Love Just Men,'" January 2, 2013, www.huffingtonpost.com/2013/01/02/kesha-bisexual-pop-star -doesnt-love-just-men_n_2396180.html.

30. Korin Miller, "Miley Cyrus Identifies as Pansexual. What Does That Mean, Exactly?" *Yahoo! Beauty*, August 28, 2015, www.yahoo.com/beauty/miley-cyrus -identifies-as-pansexual-what-does-127797473807.html.

31. See, for example, Benedict Carey, "Straight, Gay or Lying? Bisexuality Revisited," *New York Times*, July 5, 2005.

32. Joe Stokes and colleagues, "Predictors of Movement Toward Homosexuality:

A Longitudinal Study of Bisexual Men," *Journal of Sex Research*, volume 34, pp. 304–312, 1997.

33. Gerulf Rieger, Meredith Chivers, and J. Michael Bailey, "Sexual Arousal Patterns of Bisexual Men," *Psychological Science*, volume 16, pp. 579–584, 2005. The quote is from page 582.

34. National Public Radio, "Bisexuality Study," *Day to Day*, July 5, 2005, www.npr .org/templates/story/story.php?storyId=4730109.

35. A. M. Rosenthal, J. Michael Bailey, and colleagues, "The Male Bisexuality Debate Revisited: Some Bisexual Men Have Bisexual Arousal Patterns," *Archives of Sexual Behavior*, volume 41, pp. 135–147, 2012.

36. However, the more recent article *was* mentioned in an article in the *New York Times* Sunday magazine—more than two years after publication. See Benoit Denizet-Lewis, "The Scientific Quest to Prove Bisexuality Exists," March 20, 2014, www.nytimes.com/2014/03/23/magazine/the-scientific-quest-to-prove -bisexuality-exists.html.

37. Lisa Diamond, "Was It a Phase? Young Women's Relinquishment of Lesbian/ Bisexual Identities over a 5-Year Period," *Journal of Personality and Social Psychology*, volume 84, pp. 352–364, 2003.

38. See, for example, Cindy Hazan and Phillip Shaver, "Romantic Love Conceptualized as an Attachment Process," *Journal of Personality and Social Psychology*, volume 52, pp. 511–524, 1987; and Cindy Hazan and Phillip Shaver, "Love and Work: An Attachment-Theoretical Perspective," *Journal of Personality and Social Psychology*, volume 59, pp. 270–280, 1990.

39. Lisa Diamond, "What Does Sexual Orientation Orient? A Biobehavioral Model Distinguishing Romantic Love and Sexual Desire," *Psychological Review*, volume 110, pp. 173–192, 2003. The quotation comes from page 175.

40. Michael Marshal and colleagues, "Suicidality and Depression Disparities Between Sexual Minority and Heterosexual Youth: A Meta-analytic Review," *Journal of Adolescent Health*, volume 49, pp. 115–123, 2011. See also Alexa Martin-Storey and Robert Crosnoe, "Sexual Minority Status, Peer Harassment and Adolescent Depression," *Journal of Adolescence*, volume 35, pp. 1001–1011, 2012.

41. Mark Hatzenbuehler, "The Social Environment and Suicide Attempts in Lesbian, Gay, and Bisexual Youth," *Pediatrics*, volume 127, pp. 896–903, 2011.

42. Michael Marshal and colleagues, "Sexual Orientation and Adolescent Substance Use: A Meta-analysis and Methodological Review," *Addiction*, volume 103, pp. 546–556, 2008.

43. Elizabeth McConnell and colleagues, "Typologies of Social Support and Associations with Mental Health Outcomes Among LGBT Youth," *LGBT Health*, volume 2, pp. 55–61, 2015; and also Dorothy Espelage and colleagues, "Homophobic Teasing, Psychological Outcomes, and Sexual Orientation Among High School Students: What Influence Do Parents and Schools Have?" *School Psychology Review*, volume 37, pp. 202–216, 2008; and also Caitlin Ryan and colleagues, "Family Acceptance in Adolescence and the Health of LGBT Young Adults," *Journal of Child and Adolescent Psychiatric Nursing*, volume 23, pp. 205–213, 2010.

44. Ian Moss, "Ending Reparative Therapy in Minors: An Appropriate Legislative Response," *Family Court Review*, volume 52, pp. 316–329, 2014.

45. Ron de Graaf and colleagues, "Suicidality and Sexual Orientation: Differences Between Men and Women in a General Population-Based Sample from the Netherlands," *Archives of Sexual Behavior*, volume 35, pp. 253–262, 2006.

Chapter 11: Intersex and Transgender

1. See for example Margaret Corey and colleagues, "A Case of XX/XY Mosaicism," *American Journal of Human Genetics*, volume 19, pp. 378–387, 1967; see also Nathalie Josso and colleagues, "True Hermaphroditism with XX/XY Mosaicism, Probably Due to Double Fertilization of the Ovum," *Journal of Clinical Endocrinology & Metabolism*, volume 25, pp. 114–126, 1965.

2. More precisely, an intersex individual is one in whom the chromosomal sex is inconsistent with phenotypic sex—for example, an XY individual who appears to be female due to complete androgen insensitivity—or in which the phenotype is not classifiable as either male or female—for example, an XX/XY individual who has both an ovary and a testicle. This definition is taken from my paper "How Common is Intersex? a Response to Anne Fausto-Sterling," *Journal of Sex Research*, volume 39, pp. 174–178, 2002.

3. The exact figure was 0.018 percent, or 1.8 out of every 10,000 live births. See my article "How common is intersex?" (previous citation).

4. Milton Diamond and H. K. Sigmundson, "Sex Reassignment at Birth: Long-Term Review and Clinical Implications," *Archives of Pediatrics and Adolescent Medicine*, volume 151, pp. 298–304, 1997. Much more information about "the boy who was raised as a girl" is provided in John Colapinto's book *As Nature Made Him: The Boy Who Was Raised as a Girl* (New York: Harper, 2006).

5. This quote is not found in Reiner's scholarly paper but is taken from J. Michael Bailey, *The Man Who Would Be Queen: The Science of Gender-Bending and Transsexualism* (Washington, DC: National Academies Press, 2003), p. 49.

6. Steve Friess, "Mike Penner, Christine Daniels: A Tragic Love Story," *LA Weekly*, August 19, 2010.

7. Mike Penner, "Old Mike, New Christine," *Los Angeles Times*, April 26, 2007.

8. Rick Reilly, "Extreme Makeover," *Sports Illustrated*, July 2, 2007.

9. All quotes in this paragraph come from Steve Friess' article for *LA Weekly*, "Mike Penner, Christine Daniels: A Tragic Love Story," August 19, 2010.

10. Friess, "Mike Penner, Christine Daniels," previous citation.

11. Friess, previous citation.

12. Friess, previous citation.

13. Friess, previous citation

14. Friess, previous citation.

15. Karine Schwarz and colleagues, "Neural Correlates of Psychosis and Gender Dysphoria in an Adult Male," *Archives of Sexual Behavior*, volume 45, pp. 761–765, 2016.

16. For more about the transgender activists' successful lobbying for the ouster of Dr. Zucker, see Jesse Singal, "How the Fight over Transgender Kids Got a Leading Sex Researcher Fired," *New York Magazine*, February 7, 2016, http://nymag.com/scienceofus/2016/02/fight-over-trans-kids-got-a-researcher-fired.html.

17. See, for example, Kelley Drummond and colleagues, "A Follow-up Study of Girls with Gender Identity Disorder," *Developmental Psychology*, volume 44, pp. 34–45, 2008; Devita Singh, "A Follow-up Study of Boys with Gender Identity Disorder" Ph.D. dissertation, University of Toronto, 2012, online at http://images.nymag.com/images/2/daily/2016/01/SINGH-DISSERTATION.pdf; and Madeleine Wallien and Peggy Cohen Kettenis, "Psychosexual Outcome of Gender-Dysphoric Children," *Journal of the American Academy of Child and Adolescent Psychiatry*, volume 47, pp. 1413–1423, 2008. For a careful look at what factors predict which child will persist in the belief that they are transgender

("persistence"), vs. which child will not persist ("desistence"), see Thomas Steensma and colleagues, "Factors Associated with Desistence and Persistence of Childhood Gender Dysphoria: A Quantitative Follow-up Study," *Journal of the American Academy of Child & Adolescent Psychiatry*, volume 52, pp. 582–590, 2013.

18. Bailey, *The Man Who Would Be Queen*, p. 32.

19. Bailey, *The Man Who Would Be Queen*, Part III, "Women Who Once Were Boys."

20. Bailey, *The Man Who Would Be Queen*, pp. 197–198.

21. Bailey, *The Man Who Would Be Queen*, p. 185.

22. These data are taken from Cecilia Dhejne and colleagues, "Long-Term Follow-up of Transsexual Persons Undergoing Sex Reassignment Surgery: Cohort Study from Sweden," *PLOS One*, 2011, full text online at http://journals.plos.org /plosone/article/asset?id=10.1371/journal.pone.0016885.PDF.

23. Lauren Hare and colleagues, "Androgen Receptor Repeat Length Polymorphism Associated with Male-to-Female Transsexualism," *Biological Psychiatry*, volume 65, pp. 93–96, 2009.

24. Bailey, *The Man Who Would Be Queen*, p. 178.

25. Sebastian Schagen, Ray Blanchard, and colleagues, "Sibling Sex Ratio and Birth Order in Early-Onset Gender Dysphoric Adolescents," *Archives of Sexual Behavior*, volume 41, pp. 541–549, 2012.

26. Thomas Steensma and colleagues, "Factors Associated with Desistence and Persistence of Childhood Gender Dysphoria: A Quantitative Follow-up Study," *Journal of the American Academy of Child & Adolescent Psychiatry*, volume 52, pp. 582–590, 2013. Table 1 of this paper indicates that of the seventy-nine boys, twenty-three were persisters and fifty-six were desisters. $^{23}/_{79}$ = 29 percent. Of the forty-eight girls, twenty-four were persisters and twenty-four were desisters.

27. Kelley Drummond and colleagues, "A Follow-up Study of Girls with Gender Identity Disorder," *Developmental Psychology*, volume 44, pp. 34–45, 2008.

28. Timo Nieder and colleagues, "Age of Onset and Sexual Orientation in Transsexual Male-to-Females," *Journal of Sexual Medicine*, volume 8, pp. 783–791, 2011.

29. Amy Ellis Nutt, *Becoming Nicole: the Transformation of an American Family* (New York: Random House, 2015), p. 29.

30. Nutt, p. 95.

31. Jay Prosser, *Second Skins: The Body Narratives of Transsexuality* (New York: Columbia University Press, 1998), p. 69.

32. Marco Colizzi and colleagues, "Transsexual Patients' Psychiatric Comorbidity and Positive Effect of Cross-Hormonal Treatment on Mental Health: Results from a Longitudinal Study," *Psychoneuroendocrinology*, volume 39, pp. 65–73, 2014. See also Gunter Heylens and colleagues, "Effects of Different Steps in Gender Reassignment Therapy on Psychopathology: A Prospective Study of Persons with a Gender Identity Disorder," *Journal of Sexual Medicine*, volume 11, pp. 119–126, 2014.

33. Kenneth Zucker, Anne Lawrence, and B. P. C. Kreukels, "Gender Dysphoria in Adults," *Annual Review of Clinical Psychology*, volume 12, pp. 217–247, 2016. The quote is from page 237.

34. J. Eldh and colleagues, "Long-Term Follow up After Sex Reassignment Surgery," *Scandinavian Journal of Plastic and Reconstructive Surgery*, volume 31, pp. 39–45, 1997; T. Sørensen and P. Hertoft, "Male and Female Transsexualism: The Danish Experiences with 37 Patients," *Archives of Sexual Behavior*, volume 11, pp. 133–

155, 1982; P. J. van Kesteren and colleagues, "Mortality and Morbidity in Transsexual Subjects Treated with Cross-Sex Hormones," *Clinical Endocrinology*, volume 47, pp. 337–342, 1997; and L. J. Gooren and colleagues, "Long-Term Treatment of Transsexuals with Cross-Sex Hormones," *Journal of Clinical Endocrinology and Metabolism*, volume 93, pp. 19–25, 2008. See also Arnold Grossman and Anthony D'Augelli, "Transgender Youth and Life-Threatening Behaviors," *Suicide and Life-Threatening Behavior*, volume 37, pp. 527–537, 2007.

35. Dhejne and colleagues, "Long-Term Follow-up of Transsexual Persons," figure 1.

36. Kenneth Zucker and colleagues, "A Developmental, Biopsychosocial Model for the Treatment of Children with Gender Identity Disorder," *Journal of Homosexuality*, volume 59, pp. 369–397, 2012.

37. Quoted in Erin Anderssen, "Gender Identity Debate Swirls over CAMH Psychologist, Transgender Program," *Globe and Mail*, February 18, 2016.

38. Anderssen, "Gender Identity Debate."

39. Zucker, "Developmental, Biopsychosocial Model" (cited above).

Chapter 12: The Male/Female Mistake

1. Tina Susman, "Steubenville Rape: More Charges Possible with Grand Jury Probe," *Los Angeles Times*, March 27, 2013.

2. Lynn Messina, "I Don't Want My Preschooler to Be a 'Gentleman,'" *New York Times*, January 10, 2013.

3. For a sense of the controversy surrounding the policy of affirmative consent, you might start by reading Conor Friedersdorf, "Why One Male College Student Abandoned Affirmative Consent," *The Atlantic*, October 20, 2014; and also Sandy Keenan, "Affirmative Consent: Are Students Really Asking?" *New York Times*, July 28, 2015.

4. Richard Oppel, "Ohio Teenagers Guilty in Rape That Social Media Brought to Light," *New York Times*, March 17, 2013.

5. This summary of the career of Judith Butler is drawn from Gabriele Kuby, *The Global Sexual Revolution*, translated by James Kirchner (Kettering, OH: Angelico, 2015), pp. 47–48.

6. This quote is from the preamble to the Yogyakarta Principles, drawn up at an international conference in Indonesia in November 2006, as quoted in Kuby, *Global Sexual Revolution*, p. 67.

7. Jennifer Yunger and colleagues, "Does Gender Identity Influence Children's Psychological Well-being?" *Developmental Psychology*, volume 40, pp. 572–582, 2004; see especially table 4.

8. For more on the "trans revolution," see, for example, Vanessa Baird, "The Trans Revolution," *New Internationalist*, October 2015, https://newint.org/features/2015/10/01/the-trans-revolution-keynote/.

9. Lionel Shriver, "Gender—Good for Nothing," *Prospect*, April 21, 2016. The exact quote from Shriver's essay is "In this would-be enlightened age, in which primary schools hold 'Transgender Days' the way they used to sponsor bake sales, we urge children to see their genders as flexible, and to choose to be boys or girls or something in-between."

10. Elizabeth Reis, "Pronoun Privilege," *New York Times*, September 25, 2016.

11. Amanda Datnow, Lea Hubbard, and Elisabeth Woody, *Is Single Gender Schooling Viable in the Public Sector?* (New York: Ford Foundation, 2001), p. 51.

12. Datnow, Hubbard, and Woody, p. 7.

13. In 2014—the latest year for which data are available—40.2 percent of births in

the United States were to unmarried women. See Brady Hamilton and colleagues, "Births: Final Data for 2014," *National Vital Statistics Reports*, volume 64, number 12, December 2015, www.cdc.gov/nchs/data/nvsr/nvsr64/nvsr64_12 .pdf.

14. In 2016, according to the United States Census Bureau, there were roughly 125,819,000 households in the United States (see "America's Families and Living Arrangements: 2016: Households," Table H1, www.census.gov/hhes/families /data/cps2016H.html). Of those 125,819,000 households, roughly 23,772,000 households were married couples with children under eighteen years of age (see "America's Families and Living Arrangements: 2016: Family Households," Table F1, www.census.gov/hhes/families/data/cps2016F.html). If you divide 125,819,000 by 23,772,000, the result is 18.9 percent, i.e., less than 20 percent.

15. My discussion of the California teacher who tried to instruct boys about being a man is drawn from my discussion in chapter 8 of my book *Boys Adrift*, revised edition (New York: Basic Books, 2015).

16. The original French was *On ne naît pas femme: on le devient*. In the first English translation of *The Second Sex*, the translator, H. M. Parshley, translated this as "One is not born, but rather becomes, a woman." As a more recent translator, Constance Borde, has observed, there is no indefinite article in the original French, so a more accurate translation might arguably be "one is not born, but rather becomes, woman." For more on why this matters, see Simone de Beauvoir, *The Second Sex*, translated by Constance Borde (New York: Vintage, 2011), p. xviii.

17. This quotation is from Charlotte Allen's article "The Transgender Triumph," *Weekly Standard*, March 2, 2015.

18. For a feminist analysis of the problems with the word "TERF," see Rebecca Reilly-Cooper, "The Word 'TERF,'" November 1, 2016, https://rebeccarc .com/2016/11/01/the-word-terf/.

19. At least four women's colleges now admit transwomen, i.e., males who have transitioned to the female role: Mount Holyoke, Mills College, Simmons College, and Bryn Mawr. See Allen, "Transgender Triumph."

20. Quoted in Allen, "The Transgender Triumph."

21. Elinor Burkitt, "What Makes a Woman?" *New York Times*, June 6, 2015.

22. Burkitt, "What Makes a Woman?"

23. Again, see the article by Jane Goodall and her associates in the *American Journal of Physical Anthropology*, "Patterns of Predation by Chimpanzees on Red Colobus Monkeys in Gombe National Park, 1982–1991," volume 94, pp. 213–228, 1994 (I cited this article in chapter 4). They found that adolescent male and adult male chimps often kill colobus monkeys. Goodall and her colleagues never saw an *adolescent* female chimp kill a monkey, and even adult female chimps rarely killed monkeys. The anthropologists identified fifteen different male chimps each of whom killed 3 or more monkeys and nine male chimps each of whom killed more than 10 monkeys. One male killed 76 monkeys. By contrast, only two female chimps killed more than 2 monkeys: one female killed 4 monkeys, and one (a female who never mated or became pregnant) killed 10 monkeys. See their Table 3, p. 220.

24. For this point—that gender is not "assigned" at birth, it is *recognized* at birth—I am grateful to Katherine Kersten's article for *First Things*, "Transgender Conformity," December 2016, online at www.firstthings.com/article/2016/12 /transgender-conformity.

25. Quoted in Kuby, *Global Sexual Revolution*, p. 94.

26. Shriver, "Gender—Good for Nothing."

27. See for example Lisa Selin Davis, "My Daughter Is Not Transgender. She's a Tomboy," *New York Times*, April 18, 2017.

28. American Psychiatric Association, *Diagnostic and Statistical Manual of Mental Disorders*, 4th edition (Washington, DC: American Psychiatric Association, 1994), p. 535.

29. A. Bakker and colleagues, "Prevalence of Transsexualism in the Netherlands," *Acta Psychiatrica Scandinavica*, volume 87, pp. 237–238, 1993.

30. Jan Hoffman, "Estimate of U.S. Transgender Population Doubles to 1.4 million Adults," *New York Times*, June 30, 2016.

31. Abbas Hyderi and colleagues, "Transgender Patients: Providing Sensitive Care," *Journal of Family Practice*, volume 65, pp. 450–461, 2016. The estimate of "0.3% to 5%" prevalence is on the opening page, p. 450.

32. Lindsay Collin and colleagues, "Prevalence of Transgender Depends on the 'Case' Definition: A Systematic Review," *Journal of Sexual Medicine*, volume 13, pp. 613–626, 2016.

33. The breakthrough article in this regard—the article that really changed the way people thought about gender, crystallizing the emerging understanding of gender as being two-dimensional rather than one-dimensional—was Alfred Heilbrun's article, "Measurement of Masculine and Feminine Sex Identities as Independent Dimensions," *Journal of Consulting and Clinical Psychology*, volume 44, pp. 183–190, 1976.

34. The figures on these pages—one-dimensional and two-dimensional—as well as much of the discussion accompanying those figures, are taken from chapter 7 of my book *Girls on the Edge* (New York: Basic Books, 2010).

35. If you're not familiar with group contrast effects, you will find a good introduction to the topic in Judith Rich Harris' book *The Nurture Assumption: Why Children Turn Out the Way They Do*, 2nd edition (New York: Simon & Schuster, 2009), chapter 7, "Us and Them," pp. 115–135.

36. For discussion of some scholarly research on group contrast effects vis-à-vis girl/boy groups, please see my discussion of this topic in my book *Girls on the Edge* (New York: Basic Books, 2010), pp. 174–177.

37. This story from Avon Old Farms is adapted from chapter 7 of my book *Boys Adrift*, 2nd edition (New York: Basic Books, 2016).

38. Heather Haupt, *Knights in Training: Ten Principles for Raising Honorable, Courageous, and Compassionate Boys* (New York: Tarcher Perigee, 2017).

39. David Gilmore, *Manhood in the Making: Cultural Concepts of Masculinity* (New Haven: Yale University Press, 1990), pp. 14–15.

40. Gilmore, p. 25.

41. This story took place in Thunder Bay in 2001, before the reform of youth justice laws in Canada. Today a Canadian boy would generally not be sent to a secure residential facility for a first-offense nonviolent crime (without bodily injury to the victim). The Youth Criminal Justice Act (YCJA) is the Canadian law that now applies to kids aged twelve to seventeen years. Prior to the YCJA, the Young Offenders Act (YOA) governed Canada's youth justice system. Under the YOA, Canada had one of the highest youth custody rates among Western countries, higher even than the United States. On April 1, 2003, the YCJA replaced the YOA. For more on this point, see JoAnn Miller-Reid, "Transforming Ontario's Youth Justice System to Improve Outcomes for Youth," presentation at the IPAC Annual Conference 2015, online at www.ipac.ca/documents/adjudicated-miller-reid.pdf.

42. The book that resulted from this conference was titled *Hardwired to Connect*, jointly sponsored by the YMCA of the USA, Dartmouth Medical School, and the Institute for American Values. The authors included child psychiatrist Elizabeth Berger, legendary pediatrician Dr. T. Berry Brazelton, Harvard professor Robert Coles, and Stephen Suomi of the National Institutes of Health, among others. The lead authors were Kathleen Kovner Kline and Arthur Maerlender, both of Dartmouth Medical School. This quote comes from page 24.

43. *Hardwired to Connect*, p. 24.

44. *Hardwired to Connect*, pp. 24 and 57.

45. You can access every article in the special edition, free of charge, at http:// onlinelibrary.wiley.com/doi/10.1002/jnr.v95.1-2/issuetoc.

46. Larry Cahill, "An Idea Whose Time Has Come," *Journal of Neuroscience Research*, volume 95, pp. 12–13, 2017.

Extra Stuff: Sex Differences in Hearing

1. Dennis McFadden, "Sex Differences in the Auditory System," *Developmental Neuropsychology*, volume 14, pp. 261–298, 1998. The quote is from page 262.

2. Stanley Stevens, "Neural Events and the Psychophysical Law," *Science*, volume 170, pp. 1043–1050, 1970.

3. Elad Sagi and colleagues, "Identification Variability as a Measure of Loudness: An Application to Gender Differences," *Canadian Journal of Experimental Psychology*, volume 61, pp. 64–70, 2007. To be precise: the ratio of the men's value to the women's value was 0.3053 to 0.2218. The ratio 0.3053/0.2218 = 1.376, so the men's value was 37.6 percent higher, or about 38 percent higher, than the value for women. I am grateful to Dr. Norwich for his personal communication of January 2, 2017, clarifying these issues for me.

4. Lisa D'Alessandro and Kenneth Norwich, "Loudness Adaptation Measured by the Simultaneous Dichotic Loudness Balance Technique Differs Between Genders," *Hearing Research*, volume 247, pp. 122–127, 2009. To be precise: at fifty dB, the ratio of the men's value to the women's value was 52/36, or 1.444, so the men's value was 44 percent higher than the women's value. At sixty dB, the ratio of the men's value to the women's value was 49/33, or 1.485, or about 49 percent higher, than the women's value. Again, I am grateful to Dr. Norwich for his personal communication of January 2, 2017, clarifying these issues for me.

5. This quote is from the paper by Sagi and colleagues, page 69.

6. Diane McGuinness, "Equating Individual Differences for Auditory Input," *Psychophysiology*, volume 11, pp. 115–120, 1974.

7. Colin Elliott, "Noise Tolerance and Extraversion in Children," *British Journal of Psychology*, volume 62, pp. 375–380, 1971.

8. Deanna Rogers and colleagues, "The Influence of Listener's Gender on the Acceptance of Background Noise," *Journal of the American Academy of Audiology*, volume 14, pp. 372–382, 2003.

9. Neil Weinstein, "Individual Differences in Reactions to Noise: A Longitudinal Study in a College Dormitory," *Journal of Applied Psychology*, volume 63, pp. 458–466, 1978.

10. Dr. Lise Eliot published an article titled "Single-Sex Education and the Brain" (*Sex Roles*, volume 69, pp. 363–381, 2013) in which she vigorously attacked my claim in the first edition of *Why Gender Matters* that girls and boys differ in regard to hearing. In her effort to refute my claim regarding gender differences in hearing, Dr. Eliot cited a 2008 blog post by a linguist at the University of

Pennsylvania, Dr. Mark Liberman, "Liberman on Sax on Liberman on Sax on Hearing," *Language Log*, May 19, 2008, http://languagelog.ldc.upenn.edu /nll/?p=171. In his post Dr. Liberman placed great weight on questionnaires administered by German investigators Zimmer and Ellermeier (1998) and Ellermeier, Eigenstetter, and Zimmer (2001). These German investigators, in turn, based their German-language questionnaire on Weinstein's 1978 English-language questionnaire, which I have already described in the text. Ellermeier, Eigenstetter, and Zimmer administered a questionnaire assessing noise sensitivity to sixty-one undergraduates. They were startled to find that most of the respondents who were sensitive to noise were women, while most of the respondents who were not sensitive to noise were men. They asserted that their finding of gender differences in noise sensitivity was "atypical." In support of this assertion, they cited their own previous experience as well as three previous studies by other authors, none of which had found any gender difference in noise sensitivity. One of these studies was Weinstein (1978), the shortcomings of which I have already noted in the text. The second study cited by Ellermeier and colleagues is Moreira and Bryan (1972). Although it is true that Moreira and Bryan did not find gender differences in noise sensitivity, Ellermeier and colleagues fail to note that Moreira and Bryan had only five women in their study. Moreira and Bryan themselves acknowledged that "with only five of the 34 subjects being female any correlation is unlikely as the sample size is too small" (p. 455).

The third study cited by Ellermeier and colleagues is Taylor (1984), entitled "A Path Model of Aircraft Noise Annoyance." But Taylor's paper is not original empirical research at all; rather it is a reanalysis of data published over the previous two decades, going back to 1963 (Londoners disturbed by aircraft flying overhead). Taylor's analysis is based on the assumption that noise sensitivity is unrelated to, and independent of, the gender of the subject. Taylor finds that noise sensitivity is a highly significant predictor of whether someone is annoyed by aircraft flying overhead. No doubt this is accurate, but Taylor then excludes that variance from his statistical model, finding that the sex of the subject does not account for any *additional* variance in the data. Taylor's analysis is consistent with the possibility that noise sensitivity covaried with female sex. In any case, Taylor does not provide sufficient information to allow the reader to re-create his analysis of the 1963 data from London alongside more recent data (from the 1970s) from the United States.

So the three papers cited by Ellermeier and colleagues in support of their claim that gender differences in noise sensitivity are "atypical" actually provide very weak support for that claim. Ellermeier and colleagues also cite their own previous experience with their own questionnaire—a German-language questionnaire (Zimmer and Ellermeier, 1998) that adheres closely to the English-language model provided by Weinstein (1978). For example, one of the items on their questionnaire reads, "If there's noise where I am trying to work, that makes me aggressive" ("Geräusche an meinem Arbeitsplatz machen mich aggressiv"). A respondent must agree with that statement in order to be coded as "noise-sensitive."

But as I have already noted, introspective questionnaires such as these may reflect the social construction of gender—such as a woman's reluctance to admit that she gets angry or "aggressive" when other people are making noise—and thereby conceal or confuse the underlying issue of noise sensitivity. A woman might be less likely than a man, on average, to agree with any statement in the format "If X happens, that makes me aggressive." Zimmer and Ellermeier (1998), like Weinstein before them, show no awareness of how their questionnaire is confounded by the social construction of gender and the corresponding sex differences in the willingness of subjects to admit that noise makes them "aggressive."

These are the studies on which Dr. Liberman relied in his blog post cited by Dr. Eliot. Are we supposed to accept these subjective surveys in favor of more objective psychophysical measures, such as those employed by the researchers I have cited here? If so, why? These are some of the questions Eliot should have addressed but didn't.

Looking back, we can understand why Ellermeier, Eigenstetter, and Zimmer were surprised to discover that the women in their study scored higher on noise sensitivity than the men did. In view of the fact that Ellermeier and colleagues were using such a biased questionnaire, in which a person had to admit to being "aggressive" in order to qualify as being sensitive to noise, it is indeed surprising that more women than men were scored as noise sensitive. It's possible that women in 2001 were more willing to describe themselves as being "aggressive" than women had been a decade earlier. We just don't know. The take-home message for researchers seems to be that you shouldn't rely on subjects' introspection about what makes them feel "aggressive" if you want to measure noise sensitivity. Instead, use psychophysical measures that assess noise sensitivity more directly.

Here are the references cited in this note: Wolfgang Ellermeier, Monika Eigenstetter, and Karin Zimmer, "Psychoacoustic Correlates of Individual Noise Sensitivity," *Journal of the Acoustical Society of America*, volume 109, pp. 1464–1473, 2001; Naomi Moreira and M. Bryan, "Noise Annoyance Susceptibility," *Journal of Sound and Vibration*, volume 21, pp. 449–462, 1972; S. M. Taylor, "A Path Model of Aircraft Noise Annoyance," *Journal of Sound and Vibration*, volume 96, pp. 243–260, 1984; Karin Zimmer and Wolfgang Ellermeier, "Konstruktion und Evaluation eines Fragebogens zur Erfassung der individuellen Lärmempfindlichkeit" ["Construction and Evaluation of a Noise Sensitivity Questionnaire"] *Diagnostica*, volume 44, pp. 11–20, 1998.

11. David DeBonis and Deborah Moncrieff, "Auditory Processing Disorders: An Update for Speech-Language Pathologists," *American Journal of Speech-Language Pathology*, volume 17, pp. 4–18, 2008.

Extra Stuff: Sex Differences in Vision

1. In some cases the researchers gave children a choice of just a few toys to play with. See, for example, Sheri Berenbaum and Melissa Hines, "Early Androgens Are Related to Childhood Sex-Typed Toy Preferences," *Psychological Science*, volume 3, pp. 203–206, 1992. In other cases investigators interviewed children and/or parents and asked them what kind of toys they preferred. See, for example (in chronological order), Brian Sutton-Smith and Benjamin Rosenberg, "Development of Sex Differences in Play Choices During Preadolescence," *Child Development*, volume 34, pp. 119–126, 1963; Jane Connor and Lisa Serbin, "Behaviorally-Based Masculine- and Feminine-Activity Preference Scales for Preschoolers," *Child Development*, volume 48, pp. 1411–1416, 1977; Peter Smith and Linda Daglish, "Sex Differences in Parent and Infant Behavior in the Home," *Child Development*, volume 48, pp. 1250–1254, 1977; David Perry, Adam White, and Louise Perry, "Does Early Sex Typing Result from Children's

Attempts to Match Their Behavior to Sex Role Stereotypes?" *Child Development*, volume 55, pp. 2114–2121, 1984; D. Bruce Carter and Gary Levy, "Cognitive Aspects of Early Sex-Role Development: The Influence of Gender Schemas on Preschoolers' Memories and Preferences for Sex-Typed Toys and Activities," *Child Development*, volume 59 pp. 782–792, 1988.

2. Both figures here are taken from the paper by Janice Hassett, Erin Siebert, and Kim Wallen, "Sex Differences in Rhesus Monkey Toy Preferences Parallel Those of Children," *Hormones and Behavior*, volume 54, pp. 359–364, 2008. For the figure depicting toy preferences of children, Hassert and colleagues drew on data originally published by Sheri Berenbaum and Melissa Hines in their paper "Early Androgens Are Related to Childhood Sex-Typed Toy Preferences," *Psychological Science*, volume 3, pp. 203–206, 1992.

3. Janice Hassett, Erin Siebert, and Kim Wallen, "Sex Differences in Rhesus Monkey Toy Preferences Parallel Those of Children," *Hormones and Behavior*, volume 54, pp. 359–364, 2008.

4. There is a principle in logic known as "Occam's Razor," expressed this way by Isaac Newton in the *Principia Mathematica* (1687): "To the same natural effects we must, as far as possible, assign the same causes." Whatever explanation one invokes to explain the fact that male monkeys prefer trucks over dolls should logically be invoked to explain the same main effect in human children. Because the social construction of gender cannot be invoked to explain this finding in monkeys, it cannot (without violating Occam's Razor) be invoked as the primary explanation for this finding in humans.

5. Melvin Konner, *The Evolution of Childhood: Relationships, Emotion, Mind* (Cambridge, MA: Harvard University Press, 2010), p. 675.

6. I am borrowing the title of this section from the letter on this subject written by Melissa Hines and Gerianne Alexander, "Monkeys, Girls, Boys and Toys," *Hormones and Behavior*, volume 54, pp. 478–479, 2008.

7. Gerianne Alexander and Melissa Hines, "Sex Differences in Response to Children's Toys in Nonhuman Primates," *Evolution and Human Behavior*, volume 23, pp. 467–479, 2002.

8. Gerianne Alexander, "An Evolutionary Perspective of Sex-Typed Toy Preferences: Pink, Blue, and the Brain," *Archives of Sexual Behavior*, volume 32, pp. 7–14, 2003.

9. Leslie Ungerleider and Mortimer Mishkin are the neuroscientists most often credited with being the first—in the early 1980s—to recognize explicitly the anatomical distinction between the "what" system and the "where" system. See, for example, their paper (cowritten with Kathleen Macko) entitled "Object Vision and Spatial Vision: Two Cortical Pathways," *Trends in Neuroscience*, volume 6, pp. 414–417, 1983.

10. For a review of this literature, please see the article by Melvyn Goodale and David Westwood, "An Evolving View of Duplex Vision: Separate But Interacting Cortical Pathways for Perception and Action," *Current Opinion in Neurobiology*, volume 14, pp. 203–211, 2004.

11. Gerianne Alexander, Teresa Wilcox, and Rebecca Woods, "Sex Differences in Infants' Visual Interest in Toys," *Archives of Sexual Behavior*, volume 38, pp. 427–433, 2009. For more information on sex differences in the vision of babies, see the article by Anna Horwood and Patricia Riddell, "Gender Differences in Early Accommodation and Vergence Development," *Ophthalmic and Physiological Optics*, volume 28, pp. 115–126, 2009.

12. Robert Handa and Robert McGivern, "Steroid Hormones, Receptors, and

Perceptual and Cognitive Sex Differences in the Visual System," *Current Eye Research*, volume 40, pp. 110–127, 2015. The quote is from page 116. These authors cite seven different studies in support of this statement (their references 82 through 88).

13. Robert McGivern and colleagues, "Men and Women Exhibit a Differential Bias for Processing Movement Versus Objects," *PLOS One*, March 14, 2012, DOI: 10.1371/journal.pone.0032238, www.plosone.org/article /info%3Adoi%2F10.1371%2Fjournal.pone.0032238.

14. Melissa Hines and colleagues, "Spatial Abilities Following Prenatal Androgen Abnormality: Targeting and Mental Rotations Performance in Individuals with Congenital Adrenal Hyperplasia," *Psychoneuroendocrinology*, volume 28, pp. 1010–1026, 2003.

15. Katrin Amunts and colleagues, "Gender-Specific Left-Right Asymmetries in Human Visual Cortex," *Journal of Neuroscience*, volume 27, pp. 1356–1364, 2007, full text available at no charge at this link: www.jneurosci.org/cgi/content /full/27/6/1356.

16. John Vanston and Lars Strother, "Sex Differences in the Human Visual System," *Journal of Neuroscience Research*, volume 95, pp. 617–625, 2017.

17. At most schools of education it's politically incorrect even to suggest that best practices for teaching the subject areas might be different for girls and for boys. Two notable exceptions to this unfortunate rule are Stetson University in DeLand, Florida, and the University of Nevada at Reno.

ACKNOWLEDGMENTS

My first debt is to the parents and children who chose me as their family doctor in Poolesville, Maryland, over the eighteen-plus years that I practiced there. It's a great privilege to be a family doctor: an extraordinary intimacy to follow the same child from the newborn nursery through toddlerhood, through childhood and into adolescence. Because I lived and worked in the same small town for more than eighteen years, some of the children I first saw as babies were teenagers when my family and I moved to Pennsylvania. I saw the results of different parenting styles first-hand in more than two thousand children.

My next debt is to administrators at the more than four hundred schools I visited between 2001 and 2017, who invited me to visit their schools. Talking with students, meeting with teachers and parents, and listening to school leaders, I learned about different approaches to gender issues in every imaginable setting: single-sex and coed, urban and suburban and rural, affluent and low-income, North American and international.

I am grateful to the scholars who took the time to review relevant sections of the manuscript and offer their corrections and suggestions. J. Michael Bailey was kind enough to read chapters 10 and 11 and offer a detailed critique, which was immensely helpful. Pamela Dalton read and corrected my discussion of sex differences in smell. Kenneth Norwich provided important feedback on my discussion of sex differences in hearing. My medical school classmate Dr. Marc Rosen, now a professor at Yale Medical School, brought me up to speed on the latest research on the androgen receptor gene. Judge John Romero reviewed and corrected my recollection of his remarks at the conference in Albuquerque. Jerome Kagan and Pat Sexton both reviewed chapter 9 for the first edition. My thanks go to Cornell professor John Bishop for providing me with unpublished data from his study of what's "cool" for middle school girls and boys. My brother Dr. Steven Sax offered many useful comments and corrections. I also thank Murray Savar for his thoughtful insights. Any errors that remain are my responsibility.

Back in 2002, I sent a book proposal to a literary agent named Felicia Eth. She took a chance on an unknown and unpublished family doctor. We have now done four books together. I am grateful to her for her judgment, experience, and patience.

My editor at Doubleday for the first edition, Adam Bellow, did a careful reading of the manuscript and made many helpful suggestions on literary matters large and small. The editor for the second edition, Donna Loffredo, likewise read the new manuscript with care and made many wise comments and suggestions.

My late mother, Dr. Janet Sax, inspired my interest in gender differences as a child, with stories across the dinner table from her pediatric practice about differences she observed between girls and boys in development, behavior, and motivation. My late father, Harry Sax, encouraged me at every step of this project.

When the first edition of this book was published in 2005, my wife, Katie, and I had been married for fifteen years and we had no children. We thought we were infertile. But then our one and only child was born in 2006. The experience of being a father changed me, as I imagine it changes every man. It made me more humble, opening up to me vast areas of knowledge of which I was previously completely ignorant: how to change a diaper, how to rock a child to sleep, how to dress an American Girl doll. Watching my wife become a wonderful mother has been a joy. Watching my daughter, Sarah, grow to become a young woman, and helping her on that journey in some small way, has been the most rewarding experience of my life.

When I counsel depressed patients, they sometimes say something along the following lines: "Life is a series of disappointments, with long stretches of boredom in between. And then you die. So what's the point. Why bother? Why get out of bed in the morning?"

It's a fair question. For me personally, the answer I give myself begins with: for Katie and for Sarah. That's why.

PERMISSIONS

Chapter 2: "Wedding Poem for Schele and Phil" from *Playing the Black Piano: Poems* by Bill Holm (Minneapolis: Milkweed Editions, 2004). Copyright © 2004 by Bill Holm. Reprinted with permission from Milkweed Editions, www.milkweed.org.

The story of Andrew Phillips, and his drawing of the dragon being killed (or not?) by the laser, is reproduced with his permission.

Chapter 3: The photograph of the girl rappelling down the cliff at Freycinet is reproduced courtesy of St. Michael's Collegiate School, Tasmania, with gracious permission of the girl and her parents.

Chapter 4: The photograph of "Jeffrey" holding the Ndebele javelin in one hand and the dead bird in the other is reproduced with his permission.

Chapter 5: The figure showing brain development for girls and boys, as a function of age in years, is reprinted from *NeuroImage*, volume 36, Rhoshel Lenroot and colleagues, "Sexual Dimorphism of Brain Developmental Trajectories During Childhood and Adolescence," Figure 2(a), pp. 1065–1073, © 2007, with permission from Elsevier.

Dr. Edgerton's photo, "Making Applesauce at MIT," is reproduced with permission of the Harold and Esther Edgerton Family Foundation.

Chapter 6: The figure showing the proportion of teenage females and males who have had sexual intercourse is Figure 1 from Gladys Martinez and colleagues, "Teenagers in the United States: Sexual Activity, Contraceptive Use, and Childbearing, 2006–2010 National Survey of Family Growth," Hyattsville, Maryland: National Center for Health Statistics, *Vital Health Statistics*, volume 23, number 31, 2011. This figure, like all publications of the National Center for Health Statistics, is in the public domain.

Chapter 11: The figure showing death from any cause as a function of time after sex reassignment is Figure 1 from Cecilia Dhejne and colleagues, "Long-Term Follow-Up of Transsexual Persons Undergoing Sex Reassignment Surgery: Cohort Study From Sweden," *PLOS One*, 2011, full text online at no charge at http://journals.plos.org/plosone/article/asset?id=10.1371/journal.pone.0016885.PDF. This is an open-access article distributed under the terms of the Creative Commons Attribution License, which permits unrestricted use, distribution, and reproduction in any medium, provided the original author and source are credited.

Chapter 12: The photograph of the boy and the baby on page 304 is reproduced with permission of University School in Hunting Valley, Ohio, and with permission of the boy, who is now a young man.

Extra Stuff: Sex Differences in Hearing: The figure titled "Comfortable Loudness Hearing Level" is reproduced from the article by Diane McGuinness titled "Equating

INDEX

Leonard Sax, M.D., Ph.D., graduated Phi Beta Kappa from the Massachusetts Institute of Technology (MIT) at the age of nineteen and then went on to the University of Pennsylvania, where he earned both a Ph.D. in psychology and an M.D. He completed a three-year residency in family practice in Lancaster, Pennsylvania. For nineteen years, Dr. Sax was a practicing family physician in Maryland, just outside Washington, DC. He now sees patients in West Chester, Pennsylvania (west of Philadelphia). In 2005 Doubleday published his first book, *Why Gender Matters*; this book is the second edition. His second book, *Boys Adrift*, was published in 2007. His third book, *Girls on the Edge*, was published in 2010. His fourth book, *The Collapse of Parenting*, was published by Basic Books in December 2015 and became a *New York Times* bestseller.

Dr. Sax has spoken on issues of child and adolescent development not only in the United States but also in Australia, Bermuda, Canada, England, Germany, Italy, Mexico, New Zealand, Scotland, Spain, and Switzerland. He has visited more than four hundred schools since 2001. He has appeared on the *TODAY* show, CNN, National Public Radio, Fox News, PBS, the Canadian Broadcasting Corporation, the British Broadcasting Corporation, the Australian Broadcasting Corporation, New Zealand Television, and many other national and international media.

Find him online at leonardsax.com.